A Cotswold Village; or, Country Life and Pursuits in Gloucestershire

J. Arthur Gibbs

"Frontispiece. J. ARTHUR GIBBS."

A COTSWOLD VILLAGE

OR COUNTRY LIFE AND PURSUITS IN GLOUCESTERSHIRE

BY J. ARTHUR GIBBS

"Go, little booke; God send thee good passage,
And specially let this be thy prayere
Unto them all that thee will read or hear,
Where thou art wrong after their help to call,
Thee to correct in any part or all."

GEOFFREY CHAUCER.

WITH ILLUSTRATIONS

1918

PREFACE TO THE THIRD EDITION.

Before the third edition of this work had been published the author passed away, from sudden failure of the heart, at the early age of thirty-one. Two or three biographical notices, written by those who highly appreciated him and who deeply mourn his loss, have already appeared in the newspapers; and I therefore wish to add only a few words about one whose kind smile of welcome will greet us no more in this life.

Joseph Arthur Gibbs was one of those rare natures who combine a love of outdoor life, cricket and sport of every kind, with a refined and scholarly taste for literature. He had, like his father, a keen observation for every detail in nature; and from a habit of patient watchfulness he acquired great knowledge of natural history. From his grandfather, the late Sir Arthur Hallam Elton, he inherited his taste for literary work and the deep poetical feeling which are revealed so clearly in his book. On leaving Eton, he wrote a *Vale*, of which his tutor, Mr. Luxmoore, expressed his high appreciation; and later on, when, after leaving Oxford, he was living a quiet country life, he devoted himself to literary pursuits.

He was not, however, so engrossed in his work as to ignore other duties; and he was especially interested in the villagers round his home, and ever ready to give what is of greater value than money, personal trouble and time in finding out their wants and in relieving them. His unvarying kindness and sympathy will never be forgotten at Ablington; for, as one of the villagers wrote in a letter of condolence on hearing of his death, "he went in and out as a friend among them." With all his tenderness of heart, he had a strict sense of justice and a clear judgment, and weighed carefully both sides of any question before he gave his verdict.

Arthur Gibbs went abroad at the end of March 1899 for a month's trip to Italy, and in his Journal he wrote many good descriptions of scenery and of the old towns; and the way in which he describes his last glimpse of Florence during a glorious sunset shows how greatly he appreciated its beauty. In his Journal in April he dwells on the shortness of life, and in the following solemn words he sounds a warning note:—

"Do not neglect the creeping hours of time: 'the night cometh when no man can work.' All time is wasted unless spent in work for God. The best secular way of spending the precious thing that men call time is by making always for some grand end—a great book, to show forth the wonders of creation and the infinite goodness of the Creator. You must influence for *good* if you write, and write nothing that you will regret some day or think trivial."

These words, written a month before the end came, tell their own tale. The writer of them had a deep love for all things that are "lovely, pure, and of good report"; and in his book one sees clearly the adoration he felt for that God whom he so faithfully served. There are many different kinds of work in this world, and diversities of gifts; to him was given the spirit to discern the work of God in Nature's glory, and the power to win others to see it also. He had a remarkable influence for good at Oxford, and the letters from his numerous friends and from his former tutor at Christ Church show that this influence has never been forgotten, but has left its mark not only on his college, but on the university.

Like his namesake and relative, Arthur Hallam, of immortal memory, Arthur Gibbs had attained to a purity of soul and a wisdom which were not of this world, at an earlier age than is given to many men; and so in love and faith and hope—

> "I would the great world grew like thee,
>   Who grewest not alone in power
>   And knowledge; but by year and hour
>   In reverence and charity."
> LAURA BEATRICE GIBBS.

PREFACE TO THE FIRST EDITION.

To those of my readers who have ever lived beside a stream, or in an ancient house or time-honoured college, there will always be a peculiar charm in silvery waters sparkling beneath the summer sun. To you the Gothic building, with its carved pinnacles, its warped gables, its mullioned casements and dormer windows, the old oak within, the very inglenook by the great fireplace where the old folks used to sit at home, the ivy trailing round the grey walls, the jessamine, roses, and clematis that in their proper seasons clustered round the porch,—to you all these things will have their charm as long as you live. Therefore, if these pages appeal not to some such, it will not be the subject that is wanting, but the ability of the writer.

It is not claimed for my Cotswold village that it is one whit prettier or pleasanter or better in any way than hundreds of other villages in England; I seek only to record the simple annals of a quiet, old-fashioned Gloucestershire hamlet and the country within walking distance of it. Nor do I doubt that there are manor houses far more beautiful and far richer in history even within a twenty-mile radius of my own home. For instance, the ancient house of Chavenage by Tetbury, or in the opposite direction, where the northern escarpments of the Cotswolds rise out of the beautiful Evesham Vale, those historic mediaeval houses of Southam and Postlip.

It is often said that in books like these we paint arcadias that never did and never could exist on earth. To this I would answer that there are many such abodes in country places, if only our minds are such as to realise them. And, above all, let us be optimists in literature even though we may be pessimists in life. Let us have all that is joyous and bright in our books, and leave the trials and failures for the realities of life. Let us in our literature avoid as much as possible the painful side of human nature and the pains and penalties of human weakness; let us endeavour to depict a state of existence as far as possible approaching the Utopian ideal, though not necessarily the Nirvana of the Buddhists nor the paradise of fools; let us look not downwards into the depths of black despair, but upwards into the starry heavens; let us gaze at the golden evening brightening in the west. Richard Jefferies has taught us that such a literature is possible; and if we read his best books, we may some day be granted that fuller soul he prayed for and at length obtained. Would that we could all hear, as he heard, the still small voice that whispers in the woods and among the wild flowers and the spreading foliage by the brook!

To any one who might be thinking of becoming for the time being "a tourist," and in that capacity visiting the Cotswolds, my advice is, "Don't." There is really nothing to see. There is nothing, that is to say, which may not be seen much nearer London. And I freely confess that most of the subjects included in this book are usually deemed unworthy of consideration even in the district itself. Still, there are a few who realise that every county in England is more or less a mine of interest, and for such I have written. Realising my limitations, I have not gone deeply into any single subject; my endeavour has been to touch on every branch of country life with as light a hand as possible—to amuse rather than to instruct. For, as Washington Irving delightfully sums up the matter: "It is so much pleasanter to please than to instruct, to play the companion rather than the preceptor. What, after all, is the mite of wisdom that I could throw into the mass of knowledge? or how am I sure that my sagest deductions may be safe guides for the opinions of others? But in writing to amuse, if I fail, the only evil is in my own disappointment. If, however, I can by any lucky chance rub out one wrinkle from the brow of care, or beguile the heavy heart of one moment of sorrow; if I can now and then penetrate through the gathering film of misanthropy, prompt a benevolent view of human nature, and make my reader more in good humour with his fellow beings and himself, surely, surely, I shall not then have written in vain."

The first half of Chapter II. originally appeared in the *Pall Mall Magazine*. Portions of Chapters VII. and VIII., and "The Thruster's Song," have also been published in *Baily's Magazine*. My thanks are due to the editors for permission to reproduce them. Chapter XII. owes its inspiration to Mr. Madden's excellent work on Shakespeare's connection with sport and the Cotswolds, the "Diary of Master William Silence." We have no local tradition of any kind about Shakespeare.

I am indebted to Miss E.F. Brickdale for the pen-and-ink sketches, and to Colonel Mordaunt for his beautiful photographs. Three of the photographs, however, are by H. Taunt, of Oxford, and a similar number are by Mr. Gardner, of Fairford.

September 1898.

CONTENTS

Fliers of the Hunt—A Narrow Escape—A Check—A Reliable Hound—Failure of Scent—An Excellent Tonic.

CHAPTER VII.

A COTSWOLD TROUT STREAM

Loch Leven Trout—Curious Capture of an Eel—The Author Catches a Red-Herring—Macomber Falls—A Sad Episode—South Country Streams—Course of the Coln—Charles Kingsley on Fishing—A May-Fly Stream—Evening Fishing—Dry-Fly Dogmas—Flies for the Coln—Scarcity of Poachers—An Evening Walk by the River—Spring's Delights.

CHAPTER VIII.

WHEN THE MAY-FLY IS UP

Derby Day on the Coln—A Good Sportsman—The Right Fly—Pleasures of the Country—Peregrine's Quaint Expressions—Sport with the Olive Dun—A Fine Trout—Effects of Sheep-Washing—A Good Basket—Life by the Brook—A Summer's Night—In the Heart of England.

CHAPTER IX.

BURFORD, A COTSWOLD TOWN

Curious Names—The Windrush—Burford Priory—An Empty Shell—The Kingmaker—Lord Falkland—Speaker Lenthall—Bibury Races—An Old Tradition—Valued Relics—Burford Church—Mr. Oman's Discovery—Burford during the Civil Wars.

Methods and Language of Falconry—A Flight at a Heron—
Peregrine Views a Fox.

CHAPTER XIII.

CIRENCESTER

Roman Remains—The Corinium Museum—The Church—
Cirencester House—The Park—The Abbey—The "Mop" or
Hiring Fair—A Great Hunting Centre—A Varied Country—
The Badminton Hounds—Lord Bathurst's Hounds—The
Cotswold Hounds—Charles Travess—A Born Genius—The
Cricklade Hounds—The Right Sort of Horse—The Oaksey
District—The Heythrop Hounds—A Defence of Hard
Riding—A Day in the Vale—A Hunting Poem.

CHAPTER XIV.

SPRING IN THE COTSWOLDS

Habits of Moorhens—Mallard and Swan—Nuthatches—
Woodpeckers—Humane   Traps—Badgers—Fox-terriers—
Scotch Deerhounds—Retrievers—Cray-fish—The Rookery—
Jackdaws—Foxes—Artificial Earths—Fox among Sheep—
Foxes and Fowls—Poultry Claims—Observations on Scent—
The Hygrometer—How Trout are Netted—Scarcity of
Otters—Water-Voles.

CHAPTER XV.

THE PROMISE OF MAY

Wild Flowers—Cottage Gardens—The Paths of Literature—
Description of a Horse—Beauty of Trees—Their Loss
Irreparable as the Loss of Friends—A Fine Type of
Englishman—Lines in Memory of W.D. Llewelyn.

CHAPTER XVI.

SUMMER DAYS ON THE COTSWOLDS

A Walk in the Fields—Hedgerow Flowers—The Brookside—By "the Pill"—Remarks on Gray—A Fine Piece of Miniature Scenery—The Cricket Ground—The Book of Nature—At the Ford—Habits of Observation—In the Conyger Wood—The Home of the Kingfisher—A Limestone Quarry—The Great Stone Floor of the Earth—Nature's Endless Cycle—Beauty of the Ash—Hedgehogs—Trout and Snake—Sunset on the Hills.

CHAPTER XVII.

AUTUMN

Remarks on Country Life—Thrashing—The Flail—Gipsies—Harvest Feasts—Fifty Years Ago—The Wolds in Autumn—By the Stream—Wildfowl—Migration of Birds—Lapwings—Winter Visitants—Thunderstorms—Glow-Worms—A Brilliant Meteor—Night on the Hills—The "Blowing-Stone"—Christmas Day on the Cotswolds—A Solar Halo—Hamlet Festivities—Tom Peregrine Baffled—The Mummers Play—The Victorian Era—The True Days of "Merrie England"—*Carpe Diem*.

CHAPTER XVIII.

WHEN THE SUN GOES DOWN

A Glorious Panorama—Peregrine as Secretary—The Light of Setting Suns—Conclusion.

APPENDIX.

LIST OF ILLUSTRATIONS.

CHAPTER I.

FLYING WESTWARDS.

London is becoming miserably hot and dusty; everybody who can get away is rushing off, north, south, east, and west, some to the seaside, others to pleasant country houses. Who will fly with me westwards to the land of golden sunshine and silvery trout streams, the land of breezy uplands and valleys nestling under limestone hills, where the scream of the railway whistle is seldom heard and the smoke of the factory darkens not the long summer days? Away, in the smooth "Flying Dutchman"; past Windsor's glorious towers and Eton's playing-fields; past the little village and churchyard where a century and a half ago the famous "Elegy" was written, and where, hard by "those rugged elms, that yew-tree's shade," yet rests the body of the mighty poet, Gray. How those lines run in one's head this bright summer evening, as from our railway carriage we note the great white dome of Stoke House peeping out amid the elms! whilst every field reminds us of him who wrote those lilting stanzas long, long ago.

"Ah, happy hills! ah, pleasing shade!
  Ah, fields, beloved in vain!
Where once my careless childhood strayed,
  A stranger yet to pain:
I feel the gales that from ye blow
A momentary bliss bestow;
As waving fresh their gladsome wing
My weary soul they seem to soothe,
And redolent of joy and youth,
To breathe a second spring."

But soon we are flashing past Reading, where Sutton's nursery gardens are bright with scarlet and gold, and blue and white; every flower that can be made to grow in our climate grows there, we may be sure. But there is no need of garden flowers now, when the fields and hedges, even the railway banks, are painted with the lovely blue of wild geraniums and harebells, the gold of birdsfoot trefoil and Saint John's wort, and the white and pink of convolvulus or bindweed. We are passing through some of the richest scenery in the Thames valley. There, on the right, is Mapledurham, a grand mediaeval building, surrounded by such a wealth of stately trees as you will see nowhere else. The Thames runs practically through the grounds. What a glorious carpet of gold is spread over these meadows when the buttercups are in full bloom! Now comes Pangbourne, with its lovely weir, where the big Thames trout love to lie. Pangbourne used to be one of the prettiest villages on the river; but its popularity has spoilt it.

As we pass onwards, many other country houses—Purley, Basildon, and Hardwick—with their parks and clustering cottages, add their charm to the view. There are the beautiful woods of Streatley: hanging copses clothe the sides of the hills, and pretty villages nestle amid the trees. But soon the scene changes: the glorious valley Father Thames has scooped out for himself is left behind; we are crossing the chalk uplands. On all sides are vast stretches of unfenced arable land, though here and there a tiny village with its square-towered Norman church peeps out from an oasis of green fields and stately elm trees. On the right the Chiltern Hills are seen in the background, and Wittenham Clump stands forth—a conspicuous object for miles. The country round Didcot reminds one very much of the north of France: between Calais and Paris one notices the same chalk soil, the same flat arable fields, and the same old-fashioned farmhouses and gabled cottages.

But now we have entered the grand old Berkshire vale. "Fields and hedges, hedges and fields; peace and plenty, plenty and peace. I should like to take a foreigner down the vale of Berkshire in the end of May, and ask him what he thought of old England." Thus wrote Charles Kingsley forty years ago, when times were better for Berkshire farmers. But the same old fields and the same old hedges still remain—only we do not appreciate them as much as did the author of "Westward Ho!"

Steventon, that lovely village with its gables and thatched roofs, its white cottage walls set with beams of blackest oak, its Norman church in the midst of spreading chestnuts and leafy elms, appears from the railway to be one of the most old-fashioned spots on earth. This vale is full of fine old trees; but in many places the farmers have spoilt their beauty by lopping off the lower branches because the grass will not grow under their wide-spreading foliage. It is only in the parks and woodlands that the real glory of the timber remains.

And now we may notice what a splendid hunting country is this Berkshire vale. The fields are large and entirely grass; the fences, though strong, are all "flying" ones—posts and rails, too, are frequent in the hedges. Many a fine scamper have the old Berkshire hounds enjoyed over these grassy pastures, where the Rosy Brook winds its sluggish course; and we trust they will continue to do so for many years to come. Long may that day be in coming when the sound of the horn is no longer heard in this delightful country!

High up on the hill the old White Horse soon appears in view, cut in the velvety turf of the rolling chalk downs. But, in the words of the old ballad,

> "The ould White Horse wants zettin' to rights."

He wants "scouring" badly. A stranger, if shown this old relic, the centre of a hundred legends, famous the whole world over, would find it difficult to recognise any likeness to a fiery steed in those uncertain lines of chalk. Nevertheless, this is the monument King Alfred made to commemorate his victory over the Danes at Ashdown. So the tradition of the country-side has had it for a thousand years, and shall a thousand more.

The horse is drawn as galloping. Frank Buckland took the following measurements of him: The total length is one hundred and seventy yards; his eye is four feet across; his ear fifteen yards in length; his hindleg is forty-three yards long. Doubtless the full proportions of the White Horse are not kept scoured nowadays; for a few weeks ago I was up on the hill and took some of the measurements myself. I could not make mine agree with Frank Buckland's: for instance, the ear appeared to be seven yards only in length, and not fifteen; so that it would seem that the figure is gradually growing smaller. It is the head and forelegs that want scouring worst of all. There is little sign

3

of the trench, two feet deep, which in Buckland's time formed the outline of the horse; the depth of the cutting is now only a matter of a very few inches.

The view from this hill is a very extensive one, embracing the vale from Bath almost to Reading the whole length of the Cotswold Hills, as well as the Chilterns, stretching away eastwards towards Aylesbury, and far into Buckinghamshire. Beneath your feet lie many hundred thousand acres of green pastures, varied in colour during summer and autumn by golden wheatfields bright with yellow charlock and crimson poppies. It has been said that eleven counties are visible on clear days.

The White Horse at Westbury, further down the line, represents a horse in a standing position. He reflects the utmost credit on his grooms; for not only are his shapely limbs "beautifully and wonderfully made," but the greatest care is taken of him. The Westbury horse is not in reality nearly so large as this one at Uffington, but he is a very beautiful feature of the country. I paid him a visit the other day, and was surprised to find he was very much smaller than he appears from the railway. Glancing over a recent edition of Tom Hughes' book, "The Scouring of the White Horse," I found the following lines: —

"In all likelihood the *pastime* of 1857 will be the last of his race; for is not the famous Saxon (or British) horse now scheduled to an Act of Parliament as an ancient monument which will be maintained in time to come as a piece of prosaic business, at the cost of other than Berkshire men reared within sight of the hill?"

Alas! it is too true. There has been no *pastime* since 1857.

It would have been a splendid way of commemorating the "diamond jubilee" if a scouring had been organised in 1897. Forty years have passed since the last pastime, with its backsword play and "climmin a greasy pole for a leg of mutton," its race for a pig and a cheese; and, oddly enough, the previous scouring had taken place in the year of the Queen's accession, sixty-one years ago. It would be enough to make poor Tom Hughes turn in his grave if he knew that the old White Horse had been turned out to grass, and left to look after himself for the rest of his days!

Those were grand old times when the Berkshire; Gloucestershire, and Somersetshire men amused themselves by cracking each other's heads and cudgel-playing for a gold-laced hat and a pair of buckskin breeches; when a flitch of bacon was run for by donkeys; and when, last, but not least, John Morse, of Uffington, "grinned agin another chap droo hos [horse] collars, a fine bit of spwoart, to be sure, and made the folks laaf." I here quote from Tom Hughes' book, "The Scouring of the White Horse," to which I must refer my readers for further interesting particulars.

There are some days during summer when the sunlight is so beautiful that every object is invested with a glamour and a charm not usually associated with it. Such a day was that of which we write. As we were gliding out of Swindon the sun was beginning to descend. From a Great Western express, running at the rate of sixty miles an hour through picturesque country, you may watch the sun setting amidst every variety of scenery. Now some hoary grey tower stands out against the intense brightness of the western sky; now a tracery of fine trees shades for a time the dazzling light; then suddenly the fiery furnace is revealed again, reflected perhaps in the waters of some stream or amid the reeds and sedges of a mere, where a punt is moored containing anglers in broad wideawake hats. Gradually a dark purple shade steals over the long range of chalk hills; white, clean-looking roads stand out clearly defined miles away on the horizon; the smoke that rises straight up from some ivy-covered homestead half a mile away is bluer than the evening sky — a deep azure blue. The horizon is clear in the south, but in the north-west dark, but not forbidding clouds are rising; fantastic cloudlets float high up in the firmament; rooks coming home to roost are plainly visible several miles away against the brilliant western sky.

This Great Western Railway runs through some of the finest bits of old England. Not long ago, in travelling from Chepstow to Gloucester, we were fairly amazed at the surpassing beauty of the views. It was May-day, and the weather was in keeping with the occasion. The sight of the old town of Chepstow and the silvery

Wye, as we left them behind us, was fine enough; but who can describe the magnificent panorama presented by the wide Severn at low tide? Yellow sands, glittering like gold in the dazzling sunshine, stretched away for miles; beyond these a vista of green meadows, with the distant Cotswold Hills rising out of dreamy haze; waters of chrysolite, with fields of malachite beyond; the azure sky overhead flecked with clouds of pearl and opal, and all around the pear orchards in full bloom.

While on the subject of scenery, may I enter a protest against the change the Great Western Railway has lately made in the photographs which adorn their carriages? They used to be as beautiful as one could wish; lately, however, the colouring has been lavished on them with no sparing hand. These "photo-chromes" are unnatural and impossible, whereas the old permanent photographs were very beautiful.

At Kemble, with its old manor house and stone-roofed cottages, we say good-bye to the Vale of White Horse; for we have entered the Cotswolds. Stretching from Broadway to Bath, and from Birdlip to Burford, and containing about three hundred square miles, is a vast tract of hill country, intersected by numerous narrow valleys. Probably at one period this district was a rough, uncultivated moor. It is now cultivated for the most part, and grows excellent barley. The highest point of this extensive range is eleven hundred and thirty-four feet, but the average altitude would not exceed half that height. Almost every valley has its little brook. The district is essentially a "stone country;" for all the houses and most of their roofs are built of the local limestone, which lies everywhere on these hills within a few inches of the surface. There is no difficulty in obtaining plenty of stone hereabouts. The chief characteristics of the buildings are their antiquity and Gothic quaintness. The air is sharp and bracing, and the climate, as is inevitable on the shallow, porous soil of the oolite hills, wonderfully dry and invigorating. "Lands of gold have been found, and lands of spices and precious merchandise; but this is the land of *health*" Thus wrote Richard Jefferies of the downs, and thus say we of the Cotswolds.

And now our Great Western express is gliding into Cirencester, the ancient capital of the Cotswold country. How fair the old place seems after the dirt and smoke of London! Here town and country are blended into one, and everything is clean and fresh and picturesque. The garish church, as you view it from the top of the market-place, has a charm unsurpassed by any other sacred building in the land. In what that charm lies I have often wondered. Is it the marvellous symmetry of the whole graceful pile, as the eye, glancing down the massive square tower and along the pierced battlements and elaborate pinnacles, finally rests on the empty niches and traceried oriel windows of the magnificent south porch? I cannot say in what the charm exactly consists, but this stately Gothic fane has a grandeur as impressive as it is unexpected, recalling those wondrous words of Ruskin's:

"I used to feel as much awe in gazing at the buildings as on the hills, and could believe that God had done a greater work in breathing into the narrowness of dust the mighty spirits by whom its haughty walls had been raised and its burning legends written, than in lifting the rock of granite higher than the clouds of heaven, and veiling them with their various mantle of purple flower and shadowy pine."

CHAPTER II.

A COTSWOLD VILLAGE.

The village is not a hundred miles from London, yet "far from the madding crowd's ignoble strife." A green, well-wooded valley, in the midst of those far-stretching, cold-looking Cotswold Hills, it is like an oasis in the desert.

Up above on the wolds all is bleak, dull, and uninteresting. The air up there is ever chill; walls of loose stone divide field from field, and few houses are to be seen. But down in the valley all is fertile and full of life. It is here that the old-fashioned villagers dwell. How well I remember the first time I came upon it! One fine September evening, having left all traces of railways and the ancient Roman town of Cirencester some seven long miles behind me, with wearied limbs I sought this quiet, sequestered spot. Suddenly, as I was wondering how amid these never ending hills there could be such a place as I had been told existed, I beheld it at my feet, surpassing beautiful! Below me was a small village, nestling amid a wealth of stately trees. The hand of man seemed in some bygone time to have done all that was necessary to render the place habitable, but no more. There were cottages, bridges, and farm buildings, but all were ivy clad and time worn. The very trees themselves appeared to be laden with a mantle of ivy that was more than they could bear. Many a tall fir, from base to topmost twig, was completely robed with the smooth, five-pointed leaves of this rapacious evergreen. Through the thick foliage, of elm and ash and beech, I could just see an old manor house, and round about it, as if for protection, were clustered some thirty cottages. A murmuring of waters filled my ears, and on descending the hill I came upon a silvery trout stream, which winds its way down the valley, broad and shallow, now gently gliding over smooth gravel, now dashing over moss-grown stones and rock. The cottages, like the manor house and farm buildings, are all built of the native stone, and all are gabled and picturesque. Indeed, save a few new cottages, most of the dwellings appeared to be two or three

8

hundred years old. One farmhouse I noted carefully, and I longed to tear away the ivy from the old and crumbling porch, to see if I could not discern some half-effaced inscription telling me the date of this relic of the days of "Merrie England."

This quaint old place appeared older than the rest of the buildings. On enquiry, I learnt that long, long ago, before the present manor house existed, this was the abode of the old squires of the place; but for the last hundred years it had been the home of the principal tenant and his ancestors—yeomen farmers of the old-fashioned school, with some six hundred acres of land. The present occupants appeared to be an old man of some seventy years of age and his three sons. Keen sportsmen these, who dearly love to walk for hours in pursuit of game in the autumn, on the chance of bagging an occasional brace of partridges or a wild pheasant (for everything here is wild), or, in winter, when lake and fen are frostbound, by the river and its withybeds after snipe and wildfowl—for the Cotswold stream has never been known to freeze!

In this small hamlet I noticed that there were no less than three huge barns. At first I thought they were churches, so magnificent were their proportions and so delicate and interesting their architecture. One of these barns is four hundred years old.

Fifty years ago, what with the wool from his sheep and the grain that was stored in these barns year by year, the Cotswold farmer was a rich man. Alas! *Tempora mutantur, nos et mutamur in illis!* One can picture the harvest home, annually held in the barn, in old days so cheery, but now often nothing more than a form. Here, however, in this village, I learnt that, in spite of bad times, some of the old customs have not been allowed to pass away, and right merry is the harvest home. And Christmastide is kept in real old English fashion; nor do the mummers forget to go their nightly rounds, with their strange tale of "St. George and the dragon."

As I walk down the road I come suddenly upon the manor house—the "big house" of the village. Long and somewhat low, it stands close to the road, and is of some size. Over the doorway of the porch is the following inscription, engraven on stone in a recess:—

"PLEAD THOU MY CAVSE; OH LORD."
"BY JHON COXWEL ANO DOMENY 1590."

Underneath this inscription, and immediately over the entrance, are five heads, elaborately carved in stone. In the centre is Queen Elizabeth; to the right are portrayed what I take to be the features of Henry VIII.; whilst on the left is Mary. The other two are uncertain, but they are probably Philip of Spain and James I.

"INCRIPTION ON PORCH OF MANOR HOUSE."

I was enchanted with the place. The quaint old Elizabethan gables and sombre bell-tower, the old-fashioned entrance gates, the luxuriant growth of ivy, combined together to give that air of peace, that charm which belongs so exclusively to the buildings of the middle ages. Knowing that the house was for the time being unoccupied, I walked boldly into the outer porch, meaning to go no further. But another inscription over the solid oak door encouraged me to enter:

"PORTA PATENS ESTO, NULLI CLAUDARIS HONESTO."

I therefore opened the inner door with some difficulty, for it was heavy and cumbersome, and found myself in the hall. Although nothing remarkable met my eye, I was delighted to find everything in keeping with the place. The old-fashioned furniture, the old oak, the grim portraits and quaint heraldry, all were there. I was much interested in some carved beams of black oak, which I afterwards learnt originally formed part of the magnificent roof of the village church. When the roof was under repair a few years back, these beams were thrown aside as rotten and useless, and thus found their way into the manor house. Every atom of genuine old work of this kind is deeply interesting, representing as it does the rude chiselling which hands that have long been dust in the village churchyard wrought with infinite pains. That oak roof, carved in rich tracery, resting for ages on arcades of dog-tooth Norman and graceful Early English work, had echoed back the songs of praise and prayer that rose Sunday after Sunday from the lips of successive generations of simple country folk at matins and at evensong, before the strains of the Angelus had been hushed for ever by the Reformation. And who can tell how long before the Conquest, and by what manner of men, were planted the trees destined to provide these massive beams of oak?

In the centre of the hall was a round table, with very ancient-looking, high-backed chairs scattered about, of all shapes and sizes. Portraits of various degrees of indifferent oil painting adorned the walls of the hall and staircase. Somebody appeared to have been shooting with a catapult at some of the pictures. One old gentleman had a shot through his nose; and an old fellow with a hat on, over the window, had received a pellet in the right eye![1]

> [1] The writer, in a fit of infantile insanity, being then aged about nine, was discovered in the very act of committing this assault on his ancestors some twenty years ago, in Hertfordshire.

A copy of the Magna Charta, a suit of mediaeval armour, several rusty helmets (Cromwellian and otherwise), antlers of several kinds of deer, and a variety of old swords, pistols, and guns were the objects that chiefly attracted my attention. The walls were likewise adorned with a large number of heraldic shields.

"INTERIOR OF MANOR HOUSE."

I like to see coats-of-arms and escutcheons hanging up in churches and in the halls of old country houses, for the following simple reasons. There is meaning in them—deep, mystic meaning, such as no ordinary picture can boast. Every quartering on that ancient shield emblazoned in red, black, and gold has a legend attached to it Hundreds of years ago, in those splendid mediaeval times—nay, farther back than that, in the dim, mysterious, dark ages—each of those quarterings was a device worn by some brave knight or squire on his heavy shield. It was his cognizance in the field of battle and at the tournament. It was borne at Agincourt perhaps; at Creçy, or Poitiers, or in the lists for some "faire ladye"; and it is a token of ancient chivalry, an emblem of the days that have been and never more will be. It was doubtless the sight of those eighteen great hatchments which still hang in the little church at Stoke Poges that inspired Gray to attune his harp to such lofty strains.

> "The boast of heraldry, the pomp of power,
> And all that beauty, all that wealth e'er gave,
> Await alike the inevitable hour
> The paths of glory lead but to the grave."

Among other old masters was a portrait of the "John Coxwel" who built the house, by Cornelius Jansen, dated 1613. The house did not appear remarkable either for size or grandeur; yet there is always something particularly pleasing to me to alight unexpectedly on buildings of this kind, and to find that although they are obscure and unknown, they are on a small scale as interesting to the antiquarian as Knole, Hatfield, and other more famous mediaeval houses. Some lattice windows, evidently at some time out of doors, but now on the inner walls, showed that in more recent times the house had been enlarged, and the old courtyard walled in and made part of the hall. Over one of these windows is the inscription, *"Post tenebras lux."* The part I liked best, however, was the old-fashioned passage, with its lattice windows and musty dungeon savour, leading to the ancient kitchen and to a little oak-panelled sitting-room: but, knocking my head severely against the oak beam in the doorway, I nearly brought the whole ceiling down, a catastrophe which they tell me has happened before now in this rather rickety old manor house. Opening a door on the other side of the house, I passed out into the garden. How characteristic of the place!—a broad terrace running along the whole length of the house, and beyond that a few flower beds with the old sundial in their midst Beyond these a lawn, and then grass sweeping down to the edge of the river, some hundred yards away. Beyond the river again more grass, but of a wilder description, where the rabbits are scudding about or listening with pricked ears; and in the background a magnificent hanging wood, crowning the side of the valley, with a large rookery in it. I was much struck with the different tints of the foliage; for although autumn had not yet begun to turn the leaves, the different shades of green were most striking. A gigantic ash tree on the far side of the river stood out in bold relief, its lighter leaves being in striking contrast to the dark firs in the background. Then walnut and hazel, beech and chestnut all offered infinite variety of shape and foliage. The river here had been broadened to a width of some ninety feet, and an island had been made. The place seemed to be a veritable sportsman's paradise! Dearly would Isaac Walton have loved to dwell here! From the windows of the old house he would have loved to listen to the splash of the trout, the cawing of the rooks, and the quack of the waterfowl, while all the air is filled with the cooing of doves and the songs of birds. At night he could have heard the murmuring waterfall amid a stillness only broken at intervals by the scream of the owl, the clatter of the goatsucker, or the weird barking of the foxes: for not two hundred yards from the house and practically in the garden, is a fox earth that has never been without a litter of, cubs for forty years!

In an ivy-covered house in the stable-yard I saw a very large number of foxes' noses nailed to boards of wood—as Sir Roger de Coverley used to nail them. They appeared to have been slain by one Dick Turpin, huntsman to the Vale of White Horse hounds, some thirty or forty years ago, when a quondam master of those hounds lived in this old place.

What a charm there is in an old-fashioned English garden! The great tall hollyhocks and phlox, the bright orange marigolds and large purple poppies. The beds and borders crammed with cloves and many-coloured asters, the sweet blue of the cornflower, and the little lobelias. Zinneas, too, of all colours; dahlias, tall stalks of anenome japonica, and such tangled masses of stocks! As I walked down by the old garden wall, whereon lots of roses hung their dainty heads, I thought I had never seen grass so green and fresh looking, except in certain parts of Ireland.

But the wild flowers by the silent river pleased me best of all. Such a medley of graceful, fragrant meadow-sweet, and tall, rough-leaved willow-herbs with their lovely pink flowers. Light blue scorpion-grasses and forget-me-nots were there too, not only among the sword-flags and the tall fescue-grasses by the bank, but little islands of them dotted about a over the brook. Thyme-scented water-mint, with lilac-tinted spikes and downy stalks, was almost lost amongst the taller wild flowers and the "segs" that fringed the brook-side.

There are no flowers like the wild ones; they last right through the summer and autumn—yet we can never have enough of them, never cease wondering at their marvellous delicacy and beauty.

Darting straight up stream on the wings of the soft south wind comes a kingfisher clothed in priceless jewelry, sparkling in the sun: sapphire and amethyst on his bright blue back, rubies on his ruddy breast, and diamonds round his princely neck. Monarch he is of silvery stream, and petty tyrant of the silvery fish.

I was told by a labourer that the trout ran from a quarter of a pound to three pounds, and that they average one pound in weight; that in the "may-fly" season a score of fish are often taken in the day by one rod, and that the method of taking them is by the artificial fly, well dried and deftly floated over feeding fish. These Cotswold streams are fed at intervals of about half a mile by the most beautiful springs, and from the rock comes pouring forth an everlasting supply of the purest and clearest of water. I was shown such a spring in a withybed hard by the old manor house. I saw nothing at first but a still, transparent pool, nine feet deep (they told me); it looked but three! But as I gaze at the beautiful fernlike weeds at the bottom, they are seen to be gently fanned by the water that rises—never failing even in the hottest and driest of summers—from the invisible rock below. The whole scene—the silent pool at my feet, the rich, well-timbered valley, with its marked contrast to the cold hills that overlook it—reminded me forcibly of Whyte-Melville's lines at the conclusion of the most impressive poem he ever wrote: "The Fairies' Spring":

> "And sweet to the thirsting lips of men
>   Is the spring of tears in the fairies' glen."

Out of this fairy spring was taken quite recently, but not with the "dry" fly—for no fish could be deceived in water of such stainless transparency—a trout that weighed three pounds and a half. He was far and away the most beautiful trout we ever saw; as silvery as a salmon that has just left the sea, he was a worthy denizen of the secluded depths of that crystal spring, still welling up from the pure limestone rock in the heart of the Cotswold Hills, as it has for a thousand years.

I was told that the place was still owned by the descendants of the pious John Coxwell who built the manor house and commemorated it by the quaint inscription over the porch in 1590. Doubtless the architecture of all our Elizabethan manor houses in the shape of a letter E owes its origin to the first letter in the name of that great queen.

That year was a fitting time for the building of "those haunts of ancient peace" that have ever since beautified the villages of rural England. Not two years before men's minds had been stirred to a pitch of deep religious enthusiasm by what was then regarded throughout all England as a divine miracle—the destruction of the Spanish Armada. Scarce three years had passed since the war with Scotland had terminated in the execution of the ill-fated Mary Queen of Scots. It is difficult for us, at the close of this nineteenth century, to realise the feelings of our ancestors in those times of daily terror and anxiety. And when men were daily executed, and human life was held as cheap as we now value a sheep or an ox, no wonder John Coxwell was pious, and no wonder he engraved that pious inscription over those crumbling walls.

In the year 1590 there was a lull in those tempestuous times, and men were able to turn for a while from the strife of battle and the daily fear of death and cultivate the arts of peace.

Thus this stately little manor house was reared, and many like it throughout the kingdom; and there it still stands, and will stand long after the modern building has fallen to the ground. For not without much hard toil and sweat of brow did our forefathers erect these monuments of "a day that is dead"; and they remain to testify to the solid masonry and laborious workmanship of ancient times.

The descendants of this John Coxwell live on another property of theirs some twelve miles away; it is nearly seventy years since they have inhabited this old house. I was pleased to find, however, that the present occupiers look after the labouring classes; that what rabbits are killed on the manor are not sold, but distributed in the village. There is an old ivy-clad building in the grounds, only a few paces from the manor house. This is the village club. Here squire, farmer, and labourer are accustomed to meet on equal terms. I was somewhat surprised to see on the club table the *Times*, the *Pall Mall Gazette*, and other papers. These wonderful specimens of nineteenth-century literature contrast strangely with a place that in many respects has remained unchanged for centuries.

There are few labourers in England, even in these days, who have the opportunity—if they will take it—of reading the *Times'* report of every speech made in parliament. Perhaps, some day, will come forth from this hamlet

> "Some village Hampden, that with dauntless breast
> The little tyrant of his fields withstood";

one who from earliest youth has kept himself in touch with the politics of the day, and has fitted himself to sit in the House of Commons as the representative of his class. There are still a few "little tyrants" in the fields in all parts of England, but they are very much scarcer than was the case fifty years ago.

I was much pleased with a conversation I had with an old-fashioned labouring man who, though not past middle age, appeared to be incapacitated from work owing to a "game leg," and whom I found sitting under a walnut tree in the manor grounds hard by the brook. He informed me that there was bagatelle at the club for those who liked it, and all sorts of games, and smoking concerts: that it was a question who was the best bagatelle player in the club; but that it probably lay between the squire and his head gardener, though Tom, the carter, was likely to run them close! I was glad to find so much good feeling existing among all classes of this little community, and was not surprised to learn that this was a contented and happy village.

In this description of "a Cotswold village" we have been looking on the bright side of things, and there is, thank Heaven! many a place, *mutato nomine*, that would answer to it. Alas! that there should be another side to the picture, which we would fain leave untouched.

Gloucestershire, nay England, is full of old manor houses and fair, smiling villages; but in many parts of the country we see buildings falling out of repair and deserted mansions. Would that we knew the remedy for agricultural depression! But let us not despair.

> "The future hides in it
>   Gladness and sorrow;
>   We press still thorow,
> Nought that abides in it
>   Daunting us,—onward!"

It is a sad thing when the "big house" of the village is empty. The labourers who never see their squire begin to look upon him as a sort of ogre, who exists merely to screw rents out of the land they till. Those who are dependent on land alone are often the men who do their duty best on their estates, and, poor though they may be, they are much beloved. But it is to be feared that in some parts of England men who are not suffering from the depression—rich tenants of country houses and the like—are apt to take a somewhat limited view of their duty towards their poorer neighbours. To be sure, the good ladies at the "great house" are invariably "ministering angels" to the poor in time of sickness, but even in these democratic days there is too great a gulf fixed between all classes. Let all those who are fortunate enough to live in such a place as we have attempted to describe remember that a kind word, a shake of the hand, the occasional distribution of game throughout the village, and a hundred other small kindnesses do more to win the heart of the labouring man than much talk at election times of Small Holdings, Parish Councils, or Free Education.

A tea given two or three times a year by the squire to the whole village, when the grounds are thrown open to them, does much to lighten the dulness of their existence and to cheer the monotonous round of daily toil. It is often thoughtlessness rather than poverty that prevents those who live in the large house of the village from being really loved by those around them. There are many instances of unpopular squires whose faces the cottagers never behold, and yet these men may be spending hundreds of pounds each year for the benefit of those whose affection they fail to gain.

Alas! that there should exist in so many country places that class feeling that is called Radicalism. It is perhaps fortunate that under the guise of politics what is really nothing else but bitterness and discontent is hidden and prevented from being recognised by its true name.

There are many country houses that are shut up for the greater part of the year for other reasons than agricultural depression, often because the owner, while preferring to reside elsewhere, is too proud to let the place to a stranger. This should not be. Let these rich men who own large houses and great estates live *in* those houses and *on* those estates, or endeavour to find a tenant. We repeat that the landowners who really feel the stress of bad times for the most part do their duty nobly. They have learnt it in the severe school of adversity. It is the richer class that we should like to see taking a greater interest in their humble neighbours; and their power is great. The possessor of wealth is too often the tacit upholder of the doctrine of *laissez faire*. The times we live in will no longer allow it. Let us be up and doing. In many small ways we may do much to promote good fellowship, and bitterness and discontent shall be no longer known in the rural villages of England.

"IN THE GARDEN."

19

II.

In the dead of winter these old grey houses of the Cotswolds are a little melancholy, save when the sun shines. But to every variety of scenery winter is the least becoming season of the year, though the hoar frost or a touch of snow will transform a whole village into fairyland at a moment's notice. Then the trout stream, which at other seasons of the year is a never failing attraction, running as it does for the most part through the woods, in mid winter seldom reflects the light of the sun, and looks cold and uninviting. One may learn much, it is true, of the wonders of nature in the dead time of the year by watching the great trout on the spawn beds as they pile up the gravel day by day, and store up beautiful, transparent ova, of which but a ten-thousandth part will live to replenish the stock for future years. But the delight of a clear stream is found in the spring and summer; then those cool, shaded deeps and sparkling eddies please us by their contrast to the hot, burning sun; and we love, even if we are not fishermen, to linger by the bank 'neath the shade of ash and beech and alder, and watch the wonderful life around us in the water and in the air.

As you sit sometimes on a bench hard by the Coln, watching the crystal water as it pours down the artificial fall from the miniature lake in the wild garden above, you may make a minute calculation of the day and hour that that very water which is flowing past you now will reach London Bridge, two hundred miles below. Allowing one mile an hour as the average pace of the current, ten days is, roughly speaking, the time it will take on its journey. And when one reflects that every drop that passes has its work to do, in carrying down to the sea lime and I know not how many other ingredients, and in depositing that lime and all that it picked up on its way at the bottom of the ocean, to help perhaps in forming the great rolling downs of a new continent—after this island of ours has ceased to be—one cannot but realise that in all seasons of the year a trout stream is a wonderfully interesting and instructive thing.

TO THE COLN.

Flow on, clear, fresh trout stream, emblem of purity and perfect truth; thou hast accomplished a mighty work, thou hast a mighty work to do. Who can count the millions of tons of lime that thou hast borne down to the sea in far-off Kent? Thou hast indeed "strength to remove mountains," for day by day the soil that thou hast taken from these limestone hills is being piled up at the mouth of the great historic river, and some day perchance it shall become rolling downs again. Fed by clear springs, thou shalt gradually steal thy way along the Cotswold valleys, draining foul marshes, irrigating the sweet meadows. Thou shalt turn the wheels and grind many a hundred sacks of corn ere to-morrow's sun is set. And then thou shalt change thy name. No longer silvery Coln, but mighty Thames, shalt thou be called; and many a fair scene shall gladden thy sight as thou slowly passest along towards thy goal.

Smiling meadows and Gloucestershire vales will soon give place to fair Berkshire villages, and, further on, to those glorious spires and courts of Oxford; and here shalt thou make many friends—friends who will evermore think kindly of thee, ever associate thy placid waters with all that they loved best and held dearest during their brief sojourning in those old walls which tower above thy banks. A few short miles, and thou shalt pass a quiet and sacred spot—sacred to me, and dear above all other spots; for close to that little village church of Clifton Hampden, and close to thee, we laid some years ago the mortal body of a noble man. And when thou stealest gently by, and night mists rise from off thy glassy face, be sure and drop a tear in silvery dew upon the moss-grown stone I know so well. And then pass on to Eton, fairest spot on earth. Mark well the playing-fields, the glorious trees, and Windsor towering high. Here shalt thou be loved by many a generous heart, and youth and hope and smiling faces greet thee, as they long since greeted me. Ah well! those friendships never could have been made so firm and lasting mid any other scenes save under thy wide-spreading elms, beloved Eton.

But onwards, onwards thou must glide, from scenes of tranquil beauty such as these. The flag which sails o'er Windsor's stately towers must soon be lost to sight. Thy course once more through silent fields is laid; but not for long; for, Hampton Court's fair palace passed, already canst thou hear the wondrous roar of unceasing footsteps in the busy haunts of men.

Courage! thy goal is nearly reached: already thou art great, and greater still shalt thou become. Thy once transparent waters shall be merged with salt. Thus shalt thou be given strength to bear great ships upon thy bosom, and thine eyes shall behold the greatest city of the whole wide world. Nay, more; thou shalt become the most indispensable part of that city—its very life-blood, of a value not to be measured by gold. Thou makest England what it is.

Flow on, historic waters, symbolic of all that is good, all that is great—flow on, and do thy glorious work until this world shall cease; bearing thy mighty burden down towards the sea, showing mankind what can be wrought from small beginnings by slow and patient labour day by day.

Even in winter I do not know any scene more pleasing to the eye than the sight of a Cotswold hamlet nestling amid the stately trees in the valley, if you happen to see it on a fine day. And if there has been a period of rainy, sunless weather for a month past, you are probably all the more ready to appreciate the changed appearance which everything wears. If that peaceful, bright aspect had been habitual, you would never have noticed anything remarkable to-day. It is this very changeful nature of our English climate which gives it more than half its charm.

But the great attraction of this country lies in its being one of the few spots now remaining on earth which have not only been made beautiful by God, but in which the hand of man has erected scarcely a building which is not in strict conformity and good taste. One cannot walk through these Cotswold hamlets without noticing that the architecture of the country in past ages, as well as in the present day to a certain degree, shows obedience to some of those divine laws which Ruskin has told us ought to govern all the works of man's hand.

"The spirit of sacrifice," "the lamp of truth" are manifest in the ancient churches and manor houses, as well as in the humble farmhouses, cottages, and even the tithe barns of this district. Two thirds of the buildings are old, and, as Ruskin has beautifully expressed it: "The greatest glory of a building is not in its stones, nor in its gold. Its glory is in its age, and in that deep sense of voicefulness, of stern watching, of mysterious sympathy, nay, even of approval or condemnation, which we feel in walls that have long been washed by the passing waves of humanity. It is in their lasting witness against men, in their quiet contrast with the transitional character of all things, in the strength which, through the lapse of seasons and times, and the decline and birth of dynasties, and the changing of the face of the earth, and of the limits of the sea, maintains its sculptured shapeliness for a time insuperable, connects forgotten and following ages with each other, and half constitutes the identity, as it concentrates the sympathy, of nations;—it is in that golden stain of time that we are to look for the real light and colour and preciousness of architecture; and it is not until a building has assumed this character, till it has been entrusted with the fame and hallowed by the deeds of men, till its walls have been witnesses of suffering and its pillars rise out of the shadow of death, that its existence, more lasting as it is than that of the natural objects of the world around it, can be gifted with even so much as these possess of language and of life."

If we would seek a lesson in sacrifice from the men who lived and laboured here in the remote past, we can learn many a one from those deep walls of native stone, and that laborious workmanship which was the chief characteristic of the toil of our simple ancestors. "All old work, nearly, has been hard work; it may be the hard work of children, of barbarians, of rustics, but it is always their utmost." They may have been ignorant of the sanitary laws which govern health, and ill advised in some of the sites they chose, but they grudged neither hand labour nor sweat of brow; they spent the best years of their lives in the erection of the temples where we still worship and the manor houses we still inhabit.

"A COTSWOLD MANOR HOUSE."

It is not claimed that there is much *ornamental* architecture to be found in these Cotswold buildings; it is something in these days if we can boast that there is nothing to offend the eye in a district which is less than a hundred miles from London. There is no other district of equal extent within the same radius of which as much could be said.

"Jam pauca aratro jugera regiae
Moles relinquent."

But here all the houses are picturesque, great and small alike. And there are here and there pieces of work which testify to the piety and faith of very early days: fragments of inscriptions chiselled out more than fifteen hundred years ago—such as the four stones at Chedworth, discovered some thirty years ago, together with many other interesting relics of the Roman occupation, by a gamekeeper in search of a ferret. On these stones were found the Greek letters [GREEK: Ch] and [GREEK: r], forming the sacred monogram "C.H.R." Fifteen hundred years had not obliterated this simple evidence of ancient faith, nor had the devastation of the ages

24

impaired the beauty of design, nor marred the harmony of colouring of those delicate pavements and tesserae with which these wonderful people loved to adorn their habitations. Since this strange discovery the diligent research of one man has rescued from oblivion, and the liberality of another now protects from further injury, one of the best specimens of a Roman country house to be found in England. Far away from the haunts of men, in the depths of the Chedworth woods, where no sound save the ripple of the Coln and the song of birds is heard, rude buildings and a museum have been erected; here these ancient relics are sheltered from wind and storm for the sake of those who lived and laboured in the remote past, and for the benefit and instruction of him, be he casual passer-by or pilgrim from afar, who cares to inspect them.

The ancient Roman town of Cirencester, too, affords many historical remains of the same era. But it is to the part which English hands and hearts have played towards beautifying the Cotswold district that I would fain direct attention; to the stately Abbey Church of Cirencester and its glorious south porch, with its rich fan-tracery groining within and its pierced battlements and pinnacles without; to the arched gateway of twelfth century work, the sole remnant of that once famous monastery—the mitred Abbey of St. Mary— founded by the piety of the first Henry, and overthrown by the barbarity of the last king of that name, who ordained "that all the edifices within the site and precincts of the monastery should be pulled down and carried away";—it is to the glorious windows of Fairford Church—the most beautiful specimens remaining to us of glass of the early part of the sixteenth century—and to many an ancient church and mediaeval manor house still standing throughout this wide district, "to point a moral of adorn a tale," that we must look for traces of the exquisite workmanship of English hands in bygone days, "the only witnesses, perhaps, that remain to us of the faith and fear of nations. All else for which the builders sacrificed has passed away—all their living interests and aims and achievements. We know not for what they laboured, and we see no evidence of their reward. Victory, wealth, authority, happiness—all have departed, though bought by many a bitter sacrifice. But of them, and their life, and their toil upon earth, one reward, one evidence is left to us in those grey heaps of deep-wrought stone.

They have taken with them to the grave their powers, their honours, and their errors; but they have left us their adoration." [2]

[2] Ruskin, "Seven Lamps of Architecture."

Too many of our modern buildings are a sham from beginning to end—sham marble, sham stonework, sham wallpapers, sham wainscoting, sham carpets on the ground, and sham people walking about on them: even the very bookcases are sham. In these old Cotswold houses we have the reverse. The stonework is real, and the material is the best of its kind—good, honest, native stone. The oak wainscoting is real, though patched with deal and painted white in recent times. The same pains in the carving are apparent in those parts of the house which are never seen except by the servants, as in the important rooms. And so it is with all the work of three, four, and five hundred years ago. The builders may have had their faults, their prejudices, and their ignorances,—their very simplicity may have been the means of saving them from error,—but they were at all events truthful and genuine.

In many villages throughout the Cotswolds are to be seen ancient wayside crosses of exquisite workmanship and design. These were for the most part erected in the fourteenth century. One of the best specimens of the kind stands in the market-place of old Malmesbury, hard by the ancient monastery there. The date of this cross is A.D. 1480. Leland remarks upon it as follows: "There is a right faire and costely peace of worke for poor market folks to stand dry when rayne cummeth; the men of the towne made this peace of worke in *hominum memoriâ.*" Malmesbury, by the bye, is just outside the Cotswold district.

At Calmsden—a tiny isolated hamlet near North Cerney—is a grey and weather-beaten wayside cross of beautiful Gothic workmanship, erected (men say) by the Knights Templar of Quenington; and there are ancient crosses or remnants of them at Cirencester, Eastleach, Harnhill, Rendcombe, Stow-on-the-Wold, and many other places in the district. But few of these old village crosses still stand intact in their pristine beauty. May they never suffer the terrible fate of a very beautiful one which was erected in the fourteenth century at Bristol! Pope, writing a century and a half ago, describes it as "a very fine old cross of Gothic curious work, but spoiled with the folly of *new gilding it*, that takes away all the venerable antiquity."

Happily there is no likelihood of the ancient crosses in the Cotswolds being decorated by a coating of gold. The precious metal is all too scarce there, even if the good taste of the country folk did not prohibit it.

I have spoken before of the ancient barns. Every hamlet has one or more of these grand old edifices, and there are often as many as three or four in a small village. In some of these large barns the tithe was gathered together in kind, until rather more than sixty years ago it was converted into a rent charge.

Tithe was made on all kinds of farm produce. The vicar's man went into the cornfields and placed a bough in every tenth "stook"; then the titheman came with the parson's horses and took the stuff away to the barn. The tithe for every cock in the farmyard was three eggs; for every hen, two eggs. Besides poultry, geese, pigs, and sheep, the parson had a right to his share of the milk, and even of the cheeses that were made in his parish.

In an ancient manuscript which the vicar of Bibury lately acquired, and which contains the history of his parish since the Conquest, are set down some interesting and amusing details concerning tithe and the cash compensations that had been paid time out of mind. The entries form part of a diary kept by a former incumbent, and were made nearly two hundred years ago.

"For every new Milch Cow three pence.

"For every thorough Milch Cow one penny.

"N.B. Nothing is paid for a dry cow, and therefore tithe in kind must be paid for all fatting cattle.

"For every calf weaned a half penny.

"For every calf sold four pence or *the left shoulder*.

"For every calf killed in the family four pence or *the left shoulder*.

"I have heard that one or two left shoulders of veal were paid to the widow Hignall at Arlington when she rented the tithes of Dr. Vannam, but *I have received none.*"

Then follows an annual account of the value of the tithes of the parish (about five thousand acres), from 1763 to 1802, by which it appears that the year 1800 was the best during these four decades. Here is the entry: —

"1800 The crops of this year were very deficient, but corn of all sort sold at an extraordinary high price. I made of my tithes and living this year clear £1,200; from the dearness of labourers the outgoing expenses amounted to £900 in addition."

The worst year seems to have been 1766, when the parson only got £360 clear of all expenses; but even this was not bad for those days.

The architecture of the Cotswold barns is often very beautiful. The pointed windows, massive buttresses, and elaborate pinnacles are sufficient indications of their great age and the care bestowed on the building. Some of the interiors of these Gothic structures have fine old oak roofs.

The cottages, too, though in a few instances sadly deficient in sanitary improvements and internal comfort, are not only picturesque, but strong and lasting. Many of them bear dates varying from 1600 to 1700.

It is evident that in everything they did our ancestors who lived in the Elizabethan age fully realised that they were working under the eye of "a great taskmaster." This spirit was the making of the great men of that day, and in great part laid the foundation of our national greatness. The glorious churches of Cirencester, Northleach, Burford, and Bibury, and the ancient manor houses scattered throughout the Cotswolds are fitting monuments to the men who laboured to erect them. Would that space allowed a detailed account of all these old manor houses! Enough has been said, at all events, to show that there are places little known and little cared for in England where you may still dwell without, every time you go out of doors, being forcibly reminded of the utilitarian spirit of the age.

CHAPTER III.

VILLAGE CHARACTERS.

"If there's a hole in a' your coats,
  I rede ye tent it;
A chiel's amang ye takin' notes,
  And, faith, he'll prent it."
R. BURNS.

Every village seems to possess its share of quaint, curious people; but I cannot help thinking that our little hamlet has a more varied assortment of oddities than is usually to be met with in so small a place.

First of all there is the man whom nobody ever sees. Although he has lived in robust health for the past twenty years in the very centre of the hamlet, his face is unknown to half the inhabitants. Twice only has the writer set eyes on him. When a political contest is proceeding, he becomes comparatively bold; at such times he has even been met with in the bar of the village "public," where he has been known to sit discussing the chances of the candidates like any ordinary being. But an election is absolutely necessary if this strange individual is to be drawn out of his hiding-place. The only other occasion on which we have set eyes on him was on a lovely summer's evening, just after sunset: we observed him peeping at us over a hedge, for all the world like the "Spectator" when he was staying with Sir Roger de Coverley. He is supposed to come out at sunset, like the foxes and the bats, and has been seen in the distance on bright moonlight nights striding over the Cotswold uplands. If any one approach him, he hurries away in the opposite direction; yet he is not queer in the head, but strong and in the prime of life.

Then there is that very common character "the village impostor." After having been turned away by half a dozen different farmers, because he never did a stroke of work, he manages to get on the sick-list at the "great house." Long after his ailment has been cured he

29

will be seen daily going up to the manor house for his allowance of meat; somehow or other he "can't get a job nohow." The fact is, he has got the name of being an idle scoundrel, and no farmer will take him on. It is some time before you are able to find him out; for as he goes decidedly lame as he passes you in the village street, he generally manages to persuade you that he is very ill. Like a fool, you take compassion on him, and give him an ounce of "baccy" and half a crown. For some months he hangs about where he thinks you will be passing, craving a pipe of tobacco; until one day, when you are having a talk with some other honest toiler, he will give you a hint that you are being imposed on.

When a loafer of this sort finds that he can get nothing more out of you, he moves his family and goods to some other part of the country; he then begins the old game with somebody else, borrowing a sovereign off you for the expense of moving. As for gratitude, he never thinks of it. The other day a man with a "game leg," who was, in spite of his lameness, a good example of "the village impostor," in taking his departure from our hamlet, gave out "that there was no thanks due to the big 'ouse for the benefits he had received, for it was writ in the *manor parchments* as how he was to have meat three times a week and blankets at Christmas as long as he was out of work."

It is so difficult to discriminate between the good and the bad amongst the poor, and it is impossible not to feel pity for a man who has nothing but the workhouse to look forward to, even if he has come down in the world through his own folly. To those who are living in luxury the conditions under which the poorer classes earn their daily bread, and the wretched prospect which old age or ill health presents to them, must ever offer scope for deep reflection and compassion.

At the same time it must be remembered that in spite of "hard times" and "low prices," as affecting the farmers, the agricultural labourer is better off to-day than he has ever been in past times. Food is very much cheaper and wages are higher. The farmers seem to be more liberal in bad times than in good. It is the same in all kinds of business. Except injustice there is no more hardening influence in the affairs of life than success. It seems often to dry up the milk of human kindness in the breast, and make us selfish and grasping.

"A FARMHOUSE BY THE COLN."

In the good times of farming there was doubtless much cause for discontent amongst the Cotswold labourers. The profits derived from farming were then quite large. The tendency of the age, however, was to treat the labouring man as a mere machine, instead of his being allowed to share in the general prosperity. ("Hinc illae lacrymae.") Now things are changed. Long-suffering farmers are in many cases paying wages out of their fast diminishing capital. Many of them would rather lose money than cut down the wages.

Then again agricultural labourers who are unable to find work go off to the coal mines and big towns; some go into the army; others emigrate. So that the distress is not so apparent in this district as the badness of the times would lead one to expect.

The Cotswold women obtain employment in the fields at certain seasons of the year; though poorly paid, they are usually more conscientious and hard-working than the men.

Most of the cottages are kept scrupulously clean; they have an air of homely comfort which calls forth the admiration of all strangers. The children, too, when they go to church on Sundays, are dressed with a neatness and good taste that are simply astonishing when one recalls the income of a labourer on the Cotswolds—seldom, alas! averaging more than fourteen shillings a week. A boy of twelve years of age is able to keep himself, earning about five shillings per week. Cheerful and manly little chaps they are. To watch a boy of fourteen years managing a couple of great strong cart-horses, either at the plough or with the waggons, is a sight to gladden the heart of man.

It is unfortunate that there are not more orchards attached to the gardens on the Cotswolds. The reader will doubtless remember Dr. Johnson's advice to his friends, always to have a good orchard attached to their houses. "For," said he, "I once knew a clergyman of small income who brought up a family very reputably, which he chiefly fed on *apple dumplings.*"

Talking of clergymen, I am reminded of some stories a neighbour of ours—an excellent fellow—lately told me about his parishioners on the Cotswolds. One old man being asked why he liked the vicar, made answer as follows: "Why, 'cos he be so *scratchy after souls.*" The same man lately said to the parson, "Sir, you be an hinstrument"; and being asked what he meant, he added, "An hinstrument of good in this place."

This old-fashioned Cotswold man was very fond of reciting long passages out of the Psalms: indeed, he knew half the Prayer-book by heart; and one day the hearer, being rather wearied, exclaimed, "I must go now, for it's my dinner-time." To whom replied the old man, "Oh! be off with thee, then; thee thinks more of thee belly than thee God."

An old bedridden woman was visited by the parson, and the following dialogue took place:—

"Well, Annie, how are you to-day?"

"O sir, I be so bad! My inside be that comical I don't know what to do with he; he be all on the ebb and flow."

The same clergyman knew an old Cotswold labourer who wished to get rid of the evil influence of the devil. So Hodge wrote a polite, though firm, epistle, telling his Satanic Majesty he would have no more to do with him. On being asked where he posted his letter, he replied: "A' dug a hole i' the ground, and popped un in there. He got it right enough, for he's left me alone from that day to this."

The Cotswold people are, like their country, healthy, bright, clean, and old-fashioned; and the more educated and refined a man may happen to be, the more in touch he will be with them—not because the peasants are educated and refined, so much as because they are not *half*-educated and *half*-refined, but simple, honest, god-fearing folk, who mind their own business and have not sought out many inventions. I am referring now to the labourers, because the farmers are a totally different class of men. The latter are on the whole an excellent type of what John Bull ought to be. The labouring class, however, still maintain the old characteristics. A primitive people, as often as not they are "nature's gentlemen."

In the simple matter of dress there is a striking resemblance between the garb of these country people and that of the highly educated and refined. It is an acknowledged principle, or rather, I should say, an unwritten law, in these days—at all events as far as men are concerned—that to be well dressed all that is required of us is *not to be badly dressed*. Simplicity is a *sine quâ non*; and we are further required to abstain from showing bad taste in the choice of shades and colours, and to wear nothing that does not serve a purpose. To simple country folk all these things come by nature. They never trouble their heads about what clothes they shall wear. The result is, the eye is seldom offended in old-fashioned country places by the latest inventions of tailors and hatters and the ridiculous changes of fashion in which the greater part of the civilised world is wont to delight. Here are to be seen no hideous "checks," but plain, honest clothes of corduroy or rough cloth in natural colours; no absurd little curly "billycocks," but good, strong broad-brimmed hats of black beaver in winter to keep off the rain, and of white straw in summer to keep off the heat. No white satin ties, which always look dirty, such as one sees in London and other great towns, but broad, old-fashioned scarves of many colours or of blue "birdseye" mellowed by age. The fact is that simplicity—the very essence of good taste—is apparent only in the garments of the *best*-dressed and the *poorest*-dressed people in England. This is one more proof of the truth of the old saying, "Simplicity is nature's first step, and the last of art."

The greatest character we ever possessed in the village was undoubtedly Tom Peregrine, the keeper.

> "A man, take him for all in all,
> I shall not look upon his like again."

The eldest son of the principal tenant on the manor, and belonging to a family of yeoman farmers who had been settled in the place for a hundred years, he suddenly found that "he could not a-bear farming," and took up his residence as "an independent gentleman" in a comfortable cottage at the gate of the manor house. Then he started a "sack" business—a trade which is often adopted in these parts by those who are in want of a better. The business consists in buying up odds and ends of sacks, and letting them out on hire at a handsome profit. He was always intensely fond of shooting and fishing; indeed, the following description which Sir Roger de Coverley gave the "Spectator" of a "plain country fellow who rid before them," when they were on their way to the assizes, suits him exactly. "He is a yeoman of about an hundred pounds a year; and knocks down a dinner with his gun twice or thrice a week. He would be a good neighbour if he did not destroy so many partridges: in short, he is a very sensible man, shoots flying, and has been several times foreman of the petty jury."

Perhaps with regard to the "shoots flying" the reservation should be added, that should he have seen a covey of partridges "bathering" in a ploughed field within convenient distance of a stone wall or thick fence, he might not have been averse to knocking over a brace for supper on the ground. And we had almost forgotten to explain that it was for the manor-house table that he used to knock down a dinner with his gun twice or thrice a week, and not his own—for, some years ago, he persuaded the squire to take him into his service as gamekeeper. When we came to take up our abode at the manor, we found that he was a sort of standing dish on the place. Such a keen sportsman, it was explained, was better in our service than kicking his heels about the village and on his father's farm as an independent gentleman. And so this is how Tom Peregrine came into our service. For my part I liked the man; he was so delightfully mysterious. And the place would never have been the same without him; for he became part and parcel with the trees and the fields and every living thing. Nor would the woods and the path by the brook and the breezy wolds ever have been quite the same if his quaint figure had no longer appeared suddenly there. Many a time was I startled by the sudden apparition of Tom Peregrine when out shooting on the hill; he seemed to spring up from the ground like "Herne the Hunter" —

> "Shaggy and lean and shrewd. With pointed ears
> And tail cropped short, half lurcher and half cur,
> His dog attends him."

The above lines of Cowper's exactly, describe the keeper's Irish terrier; the dog was almost as deep and mysterious as the man himself. When in the woods, Tom's attitude and gait would at times resemble the movements of a cock pheasant: now stealing along for a few yards, listening for the slightest sound of any animal stirring in the underwood; now standing on tiptoe for a time, with bated breath. Did a blackbird — that dusky sentinel of the woods — utter her characteristic note of warning, he would whisper, "Hark!" Then, after due deliberation, he would add, "'Tis a fox!" or, "There's a fox in the grove," and then he would steal gently up to try to get a glimpse of reynard. He never looked more natural than when carrying seven or eight brace of partridges, four or five hares, and a lease of pheasants; it was a labour of love to him to carry such a load back to the village after a day's shooting. In his pockets alone he could stow away more game than most men can conveniently carry on their backs.

He was the best hand at catching trout the country could produce. With a rod and line he could pull them out on days when nobody else could get a "rise." He could not understand dry-fly fishing, always using the old-fashioned sunk fly. "Muddling work," he used to call the floating method of fly fishing.

But Tom Peregrine was cleverer with the landing-net than with the rod. Any trout he could reach with the net was promptly pulled out, if we particularly wanted a fish. Then he would talk all day about any subject under the sun: politics, art, Roman antiquities, literature, and every form of sport were discussed with equal facility.

One day, when I was engaged in a slight controversy with his own father, the keeper said to me: "I shouldn't take any notice whatever of him"; then he added, with a sigh, "These Gloucestershire folk are comical people."

"Ah! 'tis a wise son that knows his own father in Gloucestershire, isn't it, Peregrine?" said I, putting the Shakespearian cart before the horse.

"Yes, it be, to be sure, to be sure," was the reply. "I can't make 'em out nohow; they're funny folk in Gloucestershire."

He gave me the following account of the "chopping" of one of our foxes: "I knew there was a fox in the grove; and there, sure enough, he was. But when he went toward the 'bruk,' the hounds come along and *give him the meeting*; and then they bowled him over. It were a very comical job; I never see such a job in all my life. I knew it would be a case," he added, with a chuckle.

The fact is, with that deadly aversion to all the vulpine race common to all keepers, he dearly loved to see a fox killed, no matter how or where; but to see one "chopped," without any of that "muddling round and messing about," as he delighted to call a hunting run, seemed to him the very acme of satisfaction and despatch.

And here it may be said that Tom Peregrine's name did not bely him. Not only were the keen brown eye and the handsome aquiline beak marked characteristics of his classic features, but in temperament and habit he bore a singular resemblance to the king of all the falcons. Who more delighted in striking down the partridge or the wild duck? What more assiduous destroyer of ground game and vermin ever existed than Tom Peregrine? There never was a man so happily named and so eminently fitted to fulfil the destinies of a gamekeeper.

Who loves to trap the wily stoat?
Who loves the plover's piping note?
Who loves to wring the weasel's throat?
   Tom Peregrine.

What time the wintry woods we walk,
No need have we of lure or hawk;
Have we not Tom to *tower* and talk?
   Tom Peregrine?

When to the withybed we spy,
A hungry hern or mallard fly,
"Bedad! we'll bag un by and by,"
   Tom Peregrine.

"Creep *up wind*, sir, without a sound,
And bide thy time neath yonder 'mound,'
Then knock un over on the ground,"
   Tom Peregrine.

And so one might go on *ad infinitum*.

A more amusing companion or keener fisherman never stepped. He had all sorts of quaint Gloucestershire expressions, which rolled out one after the other during a day's fishing or shooting. Then he was very fond of reading amusing pieces at village entertainments, often copying the broad Gloucestershire dialect; apparently he was not aware that his own brogue smacked somewhat of Gloucestershire too. At home in his own house he was most friendly and hospitable. If he could get you to "step in," he would offer you gooseberry, ginger, cowslip, and currant wine, sloe gin, as well as the juice of the elder, the blackberry, the grape, and countless other home-brewed vintages, which the good dames of Gloucestershire pride themselves on preparing with such skill. Very excellent some of these home-made drinks are.

The British farmer is remarkably fond of a lord. If you wanted to put him into a good temper for a month, the best plan would be to ask a lord to shoot over his land, and tell him privately to make a great point of shaking the honest yeoman by the hand, and all that kind of thing. By the bye, I was once told by a coachman that he was sure the Bicester hounds were a first-rate pack, for he had seen in the papers that no less than four lords hunted with them. There is little harm in this extraordinarily widespread admiration for titles; it is common to all nations. We can all love a lord, provided that he be a gentleman. The gentlemen of England, whether titled or untitled, are in thought and feeling a very high type of the human race. But the man I like best to meet is he who either by natural insight or by the trained habit of his mind is able to look upon all mortals with eyes unprejudiced by outward show and circumstance, judging them by character alone. Such a man may not be understood or be awarded the credit due to him as "lord of the lion heart" and despiser of sycophants and cringers. The habit of mind, nevertheless, is worth cultivating; it will be so very useful some day, when mortal garments have been put off and the vast inequalities of destiny adjusted, and we all stand unclothed before the Judge.

Tom Peregrine was not a "great frequenter of the church"; indeed, both father and son often remarked to me that "'Twas a pity there was not a chapel of ease put up in the hamlet, the village church being a full mile away." However, when Tom was ailing from any cause or other he immediately sent for the parson, and told him that he intended in future to go to church regularly every Sunday. Shakespeare would have enquired if he was troubled "about some act that had no relish of salvation in't." "Thomas, he's a terrible coward [I here quote Mrs. Peregrine]. He can't a-bear to have anything a-wrong with him; yet he don't mind killing any animal." He made a tremendous fuss about a sore finger he had at one time; and when the doctor exclaimed, like Romeo, "Courage, man; the hurt cannot be much," Tom Peregrine replied, with much the same humour as poor Mercutio: "No, 'tis not so deep as a well, nor so wide as a church door; but 'tis enough." I do not mean to infer that he quoted Shakespeare, but he used words to the same effect. If asked whether he had read Shakespeare, he might possibly have given the same reply as the young woman in *High Life Below Stairs*:

"KITTY: Shikspur? Shikspur? Who wrote it? No, I never read Shikspur.

"LADY B.: Then you have an immense pleasure to come."

Let it be said, however, that in many respects Tom was an exceedingly well-informed and clever man. The family of Peregrines were noted, like Sir Roger de Coverley, for their great friendliness to foxes; and to their credit let it be said that they have preserved them religiously for very many years. I scarcely ever heard a word of complaint from them. All honour to those who neither hunt nor care for hunting, yet who put up with a large amount of damage to crops and fences, as well as loss of poultry and ground game, and yet preserve the foxes for a sport in which they do not themselves take part.

When conversing with me on the subject of preserving foxes, old Mr. Peregrine would wax quite enthusiastic "You should put a barley rick in the Conygers, and thatch it, and there would always be a fox." he would remark. All this I hold to be distinctly creditable. For what is there to prevent a farmer from pursuing a selfish policy and warning the whole hunt off his land?

The village parson is quite a character. You do not often see the like nowadays. An excellent man in every way, and having his duty at heart, he is one of the few Tories of the old school that are left to us. Ruling his parish with a rod of iron, he is loved and respected by most of his flock. In the Parish Council, at the Board of Guardians, his word is law. He seldom goes away from the village save for his annual holiday, yet he knows all that is going on in the great metropolis, and will tell you the latest bit of gossip from Belgravia. He has a good property of his own in Somersetshire, but to his credit let it be said that his affections are entirely centred in the little Cotswold village, which he has ruled for a quarter of a century.

> "Full loth were him to curse for his tithes,
> But rather would be given out of doubt
> Unto his poore parishens about
> Of his off'ring, and eke of his substance.
> He could in little thing have suffisance.
> Wide was his parish and houses far asunder,
> But he ne left not for no rain nor thunder
> In sickness and in mischief to visit

> The farthest in his parish much and lit,
> Upon his feet, and in his hand a staff,
> This noble ensample to his sheep he gaf,
> That first he wrought and afterwards he taught."

CHAUCER.

Sermons are not so lengthy in our church as they were three hundred years ago. Rudder mentions that a parson of the name of Winnington used to preach here for two hours at a time, regularly turning the hour-glass; for in those days hour-glasses were placed near the pulpit, and the clergy used to vie with each other as to who could preach the longest. I do not know if Mr. Barrow was ever surpassed in this respect. History relates that he succeeded in emptying his church of the whole congregation, including the Lord Mayor and Aldermen of London—one man only (an apprentice) remaining to the bitter end. Misguided laymen used to amuse themselves in the same way. Fozbrooke mentions that one Will Hulcote, a zealous lay preacher after the Reformation, used to mount the pulpit in a velvet bonnet, a damask gown, and a gold chain. What an ass he must have looked! This reminds me that at the age of twenty-four I accepted the office of churchwarden of a certain country parish. I do not recommend any of my readers to become churchwardens. You become a sort of acting aide-de-camp to the parson, liable to be called out on duty at a moment's notice. No; a young man might with some advantage to others and credit to himself take upon himself the office of Parish Councillor, Poor Law Guardian, Inspector of Lunatic Asylums, High Sheriff, or even Public Hangman; but save, oh, save us from being churchwardens! To be obliged to attend those terrible institutions called "vestry meetings," and to receive each year an examination paper from the archdeacon of the diocese propounding such questions as, "Do you attend church regularly? If not, why not?" etc., etc., is the natural destiny of the churchwarden, and is more than human nature can stand: in short, my advice to those thinking of becoming churchwardens is, "Don't," with a very big *D*.

According to the "Diary of Master William Silence," in the olden times a pedlar would occasionally arrive at the church door during the sermon, and proceed to advertise his wares at the top of his voice. Whereupon the parson, speedily deserted by the female portion of his congregation and by not a few of the other sex, was obliged to bring his discourse to a somewhat inglorious conclusion.

We learn from the same work that the churchwardens were in the habit of disbursing large sums for the destruction of foxes. When a fox was marked to ground the church bell was rung as a signal, summoning every man who owned a pickaxe, a gun, or a terrier dog, to lend a hand in destroying him. We are talking of two or three hundred years ago, when the stag was the animal usually hunted by hounds on the Cotswolds and in other parts of England.

Our village is a favourite meet of the V.W.H. foxhounds. An amusing story is told of a former tenant of the court house—a London gentleman, who rented the place for a time. He is reported to have made a special request to the master of the hounds, that when the meet was held at "the Court," "his lordship" would make the fox pass in front of the drawing-room windows, "For," said he, "I have several friends coming from London to see the hunt."

In a hunting district such as this the owners and occupiers of the various country houses are usually enthusiastic devotees of the chase. The present holder of the "liberty" adjoining us is a fox-hunter of the old school. An excellent sportsman and a wonderful judge of a horse, he dines in pink the best part of the year, drives his four-in-hand with some skill, and wears the old-fashioned low-crowned beaver hat.

We have many other interesting characters in our village; human nature varies so delightfully that just as with faces so each individual character has something to distinguish it from the rest of the world. The old-fashioned autocratic farmer of the old school is there of course, and a rare good specimen he is of a race that has almost disappeared. Then we have the village lunatic, whose mania is "religious enthusiasm." If you go to call on him, he will ask you "if you are saved," and explain to you how his own salvation was brought about. Unfortunately one of his hobbies is to keep fowls and pigs in his house so that fleas are more or less numerous there, and your visits are consequently few and far between.

The village "quack," who professes to cure every complaint under the sun, either in mankind, horses, dogs, or anything else by means of herbs, buttonholes you sometimes in the village street. If once he starts talking, you know that you are "booked" for the day. He is rather a "bore," and is uncommonly fond of quoting the Scriptures in support of his theories. But there is something about the man one cannot help liking. His wonderful infallibility in curing disease is set down by himself to divine inspiration. Many a vision has he seen. Unfortunately his doctrines, though excellent in theory, are seldom successful in practice. An excellent prescription which I am informed completely cured a man of indigestion is one of his mixtures "last thing at night" and the first chapter of St. John carefully perused and digested on top.

I called on the old gentleman the other day, and persuaded him to give me a short lecture. The following is the gist of what he said: "First of all you must know that the elder is good for anything in the world, but especially for swellings. If you put some of the leaves on your face, they will cure toothache in five minutes. Then for the nerves there's nothing like the berries of ivy. Yarrow makes a splendid ointment; and be sure and remember Solomon's seal for bruises, and comfrey for 'hurts' and broken bones. Camomile cures indigestion, and ash-tree buds make a stout man thin. Soak some ash leaves in hot water, and you will have a drink that is better than any tea, and destroys the 'gravel.' Walnut-tree bark is a splendid emetic; and mountain flax, which grows everywhere on the Cotswolds, is uncommon good for the 'innards.' 'Ettles [nettles] is good for stings. Damp them and rub them on to a 'wapse' sting, and they will take away the pain directly." On my suggesting that stinging nettles were rather a desperate remedy, he assured me that "they acted as a blister, and counteracted the 'wapse.' Now, I'll tell you an uncommon good thing to preserve the teeth," he went on, "and that is to *brush* them once or twice a week. You buys a brush at the chymists, you know; they makes them specially for it. Oh, 'tis a capital good thing to cleanse the teeth occasionally!"

He wound up by telling me a story of a celebrated doctor who left a sealed book not to be opened till after his death, when it was to be sold at auction. It fetched six hundred pounds. The man who paid this sum was horrified on opening it to find it only contained the following excellent piece of advice: "Always remember to keep the feet warm and the head cool."

As I said good-bye, and thanked him for his lecture, he said: "Those doctors' chemicals destroy the 'innards.' And be sure and put down rue for the heart; and burdock, 'tis splendid for the liver."

Nor must mention be omitted of old Isaac Sly, a half-witted labouring fellow with a squint in one eye and blind of the other, who at first sight might appear a bad man to meet on a dark night, but is harmless enough when you know him; he haunts the lanes at certain seasons of the year, carrying an enormous flag, and invariably greets you with the intelligence that he will bring the flag up next Christmas the same as usual, according to time-honoured custom. He is the last vestige of the old wandering minstrels of bygone days, playing his inharmonious concertina in the hall of the manor house regularly at Christmas and at other festivals.

Nor must we forget dear, honest Mr. White, the kindest and most pompous of men, who, after fulfilling his destiny as head butler in a great establishment, and earning golden opinions from all sorts and conditions of men, finally settled down to a quiet country life in a pretty cottage in our village, where he is the life and soul of every convivial gathering and beanfeast, carving a York ham or a sirloin with great nicety and judgment. He has seen much of men and manners in his day, and has a fund of information on all kinds of subjects. Having plenty of leisure, he is a capital hand at finding the whereabouts of outlying foxes; and once earned the eternal gratitude of the whole neighbourhood by starting a fine greyhound fox, known as the "old customer," out of a decayed and hollow tree that lay in an unfrequented spot by the river. He poked him out with a long pole, and gave the "view holloa" just as the hounds had drawn all the coverts "blank," and the people's faces were as blank as the coverts; whereupon such a run was enjoyed as had not been indulged in for many a long day.

But what of our miller—our good, honest gentleman farmer and miller—now, alas! retired from active business? What can I say of him? I show you a man worthy to sit amongst kings. A little garrulous and inquisitive at times, yet a conqueror for all that in the battle of-life, and one of whom it may in truth be said,

> "And thus he bore without abuse
> The grand old name of gentleman."

As to the morals of the Gloucestershire peasants in general, and of our village in particular, it may be said that they are on the whole excellent; in one respect only they are rather casual, not to say prehistoric.

The following story gives one a very good idea of the casual nature of hamlet morals:—

A parson—I do not know of which village, but it was somewhere in this neighbourhood—paid a visit to a newly married man, to speak seriously about the exceptionally premature arrival of an heir. "This is a terrible affair," said the parson on entering the cottage. "Yaas; 'twere a bad job to be sure," replied the man. "And what will yer take to drink?"

Let it in justice be said that such episodes are the exception and not the rule.

Among the characters to be met with in our Cotswold hamlet is the village politician. Many a pleasant chat have we enjoyed in his snug cottage, whilst the honest proprietor was having his cup of tea and bread and butter after his work. Common sense he has to a remarkable degree, and a good deal more knowledge than most people give him credit for. He is a Radical of course; nine out of ten labourers are *at heart*. And a very good case he makes out for his way of thinking, if one can only put oneself in his place for a time. We have endeavoured to convert him to our way of thinking, but the strong, reflective mind,

> "Illi robur, et aes triplex
> Circa pectus erat,"

is not to be persuaded. He will be true to "the colour"; this is his final answer, even if your arguments overcome for the time being. And you cannot help liking the man for his straightforward, self-reliant nature; he is acting up to the standard he has set himself all through life.

> "This above all, to thine own self be true,
> And it must follow, as the night the day,
> Thou canst not then be false to any man."

And how many there are in the byways of England acting up to this motto, and leading the lives of heroes, though their reward is not to be found here!

There is no nobler sight on this earth than to behold men of all ages doing their duty to the best of their ability, in spite of manifold hardships and many a bitter disappointment; cheerfully and manfully confronting difficulties of all kinds, and training up children in the fear and knowledge of God. If this is not nobleness, there is no such thing on earth. And it is owing to the vast amount of real, genuine Christianity that exists among these honest folk that life is rendered on the whole so cheerful in these Cotswold villages. Many small faults the peasants doubtless possess; such are inseparable from human nature. The petty jealousies always to be found where men do congregate exist here, and as long as the earth revolves they will continue to exist; but underneath the rough, unpolished exterior there is a reef of gold, far richer than the mines of South Africa will ever produce, and as immortal as the souls in which it lies so deeply rooted and embedded.

For the best type of humanity we need not search in vain among the humble cottages of the hamlets of England. There shall we find the courageous, brave souls who "scorn delights and live laborious days,"—men who estimate their fellows at their worth, and not according to their social position. Blunt and difficult to lead, not out of hardness of heart or obstinate pigheadedness, but as Burns has put it:

> "For the glorious priviledge
> Of being independant."

A few such are to be found in all our rural villages if one looks for them; and if they are the exceptions to the general rule, it must also be remembered that men with "character" are equally rare amongst the upper and middle classes.

Talking of village politics, I shall never forget a meeting held at Northleach a few years ago. It was at a time when the balance of parties was so even that our Unionist member was returned by the bare majority of three votes, only to be unseated a few weeks afterwards on a recount. Northleach is a very Radical town, about six miles from my home; and when I agreed to take the chair, I little knew what an unpleasant job I had taken in hand. Our member for some reason or other was unable to attend. I therefore found myself at 7.30 one evening facing two hundred "red-hot" Radicals, with only one other speaker besides myself to keep the ball a-rolling. My companion was one of those professional politicians of the baser sort, who call themselves Unionists because it pays better for the working-class politician—in just the same way as ambitious young men among the upper classes sometimes become Radicals on the strength of there being more opening for them on the "Liberal" side.

Well, this fellow bellowed away in the usual ranting style for about three-quarters of an hour; his eloquence was great, but truth was "more honoured in the breach than in the observance." So that when he sat down, and my turn came, the audience, instead of being convinced, was fairly rabid. I was very young at that time, and fearfully nervous; added to which I was never much of a speaker, and, if interrupted at all, usually lost the thread of my argument.

After a bit they began shouting, "Speak up." The more they shouted the more mixed I got. When once the spirit of insubordination is roused in these fellows, it spreads like wild-fire. The din became so great I could not hear myself speak. In about five minutes there would have been a row. Suddenly a bright idea occurred to me. "Listen to me," I shouted; "as you won't hear me speak, perhaps you will allow me to sing you a song." I had a fairly strong voice, and could go up a good height; so I gave them "Tom Bowling." Directly I started you could have heard a pin drop. They gave, me a fair hearing all through; and when, as a final climax, I finished up with a prolonged B flat—a very loud and long note, which sounded to me something between a "view holloa" and the whistle of a penny

46

steamboat, but which came in nicely as a sort of *pièce de résistance*, fairly astonishing "Hodge" — their enthusiasm knew no bounds. They cheered and cheered again. Hand shaking went on all round, whilst the biggest Radical of the lot stood up and shouted, "You be a little Liberal, I know, and the other blokes 'ave 'ired [hired] you." Whether we won any votes that evening I am doubtful, but certain I am that this meeting, which started so inauspiciously, was more successful than many others in which I have taken part in a Radical place, in spite of the fact that we left it amid a shower of stones from the boys outside.

I do not think there is anything I dislike more than standing up to address a village audience on the politics of the day. Unless you happen to be a very taking speaker — which his greatest friends could not accuse the present writer of being — agricultural labourers are a most unsympathetic audience. They will sit solemnly through a long speech without even winking an eye, and your best "hits" are passed by in solemn silence. To the nervous speaker a little applause occasionally is doubtless encouraging; but if you want to get it, you must put somebody down among the audience, and pay them half a crown to make a noise.

I suppose no better fellow or more suitable candidate for a Cotswold constituency ever walked than Colonel Chester Master, of the Abbey; yet his efforts to win the seat under the new ballot act were always unavailing, saving the occasion on which he got in by three votes, and then was turned out again within a month. An unknown candidate from London — I will not say a carpet-bagger — was able to beat the local squire, entirely owing to the very fact that he was a stranger.

There is a good deal of chopping and changing about among the agricultural voters, in spite of a general determination to be true to the "yaller" colour or the "blue," as the case may be. As I passed down the village street on the day on which our last election took place, I enthusiastically exclaimed to a passer-by in whom I thought I recognised one of our erstwhile firmest supporters, "We shall have our man in for a certainty this time." "What — in the brook!" replied the turncoat, with a glance at the stream, and not without humour, his face purple with emotion. This was somewhat damping; but the hold of the paid social agitator is very great in these country places, and it is scarcely credible what extraordinary stories are circulated on the eve of an election to influence the voters. At such times even loyalty is at a discount At a Tory meeting a lecturer was showing a picture of Gibraltar, and expatiating on the English victory in 1704, when Sir George Rooke won this important stronghold from the Spaniards. "How would you like any one to come and take your land away?" exclaimed a Radical, with a great show of righteous indignation. And his sentiments received the applause of all his friends.

In these matters, and in the spirit of independence generally, country folk have much altered. No longer can it be said; as Addison quaintly puts it in the *Spectator*, that "they are so used to be dazzled with riches that they pay as much deference to the understanding of a man of estate as of a man of learning; and are very hardly brought to regard any truth, how important soever it may be, that is preached to them, when they know there are several men of five hundred a year who do not believe it."

In such-like matters the labourers now show a vast deal of common sense, and the only wonder is that whilst paying but little deference either to men of estate or men of learning, they yet allow themselves to be "bamboozled" by the promises and claptrap of the paid agitator.

Narrow and ignorant as is the Toryism commonly displayed in country districts, it is yet preferable, from the point of view of those whose motto is *aequam memento*, etc., to the impossible Utopia which the advanced Radicals invariably promise us and never effect.

A word now about the farmers of Gloucestershire.

It is often asked, How do the Cotswold farmers live in these bad times? I suppose the only reply one can give is the old saw turned upside down: They live as the fishes do in the sea; the great ones eat up the little ones. The tendency, doubtless, in all kinds of trade is for the small capitalists to go to the wall.

Some of the farmers in this district are yeoman princes, not only possessing their own freeholds, but farming a thousand or fifteen hundred acres in addition. Mr. Garne, of Aldsworth, is a fine specimen of this class. He makes a speciality of the original pure-bred Cotswold sheep, and his rams being famous, he is able to do very well, in spite of the fact that there is little demand for the old breed of sheep, the mutton being of poor quality and the wool coarse and rough. Mr. Garne carries off all the prizes at "the Royal" and other shows with his magnificent sheep. A cross between the Hampshire downs and the Cotswold sheep has been found to give excellent mutton, as well as fine and silky wool. The cross breed is gradually superseding the native sheep. Mr. Hobbs, of Maiseyhampton, is famous for his Oxford downs. These sheep are likewise superior to the Cotswold breed.

Barley does uncommonly well on the light limestone soil of these hills. The brewers are glad to get Cotswold barley for malting purposes. Fine sainfoin crops are grown, and black oats likewise do well. The shallow, porous soil requires rain at least once a week throughout the spring and summer. The better class of farmer on these hills does not have at all a bad time even in these days. Very often they lead the lives of squires, more especially in those hamlets where there is no landowner resident. Hunting, shooting, coursing, and sometimes fishing are enjoyed by most of these squireens, and they are a fine, independent class of Englishman, who get more fun out of life than many richer men, They will tell you with regard to the labourers that the following adage is still to be depended upon: —

> "Tis the same with common natures:
> Use 'em kindly they rebel;
> But be rough as nutmeg-graters,
> And the rogues obey you well."

CHAPTER IV.

THE LANGUAGE OF THE COTSWOLDS, WITH SOME ANCIENT
SONGS AND LEGENDS.

A very marked characteristic of the village peasant is his extraordinary honesty. Not one in ten would knock a pheasant on the head with his stick if he found one on his allotment among the cabbages. Rabbit poachers there are, but even these are rare; and as for housebreaking and robbery, it simply does not exist. The manor house has a tremendous nail-studded oak door, which is barred at night by ponderous clamps of iron and many other contrivances; but the old-fashioned windows could be opened by any moderately skilful burglar in half a minute. There is absolutely nothing to prevent access to the house at night, whilst in the daytime the doors are open from "morn till dewy eve." Most of the windows are innocent of shutters. When in Ireland recently, I noticed that the gates in every field were immensely strong, generally of iron, with massive pillars of stone on either side; but in spite of these precautions there was usually a gap in the hedge close by, through which one might safely have driven a waggon. This reminded one of the Cotswold manor house and its strongly barricaded oak door, surrounded by windows, which any burglar could open "as easy as a glove," as Tom Peregrine would say.

A strange-looking traveller, with slouching gait and mouldy wideawake hat, passes through the hamlet occasionally, leading a donkey in a cart. This is one of the old-fashioned hawkers. These men are usually poachers or receivers of poached goods. They are not averse to paying a small sum for a basket of trout or a few partridges, pheasants, hares or rabbits in the game season; whilst in spring they deal in a small way in the eggs of game birds. As often as not this class of man is accompanied by a couple of dogs, marvellously trained in the art of hunting the coverts and "retrieving" a pheasant or a rabbit which may be crouching in the underwood. Hares, too, are taken by dogs in the open fields. One never finds out much about these gentry from the natives. Even the keeper is reticent on the subject. "A sart of a harf-witted fellow" is Tom Peregrine's description of this very suspicious-looking traveller.

The better sort of carrier, who calls daily at the great house with all kinds of goods and parcels from the big town seven miles off, is occasionally not averse to a little poaching in the roadside fields among the hares. The carriers are a great feature of these rural villages; they are generally good fellows, though some of them are a bit too fond of the bottle on Saturday nights.

The dogs employed by poachers are taught to keep out of sight and avoid keepers and such-like folk. They know as well as the poacher himself the nature of their trade, and that the utmost secrecy must be observed. To see them trotting demurely down the road you would never think them capable of doing anything wrong. A wave of the hand and they are into the covert in a second, ready to pounce like a cat on a sitting pheasant. One short whistle and they are at their master's heels again. If in carrying game in their mouths they spied or winded a keeper, they would in all probability contrive to hide themselves or make tracks for the high road as quickly as possible, leaving their spoil in the thick underwood, "to be left till called for."

But to return once more to the honest Cotswold labourer. Occasionally a notice is put up in the village as follows: —

"There will be a dinner in the manor grounds on July —. Please bring knives and forks."

These are great occasions in a Cotswold village. Knives and forks mean meat; and a joint of mutton is not seen by the peasants more than "once in a month of Sundays." Needless to say, there is not much opportunity of studying the language of the country as long as the feast is progressing. "Silence is golden" is the motto here whilst the viands are being discussed; but afterwards, when the Homeric desire of eating and drinking has been expelled, an adjournment to the club may lead to a smoking concert, and, once started, there are very few Cotswold men who cannot sing a song of at least eighteen verses. For three hours an uninterrupted stream of music flows forth, not only solos, but occasionally duets, harmoniously chanted in parts, and rendered with the utmost pathos. It cannot be said that Gloucestershire folk are endowed with a large amount of musical talent; neither their "ears" nor their vocal chords are ever anything great, but what they lack in quality they make up in quantity, and I have listened to as many as forty songs during one evening—some of them most entertaining, others extremely dull. The songs the labourer most delights in are those which are typical of the employment in which he happens to be engaged. Some of the old ballads, handed down from father to son by oral tradition, are very excellent. The following is a very good instance of this kind of song; when sung by the carter to a good rollicking tune, it goes with a rare ring, in spite of the fact that it lasts about a quarter of an hour. There would be about a dozen verses, and the chorus is always sung twice at the end of each verse, first by the carter and then by the whole company.

"Now then, gentlemen, don't delay harmony," Farmer Peregrine keeps repeating in his old-fashioned, convivial way, and thus the ball is kept a-rolling half the night.

JIM, THE CARTER LAD.

"My name is Jim, the carter lad—
  A jolly cock am I;
I always am contented,
  Be the weather wet or dry.
I snap my finger at the snow,
  And whistle at the rain;
I've braved the storm for many a day,
  And can do so again."

(*Chorus.*)

"Crack, crack, goes my whip,
  I whistle and I sing,
I sits upon my waggon,
  I'm as happy as a king.
My horse is always willing;
  As for me, I'm never sad:

There's none can lead a jollier life
  Than Jim, the carter lad."

"My father was a carrier
  Many years ere I was born,
And used to rise at daybreak
  And go his rounds each morn.
He often took me with him,
  Especially in the spring.
I loved to sit upon the cart
  And hear my father sing.
  Crack, crack, etc."

"I never think of politics
  Or anything so great;
I care not for their high-bred talk
  About the Church and State.
I act aright to man and man,
  And that's what makes me glad;
You'll find there beats an honest heart
  In Jim, the carter lad.
  Crack, crack, etc."

"The girls, they all smile on me
  As I go driving past.
My horse is such a beauty,
  And he jogs along so fast.
We've travelled many a weary mile,
  And happy days have had;
For none can lead a jollier life
  Than Jim, the carter lad.
  Crack, crack, etc."

"So now I'll wish you all good night
  It's time I was away;
For I know my horse will weary
  If I much longer stay.
To see your smiling faces,

A Cotswold Village; or, Country Life and Pursuits in Gloucestershire

> It makes my heart quite glad.
> I hope you'll drink your kind applause
>   To Jim, the carter lad.
>   Crack, crack, etc."

The village choirs do very well as long as their organist or vicar is not too ambitious in his choice of music. There is a fatal tendency in many places to do away with the old hymns, which every one has known from a boy, and substitute the very inferior modern ones now to be found in our books. This is the greatest mistake, if I may say so. A man is far more likely to sing, and feel deeply when he is singing, those simple words and notes he learnt long ago in the nursery at home. And there is nothing finer in the world than some of our old English hymns.

I appeal to any readers who have known what it is to feel deeply; and few there are to whom this does not apply, if some of those moments of their lives, when the thoughts have soared into the higher regions of emotion, have not been those which followed the opening strain of the organ as it quietly ushered in the old evening hymn, "Abide with me, fast falls the eventide," or any other hymn of the same kind. It is the same in the vast cathedral as in the little Norman village church. There are fifty hymns in our book which would be sufficient to provide the best possible music for our country churches. The best organists realise this. Joseph Barnby always chose the old hymns; and you will hear them at Westminster and St. Paul's. The country organist, however, imagines that it is his duty to be always teaching his choir some new and difficult tune; the result in nine cases out of ten being "murder" and a rapid falling off in the congregation.

The Cotswold folk on the whole are fond of music, though they have not a large amount of talent for it. The Chedworth band still goes the round of the villages once or twice a year. These men are the descendants of the "old village musicians," who, to quote from the *Strand Musical Magazine* for September 1897, "led the Psalmody in the village church sixty years ago with stringed and wind instruments. Mr. Charles Smith, of Chedworth, remembers playing the clarionet in Handel's *Zadok the Priest*, performed there in 1838 in

54

honour of the Queen's accession." He talks of a band of twelve, made up of strings and *wood-wind*.

I am bound to say that the music produced by the Chedworth band at the present day, though decidedly creditable in such an old-world village, is rather like the Roman remains for which the district is so famous; it savours somewhat of the prehistoric. But when the band comes round and plays in the hall of our old house on Christmas Eve, I have many a pleasant chat with the Chedworth musicians; they are so delightfully enthusiastic, and so grateful for being allowed to play. When I gave them a cup of tea they kept repeating, "A thousand thanks for all your kindness, sir."

It is inevitable that men engaged day by day and year by year in such monotonous employ as agricultural labour should be somewhat lacking in acuteness and sensibility; in no class is the hereditary influence so marked. Were it otherwise, matters would be in a sorry pass in country places, for discontent would reign supreme; and once let "ambition mock their useful toil," once their sober wishes learn to stray, how would the necessary drudgery of agricultural work be accomplished at all? In spite, however, of this marked characteristic of inertness—hereditary in the first place, and fostered by the humdrum round of daily toil on the farm—there is sometimes to be found a sense of humour and a love of merriment that is quite astonishing. A good deal of what is called knowledge of the world, which one would have thought was only to be acquired in towns, nowadays penetrates into remote districts, so that country folk often have a good idea of "what's what" I once overheard the following conversation:

"Who's your new master, Dick? He's a bart., ain't he?"

"Oh no," was the reply; "he's only a *jumped-up jubilee knight!*"

Sense of humour of a kind the Cotswold labourer certainly has, even though he is quite unable to see a large number of apparently simple jokes. The diverting history of John Gilpin, for instance, read at a smoking concert, was received with scarce a smile.

Old Mr. Peregrine lately told me an instance of the extraordinary secretiveness of the labourer. Two of his men worked together in his barn day after day for several weeks. During that time they never spoke to each other, save that one of them would always say the last thing at night, "Be sure to shut the door."

Oddly enough they thoroughly appreciate the humour of the wonderful things that went on fifty and a hundred years ago. The old farmer I have just mentioned told me that he remembers when he used to go to church fifty years ago, how, after they had all been waiting half an hour, the clerk would pin a notice in the porch, "No church to-day; Parson C— — got the gout."

As with history so also with geography, the Cotswold labourer sometimes gets "a bit mixed."

"'Ow be they a-gettin' on in Durbysher?" lately enquired a man at Coln-St-Aldwyns.

To him replied a righteously indignant native of the same village, "I've 'eard as 'ow the English army 'ave killed ten thousand Durvishers (Dervishes)."

"Bedad!" answered his friend, "there won't be many left in Durbysher if they goes on a-killin' un much longer."

"THE HAMLET."

56

Another story lately told me in the same village was as follows:—

An old lady went to the stores to buy candles, and was astonished to find that owing to the Spanish-American war "candles was riz."

"Get along!" she indignantly exclaimed. *"Don't tell me they fights by candlelight"*

One of the cheeriest fellows that ever worked for us was a carter called Trinder. He was the father of *twenty-one children*—by the same wife. He never seemed to be worried in the slightest degree by domestic affairs, and was always happy and healthy and gay. This man's wages would be about twelve shillings a week: not a very large sum for a man with a score of children. Then it must be remembered that the boys would go off to work in the fields at a very early age, and by the time they were ten years old they would be keeping themselves. A large family like this would not have the crushing effect on the labouring man that it has on the poor curate or city clerk. Nevertheless, one cannot help looking upon the man as a kind of hero, when one considers the enormous number of grandchildren and descendants he will have. On being asked the other day how he had contrived to maintain such a quiverful, he answered, "I've always managed to get along all right so far; I never wanted for vittals, sir, anyhow." This was all the information he would give.

Talking of "vittals," the only meat the labouring man usually indulges in is bacon. His breakfast consists of bread and butter, and either tea or cocoa. For his dinner he relies on bread and bacon, occasionally only bread and cheese. In the winter he is home by five, and once more has tea, or cocoa, or beer. Coffee is very seldom seen in the cottages. During the short days there is nothing to do but go to bed in the evening, unless a walk of over a mile to the village inn is considered worth the trouble. But being tired and leg weary, a long walk does not usually appeal to the men after their evening meal; so to bed is the order of the day,—and, thank Heaven! "the sleep of a labouring man is sweet." In the longer days of spring and summer there is plenty to do in the allotments; and on the whole the allotments acts have been a great blessing to the labourers.

It is during the three winter months that penny readings and smoking concerts are so much appreciated in the country. Too much cannot be done in this way to brighten the life of the village during the cold, dark days of December and January, for the labouring man hates reading above all things.

Perhaps the fact that these simple folk do not read the newspapers, or only read those parts in which they have a direct interest—such as paragraphs indulging in socialistic castles in the air—has its advantages, inasmuch as it allows their common sense full play in all other matters, unhampered as it is (except in this one weak point of socialism) by the prejudices of the day. So that if one wanted to get an unprejudiced opinion on some great question of right or wrong, in the consideration of which common sense alone was required— such a question, for instance, as is occasionally cropping up in these times in our foreign policy—one would have to go to the very best men in the country, namely, those amongst the educated classes who think for themselves, or to men of the so-called lowest strata of society, such as these honest Cotswold labourers; because there is scarcely one man in ten among the reading public who is not biassed and confused by the manifold contradictions and political claptrap of the daily papers, and led away by side issues from a clear understanding of the rights of every case. Our free press is doubtless a grand institution. As with individuals, however, so ought it to be with nations. Let us, in our criticisms of the policy of those who watch over the destinies of other countries, whilst firmly upholding our rights, strictly adhere to the principle of *noblesse oblige*. The press is every day becoming more and more powerful for good or evil; its influence on men's minds has become so marked that it may with truth be said that the press rules public opinion rather than that public opinion rules the press. But the writers of the day will only fulfil their destiny aright by approaching every question in a broad and tolerant spirit, and by a firm reliance, in spite of the prejudices of the moment, on the ancient faith of *noblesse oblige*. However, the unanimity recently shown by the press in upholding our rights at Fashoda was absolutely splendid.

The origin of the names of the fields in this district is difficult to trace. Many a farm has its "barrow ground," called after some old burial mound situated there; and many names like Ladbarrow, Cocklebarrow, etc., have the same derivation. "Buryclose," too, is a name often to be found in the villages; and skeletons are sometimes dug up in meadows so called. A copse, called Deadman's Acre, is supposed to have received its name from the fact that a man died there, having sworn that he would reap an acre of corn with a sickle in a day or perish in the attempt. It is more likely, however, to be connected with the barrows, which are plentiful thereabouts.

Oliver Cromwell's memory is still very much respected among the labouring folk. Every possible work is attributed to his hand, and even the names of places are set down to his inventive genius. Thus they tell you that when he passed through Aldsworth he did not think very much of the village (it is certainly a very dull little place), so he snapped his fingers and exclaimed, "That's all 'e's worth!" On arriving at Ready Token, where was an ancient inn, he found it full of guests; he therefore exclaimed, "It's already taken!" Was ever such nonsense heard? Yet these good folk believe every tradition of this kind, and delight in telling you such stories. Ready Token is a bleak spot, standing very high, and having a clump of trees on it; it is therefore conspicuous for miles; so that when this country was an open moor, Ready Token was very useful as a landmark to travellers. Mr. Sawyer thinks the name is a corruption from the Celtic word "rhydd" and the Saxon "tacen," meaning "the way to the ford," the place being on the road to Fairford, where the Coln is crossed.

One of the chief traditions of this locality, and one that doubtless has more truth in it than most of the stories the natives tell you, relates that two hundred years ago people were frequently murdered at Ready Token inn when returning with their pockets full of money from the big fairs at Gloucester or Oxford. A labouring friend of mine was telling me the other day of the wonderful disappearance of a packman and a "jewelrer," as he called him. For very many years nothing was heard of them, but about twenty years ago some "skellingtons" were dug up on the exact spot where the inn stood, so their disappearance was accounted for.

This same man told me the following story about the origin of Hangman's Stone, near Northleach:—

"A man stole a 'ship' [sheep], and carried it tied to his neck and shoulders by a rope. Feeling rather tired, he put the 'ship' down on top of the 'stwun' [stone] to rest a bit; but suddenly it rolled off the other side, and hung him—broke his neck."

Hangman's Stone may be seen to this day. The real origin of the name may be found in Fozbrooke's History of Gloucestershire. It was the place of execution in Roman times.

"As illuminations in cases of joy, dismissal from the house in quarrels, wishing joy on New Year's Day, king and queen on twelfth day (from the Saturnalia), holding up the hand in sign of assent, shaking hands, etc., are Roman customs, so were executions just out of the town, where also the executioner resided. In Anglo-Saxon times this officer was a man of high dignity."

A very common name in Gloucestershire for a field or wood is "conyger" or "conygre." It means the abode of conies or rabbits.

Some farms have their "camp ground"; and there, sure enough, if one examines it carefully, will be found traces of some ancient British camp, with its old rampart running round it. But what can be the derivation of such names as Horsecollar Bush Furlong, Smoke Acre Furlong, West Chester Hull, Cracklands, Crane Furlong, Sunday's Hill, Latheram, Stoopstone Furlong, Pig Bush Furlong, and Barelegged Bush?

Names like Pitchwells, where there is a spring; Breakfast Bush Ground, where no doubt Hodge has had his breakfast for centuries under shelter of a certain bush; Rickbushes, and Longlands are all more or less easy to trace. Furzey Leaze, Furzey Ground, Moor Hill, Ridged Lands, and the Pikes are all names connected with the nature of the fields or their locality.

Leaze is the provincial name for a pasture, and Furzey Leaze would be a rough "ground," where gorse was sprinkled about. The Pikes would be a field abutting on an old turnpike gate. The word "turnpike" is never used in Gloucestershire; it is always "the pike."

A field is a "ground," and a fence or stone wall is a "mound." The Cotswold folk do not talk about houses; they stick to the old Saxon termination, and call their dwellings "housen"; they also use the Anglo-Saxon "hire" for hear. The word "bowssen," too, is very frequently heard in these parts; it is a provincialism for a stall or shed where oxen are kept. "Boose" is the word from which it originally sprang. A very expressive phrase in common use is to "quad" or "quat"; it is equivalent to the word "squat." Other words in this dialect are "sprack," an adjective meaning quick or lively; and "frem" or "frum," a word derived from the Anglo-Saxon "fram," meaning fresh or flourishing. The latter word is also used in Leicestershire. Drayton, who knew the Cotswolds, and wrote poetry about the district, uses the expression "frim pastures." "Plym" is the swelling of wood when it is immersed in water; and "thilk," another Anglo-Saxon word, means thus or the same.

A mole in the Gloucestershire dialect is an "oont" or "woont." A barrow or mound of any kind is a "tump." Anything slippery is described as "slick"; and a slice is a "sliver." "Breeds" denotes the brim of a hat, and a deaf man is said to be "dunch" or "dunny." To "glowr" is to stare—possibly connected with the word "glare."

Two red-coated sportsmen, while hunting close to our village the other day, got into a small but deep pond. They were said to have fallen into the "stank," and got "zogged" through: for a small pond is a "stank," and to be "zogged" is equivalent to being soaked.

"Hark at that dog 'yoppeting' in the covert! I'll give him a nation good 'larroping' when I catch him!" This is the sort of sentence a Gloucestershire keeper makes use of. To "larrop" is to beat. Oatmeal or porridge is always called "grouts"; and the Cotswold native does not talk of hoisting a ladder, but "highsting" is the term he uses. The steps of the ladder are the "rongs." Luncheon is "nuncheon." Other words in the dialect are "caddie" = to humbug; "cham" = to chew; "barken" = a homestead; and "bittle" = a mallet.

Fozbrooke says that the term "hopping mad" is applied to people who are very angry; but we do not happen to have heard it in Gloucestershire. Two proverbs that are in constant use amongst all classes are, "As sure as God's in Gloucestershire," and, "'Tis as long

in coming as Cotswold 'berle'" (barley). The former has reference to
the number of churches and religious houses the county used to
possess, the latter to the backward state of the crops on the exposed
Cotswold Hills. To meet a man and say, "Good-morning, nice day,"
is to "pass the time of day with him." Anything queer or mysterious
is described as "unkard" or "unket"; perhaps this word is a
provincialism for "uncouth." A narrow lane or path between two
walls is a "tuer" in Gloucestershire vernacular. Another local word I
have not heard elsewhere is "eckle," meaning a green woodpecker or
yaffel. The original spelling of the word was "hic-wall." In these
days of education the real old-fashioned dialect is seldom heard;
among the older peasants a few are to be found who speak it, but in
twenty years' time it will be a thing of the past.

The incessant use of "do" and "did," and the changing of *o*'s into *a*'s
are two great characteristics of the Gloucestershire talk. Being
anxious to be initiated into the mysteries of the dialect, I buttonholed
a labouring friend of mine the other day, and asked him to try to
teach it to me. He is a great exponent of the language of the country,
and, like a good many others of his type, he is as well satisfied with
his pronunciation as he is with his other accomplishments. The fact
is that

> "His favourite sin
> Is pride that apes humility."

It is *your* grammar, not his, which is at fault. In the following verses
will be found the gist of what he told me: —

> "If thee true 'Glarcestershire' would know,
> I'll tell thee how us always zays un;
> Put 'I' for 'me,' and 'a' for 'o'.
> On every possible occasion.
>
> When in doubt squeeze in a 'w' —
> 'Stwuns,' not 'stones.' And don't forget, zur,
> That 'thee' must stand for 'thou' and 'you';
> 'Her' for 'she,' and *vice versâ*.
>
> Put 'v' for 'f'; for 's' put 'z';

> 'Th' and 't' we change to 'd,' —
> So dry an' kip this in thine yead,
> An' thou wills't talk as plain as we."

The student in the language of the Cotswolds should study a very ancient song entitled "George Ridler's Oven." Strange to say, there is little or nothing in it about the oven, but a good deal of the old Gloucestershire talk may be gleaned from it. It begins like this:

GEORGE RIDLER'S OVEN.

A RIGHT FAMOUS OLD GLOUCESTERSHIRE BALLAD.

> "The stwuns, the stwuns, the stwuns, the stwuns,
> The stwuns, the stwuns, the stwuns, *the stwuns*."

This is sung like the prelude to a grand orchestral performance. Beginning somewhat softly, Hodge fires away with a gravity and emotion which do him infinite credit, each succeeding repetition of the word "stwuns" being rendered with ever-increasing pathos and emphasis, until, like the final burst of an orchestral prelude, with drums, trumpets, fiddles, etc, all going at the same time, are at length ushered in the opening lines of the ballad.

> "The stwuns that built Gaarge Ridler's oven,
> And thauy qeum from the Bleakeney's Quaar;
> And Gaarge he wur a jolly ould mon,
> And his yead it graw'd above his yare.

> "One thing of Gaarge Ridler's I must commend.
> And that wur vor a notable theng;
> He mead his braags avoore he died,
> Wi' any dree brothers his zons zshou'd zeng.

> "There's Dick the treble and John the mean
> (Let every mon zing in his auwn pleace);
> And Gaarge he wur the elder brother,
> And therevoore he would zing the beass.

"Mine hostess's moid (and her neaum 'twur Nell)
A pretty wench, and I lov'd her well;
I lov'd her well—good reauzon why,
Because zshe lov'd my dog and I.

"My dog has gotten zitch a trick
To visit moids when thauy be zick;
When thauy be zick and like to die,
Oh, thether gwoes my dog and I.

"My dog is good to catch a hen,—
A duck and goose is vood vor men;
And where good company I spy,
Oh, thether gwoes my dog and I.

"Droo aal the world, owld Gaarge would bwoast,
Commend me to merry owld England mwoast;
While vools gwoes scramblin' vur and nigh,
We bides at whoam, my dog and I.

"Ov their furrin tongues let travellers brag,
Wi' their vifteen neames vor a puddin' bag;
Two tongues I knows ne'er towld a lie,
And their wearers be my dog and I.

"My mwother told I when I wur young,
If I did vollow the strong beer pwoot,
That drenk would pruv my auverdrow,
And meauk me wear a thzreadbare cwoat.

"When I hev dree zixpences under my thumb,
Oh, then I be welcome wherever I qeum;
But when I hev none, oh, then I pass by,—
'Tis poverty pearts good company.

"When I gwoes dead, as it may hap,
My greauve shall be under the good yeal tap

> In vouled earms there wool us lie,
> Cheek by jowl, my dog and I."

GLOSSARY.

stwuns = stones.	*pleace* = place.
quaar = quarry.	*pwoot* = pewter.
yare = hair.	*yeal* = ale.
avoor = before.	*qeum* = come.
auwn = own.	*graw'd* = grew.
furrin = foreign.	*braags* = brag.
greauve = grave.	*zshou'd* = should.
thauy = they.	*beass* = bass.
yead = head.	*auverdrow* = overthrow.
mead = made.	*vouled earms* = folded arms.
dree = three.	*zitch* = such.

The song itself is as old as the hills, but I have taken the liberty of appending a glossary, in order that my readers may be spared the trouble of making out the meaning of some of the words. It was a long time before it dawned upon me that "vouled earms" meant "folded arms "; "auverdrow" likewise was very perplexing. Like many of the old ballads, it sounds like a rigmarole from beginning to end; but there is really a great deal more in it than meets the eye. George Ridler is no less a personage than King Charles I., and the oven represents the cavalier party. (See Appendix.)

Such songs as these are deeply interesting from the fact that they are handed down by oral tradition from father to son, and written copies are never seen in the villages. The same applies to the play the mummers act at Christmas-time; all has to be learnt from the preceding generation of country folk. But the great feature of our smoking concerts and village entertainments has always been the reading of Tom Peregrine. This noted sportsman, who writes one of the best hands I ever saw, has kindly copied out a recitation he lately gave us. It relates to the adventures of one Roger Plowman, a Cotswold man who went to London, and is taken from a book, compiled some years ago by some Ciceter men, entitled "Roger Plowman's Excursion to London." It was read at a harvest home given by old Mr. Peregrine in his huge barn, an entertainment which lasted from six o'clock till twelve. I trust none of my readers will be any the worse for reading it. Tom Peregrine declares that when he first gave it at a penny reading some years ago, one or two of the audience had to be carried out in hysterics—they laughed so much; and another man fell backwards off his chair, owing to the extreme comicality of it. The truth is, our versatile keeper is a wonderful reader, and speaking as he does the true Gloucestershire accent, in the same way as some of the squires spoke it a century or more ago, it is extremely amusing to hear him copying the still broader dialect of the labouring class. He has a tremendous sense of humour, and his epithet for anything amusing is "Foolish." "'Tis a splendid tale; 'tis so desperate foolish," he would often say.

ROGER PLOWMAN'S JOURNEY TO LONDON.

Monday marnin' I wur to start early. Aal the village know'd I wur a-gwain, an' sum sed as how I shood be murthur'd avoor I cum back. On Sunday I called at the manur 'ouse an' asked cook if she hed any message vor Sairy Jane. She sed:

"Tell Sairy Jane to look well arter 'e, Roger, vor you'll get lost, tuck in, an' done vor."

"Rest easy in yer mind, cook," I zed; "Roger is toughish, an' he'll see thet the honour o' the old county is well show'd out and kep' up."

Cook wished me a pleasant holiday.

I started early on Monday marnin', 'tarmined to see as much as possible. I wur to walk into Cizzeter, an' vram thur goo by train to Lunnon.

I wur delighted wi' Cizzeter. The shops an' buildin's round the market-pleace wur vine; an' the church wur grand; didn't look as how he wur built by the same sort of peeple as put the shops up.

When the Roomans an' anshunt Britons went to church arm-in-arm it wur always Whitsuntide, an' arter church vetched their banners out wi' brass eagles on, an' hed a morris dance in the market-pleace. The anshunt Britons never hed any tailory done, but thay wur all artists wi' the paint pot. The Consarvatives painted thurselves bloo, and the Radicals yaller, an' thay as danced the longest, the Roomans sent to Parlyment to rool the roost.

I wur show'd the pleace wur the peeple started vor Lunnon. I walked in, an' thur wur a hole in the purtition, an' I seed the peeple a-payin' thur money vor bits o' pasteboord. I axed the mon if he could take I to Lunnon.

He sed, "Fust, second, or thurd?"

I sed, "Fust o' course, not arter; vor Sairy Jane ull be waitin'."

He sed 'twer moor ner a pound to pay.

I sed the paason sed 'twer about eight shillin'.

"That's thurd class," he sed; an' that thay ud aal be in Lunnon at the same time.

So I paid thurd class, an' he shuved out sum pasteboord, an' I put it in my pocket, an' walked out; an' thur wur a row o' carridges waitin' vor Lunnon; an' off we went as fast as a racehoss.

I heerd sum say thay wur off to Cheltenham, Gloucester, Tewkesbury, North Wales; an' I sed to meself, "I be on the rong road. Dang the buttons o' that little pasteboord seller! he warn't a 'safe mon' to hev to do wi'."

I enquired if the peeple hed much washin' to do for the railway about here, an' thay wanted to know what I required to know vor.

I sed because thur war such a long clothesline put up aal the way along. An' thay aal bust out a-larfin,' an' sed 'twur the tallergraph;

67

an' one sed as how if the Girt Western thought as how 'twould pay better, thay ud soon shet up shop, an' take in washin'.

Never in aal me life did I go at such a rate under and awver bridges an droo holes in the 'ills. We wur soon at Swindon, wur a lot wur at work as black as tinkers. We aal hed to get out, an' a chap in green clothes sed we shood hev to wait ten minits.

Thur wur a lot gwain into a room, an' I seed they wur eatin' and drinkin'; so I ses to meself, "I be rayther peckish, I'll go in an' see if I can get summut." So in I goes; an' 'twer a vine pleace, wi' sum nation good-looking gurls a-waitin'.

"I'll hev a half-quartern loaf," I sed.

"We doan't kip a baker's shop," she sed. "Thur's cakes, an' biskits, an' sponge cakes."

"Hev 'e got sum good bacon, raythur vattish?" I sed.

"No, sur; but thur's sum good poork sausingers at sixpence."

"Hand awver the pleat, young 'ooman," I sed, "an' I'll trubble you vor the mustard, an' salt, an' that pleat o' bread an' butter, an' I'll set down an' hev a bit of a snack."

The sausingers wur very good, an' teasted moorish aal the time; but the bread an' butter wur so nation thin that I had to clap dree or vour pieces together to get a mouthful. I didn't seem to want a knife or vork, but the young 'ooman put a white-handled knife an' silver vork avoor me.

The pleat o' bread an' butter didn't hold out vor the sausingers, so I hed another pleat o' bread an' butter, an' wur getting on vine. I seem'd to want summut to wet me whistle, an' wur gwain to order a quart o' ale, when I heers a whistle an' a grunt vram a steamer, an' out I goos; an', begum! he wur off.

I beckuned to the chap to stop the train, wi' me vork as I hed jest stuck into the last sausinger. I hed clapt a good mouthful in, or I could hev hollur'd loud enough vor him to heer. The train didn't stop, an' the vellers in green laughed to see I wur left in the lurch, as

I tell'd them that Sairy Jane would be sure to meet the Lunnon train. Thay sed I could go in an' vinish the sausingers now, an' that wur what I intended to do.

I asked the young 'ooman for a bottle o' ale, when she put a tallish bottle down wi' a beg head; an' as I wur dry I knocked the neck off, an' the ale kum a-fizzing out like ginger pop,—an' 'twer no use to try to stop the fizzle. I had aal I could get in a glass, an' it zeemed goodish. She soon run back wi' another bottle in her hand, an' I tell'd her 'twer pop she hed put down.

"What hev you bin an' dun, sur?" she sed; "that wur a bottle o' Moses's shampane, at seven shillin's an' sixpence a bottle."

I tell'd her I know'd 'twer nothin' but pop, as it fizzled so. Thur wur two or dree gentlemen in, an' thay larfed at the fizzle an' I. It seemed to meak me veel merryish, an' I zed, "What's to pay, young 'ooman?"

She sed, "Thirteen shillin's, sur."

"Thirteen scaramouches!" I sed. "What vor?"

"Seven sausingers, dree and sixpence; twenty-vour slices o' bread an' butter, two shillin's; an' a bottle of shampane, seven and sixpence;—kums to thirteen shillin's," she sed.

"Yer tell'd me as how the sausingers wur sixpence," I sed; "an' the slices o' bread ud cut off a tuppeny loaf."

She sed the sausingers wur sixpence each, an' twenty-vour slices o' bread an' butter wur a penny each—two shillin's.

I sed, "Do 'e call that reysonable, young 'ooman? 'cause I bain't a-gwain to pay thirteen shillin's vor't, an' lose me train, an' disappoint Sairy Jane. Thirteen shillin's vor two or dree sausingers, a few slices o' bread an' butter, an' a bottle o' pop—not vor Roger, if he knows it"

Up kums a chap an' ses, "Be you gwain to pay vor wat you hev hed?"

"To be sure I be. Thur's sixpence vor the sausingers, tuppence vor bread an' butter, an' dreppence the pop,—that meaks 'levenpence"; an' I drows down a shillin', and ses, "Thur's the odd penny vor the young 'ooman as waited upon me."

"You hed thirteen shillin's worth o' grub an' shampane, an' you'll hev to pay twelve shillin's moor or I shall take 'e away an' lock 'e up vor the night," he sed.

"Do 'e thenk as how you could do aal that, young man?" I sed. "No disrespect to 'e though, vor that don't argify; but I could ketch hold on 'e by the scroff o' yer neck an' the seat o' yer breeches, an' pitch 'e slick into the roadway among the iron."

"Look heer, Meyster Turmot, you'll hev to pay twelve shillin' moor avoor you gwoes out o' heer, or Lunnon won't hold 'e to-night."

I know'd Sairy Jane ud be a-waitin', an' as he sed the train were moast ready, I drows down a suverin', an' hed the change, an' as I wur a-gwain out I hollurs out as how I shood remember Swindleum stashun. I heer'd the lot a-larfin, an' hed moast a mind to go in an' twirl me ground ash among um vor thur edification.

I wur soon on the road agen, a-gwain like a house a-vire, an' thur wur more clotheslines aal the way along on pwosts.

W'en we got nearish to Lunnon I seed sum girt beg round barrels painted black.[3] I axed a chap what thay wur, an' he sed that thay wur beg barrels o' stingo, an' thur wur pipes laid on to the peeple's housen vor thay to draw vram.

[3] Gasometers.

I sed that wur very good accommodashun to hev XXX laid on vor use.

We soon druv into the beggest pleace I wur ever in since I wur born'd. Thay sed 'twer Paddington, an' that I wur to get out, vor they wurn't a-gwain to drive no furder. I hed paid to go to Lunnon, an' thay shood drive all the way when thay wur paid avoor'and.

I wur tell'd Paddington wur the Lunnon stashun by a porter, an' I look'd round vor Sairy Jane, as she sed as how her ud be heer at one o'clock; and porter sed 'twer then dree o'clock, an' likely Sairy Jane had gone away. Drat thay sausingers as mead I too late vor the train!

I set down to wait for Sairy Jane, as I didn't know her directions, an' hed left the letter she sent at whoam. Arter waitin' for a long while I started out, an' 'oped to see her in sum part o' Lunnon.

Another story Tom Peregrine is fond of reading to us relates how a labouring man was recommended to get some oxtail soup to strengthen him. He goes into the town and sees "Oxikali Soap" written up on a shop window. He buys a cake of it, makes his wife boil it up in the pot, and then proceeds to drink it for his health. When he has taken a spoonful or two and found it very unpleasant, his wife makes him finish it up, saying it is sure to do him good; and she consoles him with the assurance that all medicine is nasty.

At the harvest home in the big barn, after the applause which followed Tom Peregrine's recitation had died away, a sturdy carter stood up and sang a very old Gloucestershire song, which runs as follows:—

THE TURMUT HOWER.

"I be a turmut hower,
Vram Gloucestershire I came;
My parents be hard-working folk,
Giles Wapshaw be my name.
The vly, the vly,
The vly be on the turmut,
An' it be aal me eye, and no use to try
To keep um off the turmut.

"Zum be vond o' haymakin',
An' zum be vond o' mowin',
But of aal the trades thet I likes best

71

Gie I the turmut howin'.
The vly, etc.

"'Twas on a summer mornin',
Aal at the brake o' day,
When I tuck up my turmut hower,
An' trudged it far away.
The vly, etc.

"The vust pleace I got work at,
It wus by the job,
But if I hed my chance agen,
I'd rayther go to quod.
The vly, etc.

"The next pleace I got work at,
'Twer by the day,
Vor one old Varmer Vlower,
Who sed I wur a rippin' turmut hower.
The vly, etc.

"Sumtimes I be a-mowin',
Sumtimes I be a-plowin',
Gettin' the vurrows aal bright an' clear
Aal ready vor turmut sowin'.
The vly, etc.

"An' now my song be ended
I 'ope you won't call encore;
But if you'll kum here another night,
I'll seng it ye once more.
The vly, etc."

CHAPTER V.

ON THE WOLDS.

Time passes quickly for the sportsman who has the good fortune to dwell in the merry Cotswolds. Spring gives place to summer and autumn to winter with a rapidity which astonishes us as the years roll on.

So diversified are the amusements that each season brings round that no time of year lacks its own characteristic sport. In the spring, ere red coats and "leathers" are laid aside by the fox-hunting squire, there is the best of trout-fishing to be enjoyed in the Coln and Windrush—streams dear to the heart of the accomplished expert with the "dry" fly. In spring, too, are the local hunt races at Oaksey and Sherston, at Moreton-in-the-Marsh and Andoversford. Pleasant little country gatherings are these race meetings, albeit the *bonâ-fide* hunter has little chance of distinguishing himself between the flags in any part of England nowadays. The Lechlade Horse Show, too, is a great institution in the V.W.H. country at the close of the hunting season.

Annually at Whitsuntide for very many centuries "sports" have been held in all parts of the country. It is said that they are the *floralia* of the Romans. Included in these sports are many of those amusements of the middle ages of which Ben Jonson sang:

> "The Cotswold with the Olympic vies
> In manly games and goodly exercise."

Horse-racing is a great feature in the programme of these Whitsuntide festivities.

The "may-fly" carnival among the trout, together with lots of cricket matches, make the time pass all too quickly for those who spend the glorious summer months in the Cotswolds. By the time the Cirencester Horse Show is over, the cubs are getting strong and mischievous. Directly the corn is cut the hounds are out again in the lovely September mornings. By this time partridges are plentiful, and must be shot ere they get too wild. So year by year the ball is kept rolling in the quiet Cotswold Hills; the days go by, yet content reigns amongst all classes.

> "Far from the madding crowd's ignoble strife
> Their sober wishes never learned to stray;
> Along the cool, sequestered vale of life
> They kept the noiseless tenor of their way."

Then there is so much to do indirectly connected with sport of all kinds, if you live in a Cotswold village. Woods and fox coverts must be kept in good order, so that there may always be cover to shelter game and foxes. Cricket grounds afford unlimited scope for labour and experiment.

If you either own or rent a trout stream there is no end to the improvements that can be made with a little time and labour. Deep holes or even lakes may be dug, great stones and fir poles may be utilised, to form eddies and waterfalls and homes for the trout. By means of a little stocking with fresh blood a stream may often be turned from a worthless piece of water into a splendid fishery. There is no limit to the articles of food which can be imported. Gammari, or fresh-water shrimps, caddis and larvae, and various species of weeds which nourish insects and snails—notably the *chara flexilis* from Loch Leven—may all be procured and transplanted to your water. The beautiful springs which feed the Coln at various intervals, where the watercress grows freely, would be of great service in forming lakes; there is so much poor marshy land even in the fertile valleys that might be utilised, with advantage and profit for the purpose of trout preserving.

Talking of watercress, this is a branch of farming which appears to be somewhat neglected on the banks of the Coln. The villagers tell you that watercress, like the oyster, is good in every month with an "r" in it: so that all through the year, save in May, June, July, and August, watercress may be picked and sent to market. But the proprietor of watercress beds attaches little importance to the fact that he possesses large beds of this wholesome and reproductive plant, and you will not see it on his table once in a month of

Sundays. In London one eats watercress all the year round, more especially in the months without an "r," but it does not come from the Cotswolds.

There is not much covert shooting on these hills. The country is so open and the coverts so small and deficient in underwood that pheasant preserving on a large scale is not practicable; for this reason the preservation of foxes is the first consideration. At Stowell, Sherborne, Rendcombe, Barnsley, and Cirencester, as well as on a few other large estates, a large head of game is reared; while foxes are plentiful too. But the owners and occupiers of most of the manors are content to rely on nature to supply them with game in due season.

However, for those gunners who, like the writer, are both unskilful and unambitious, the shooting obtained on the Cotswold Hills is very enjoyable. In September from ten to twenty brace of partridges are to be picked up, together with what hares a man cares to shoot, and a few rabbits. Then landrails or corncrakes, and last, but not least, an occasional quail, are usually included in the bag. Quails are rather partial to this district; during the first fortnight of September a few are generally shot on the manor we frequent. On August 17th this year we found a nest containing five young quails about half-grown.

But the real pleasure connected with this kind of sport lies in the sense of wildness. The air is almost as good a tonic as that of the Scotch moors, whilst there is the additional satisfaction of being at home in September instead of flying away to the North, and having to put up with all the discomfort of a long railway journey each way.

There is no time of year one would sooner spend at home on Cotswold than the month of September. Nature is then at her best: the cold, bleak hills are clothed with the warmth of golden stubble; the autumnal haze now softens the landscape with those lights and shades which add so much of loveliness and sense of mystery to a hill country; the rich aftermath is full of animal life; birds of all descriptions are less wild and more easily observed than is the case later on, when the pastures and downs have been thinned by frost and there is no shelter left. Now you may see the kestrels hovering in mid air, and the great sluggish heron wending his ethereal way to the upper waters of the trout stream. You watch him till he drops suddenly from the heavens, to alight in the little valley which lies a short mile away, invisible amid the far-stretching tablelands. Occasionally, too, a marsh-harrier may be met with, but this is a *rara avis* even in these outlandish parts. Peregrine falcons are uncommon too, though one may yet see a pair of them now and then if one keeps a sharp look-out at all times and seasons. There are wimbrels and curlews that have been shot here during recent years stuffed and hung up in glass cases in old Mr. Peregrine's house.

Of other birds which are becoming scarcer year by year in England, the kingfishers are not uncommon in these parts; you will often see the brilliant little fellow dart past you as you walk by the stream in summer. Water-ousels or dippers are scarce; we have seen but one specimen in the last three years.

In September, as you walk over the fields, the Cotswolds are seen at their best. Somehow or other a country never looks so well from the roads as it appears when you are in the fields. The man who prefers the high road had better not live in the Cotswolds; for these roads, mended as they are with limestone in the more remote parts of the district, become terribly sticky in winter, while the grass fields and stubbles are generally as dry as a bone. There is but a small percentage of clay in the soil, but a good deal of lime, and five inches down is the hard rock; therefore this light, stony soil never holds the rain, but allows it to percolate rapidly through, even as a sieve. When the sun is hot after a frost the ploughs "carry" certainly, but this is because they dry so quickly; they seldom remain thoroughly wet for any length of time. Consequently, in hunting, the feet of hounds, horses, and even of foxes pick up the sticky, arable soil, instead of splashing through it, and scent is spoiled thereby. Doubtless the lime in the soil adds to its stickiness. It is amusing to watch a fox "break" covert and make his way over a plough which "carries": he travels very badly; we have seen him fail to jump a sheep hurdle at the first attempt. Fortunately for the fox, the hounds are also handicapped by these conditions, and scent is wretched. This might appear at first sight to show that the scent of foxes is chiefly given off from their feet. We can recall few occasions on which a plough that "carried" held a "burning scent." But little though we know of the mysteries of "scent," it is generally agreed that the "steaming trail" emanates chiefly from the body and breath of a fox, even though on certain days there is no evidence of any scent, save on the ground. It is probable, however, that on light ploughlands evaporation is so great when the sun is shining (unless the wind is sufficiently cold to counteract the heat of the sun and prevent rapid evaporation) that all scent from the body and breath of the fox, save that which happens to cling to the ground, is borne upwards and lost in the upper air. *The hounds therefore have to fall back on whatever scent may remain clinging to the soil*, those occasions of course excepted when the great density or gravity of the air prevents scent from rising and dispersing, and causes it to hang *breast high*.

After some years of careful experiment with the hygrometer and barometer, and after an intricate investigation of scent (that mysterious matter which is given off from the skin and breath of foxes), I have come to the conclusion that if we could get an Isaac Newton to "whip in" to a Tom Firr for about a twelvemonth, we might very likely come to know all about it. In standing on ground whereon "angels fear to tread," I am fully aware that I speak as a fool. But let me state that it is on the barometer that I now place my somewhat limited reliance on a hunting morning, and not on the hygrometer, on the weight of the column of air on a given point of the surface of the earth, rather than on the state of the evaporations, the relative humidity, and the dew point. And I have noticed that the best scenting days have been those when the thermometer has given readings from 38º up to 46º Fahrenheit in the shade. A high and steady glass, an almost imperceptible east or north-east wind, with the ground soaked with moisture and no frost during the previous night, is the only combination of conditions under which scent on the grass is a moral certainty. On the other hand, a low and unsteady glass, a warm, gusty south or west wind, with a hot sun, following a frost, or a day with cold showers, with bright, sunny intervals, or during the afternoon (but not always the morning) before a storm of wind or rain,—such are the conditions which make so many of our attempts to hunt the fox by scent a miserable farce; yet even on these days hounds may run during some part of the day. When the barometer is thoroughly unsettled there may be light local currents, perfectly imperceptible to man, yet felt by cows and sheep—currents created like winds by a variation of temperature in different parts of any given field, and which will scatter the scent and spoil the sport. These currents, rapid evaporation combined with a lack of steady atmospheric pressure, and that sticky state of soil which on ploughed land invariably follows a frost, and in a lesser degree affects grass, causing a fox to take his pad scent on with him (all the particles that do not cling to the ground having been diffused and lost in the air),—these are the curses of modern hunting fields and the chief causes of bad scenting days.

"OXEN PLOUGHING."

After September is past the shooting man will not get very much sport on the Cotswolds, as far as the partridges are concerned, for they are not numerous enough to be worth driving; they soon become as wild as they can possibly be. On Hatherop and some other estates good partridge driving is enjoyed. The farmers are very fond of shooting them under a "kite,"—this, as it is hardly necessary to explain, is an artificial representation of the hawk. It is flown high up in the air at some distance ahead of the guns. The birds, seeing what they take to be a very large and savage-looking hawk hovering above them, ready to pounce down at a moment's notice, become frightened, and lie crouching in the hedges and turnips, until they almost have to be kicked up by the sportsmen. But when once they do get up they fly straight away, nor do they come back for a long time. This mode of shooting is all very well once in a way, but if indulged in habitually it scares the birds, driving them on to other manors. Not having seen it successfully carried out, we are not fond of the method, but there are good sportsmen in these parts who advocate it. Some maintain that this cannot be called a really sportsmanlike way of shooting partridges, though there is doubtless room for two opinions on the question.

Later on in the autumn, when November frosts begin to attract snipes to the withybeds and water meadows by the Coln, the unambitious gunner may often enjoy the charm of a small and select mixed bag.

Two of us went out for an hour last winter before breakfast, having been informed that a woodcock was lying in an ash copse by the river. We got the woodcock—a somewhat *rara avis* in small, isolated coverts on the hills; in addition, the bag contained one snipe, one wild duck, two pheasants, six rabbits, a pigeon, a heron, and some moorhens. Now this was very good sport, because it was totally unexpected. The majority of shooting people might not think much of so small a bag, but it must be remembered that the charm of this kind of shooting is its wildness. It seems rather hard to kill herons, but anybody who has tried to preserve trout will agree that herons are the greatest enemies with which the trout-fisher has to contend. One heron will clear a shallow stream in a very short time. When the floods are out, trout fall a ready prey to these rapacious birds. The kingfishers likewise have a very good time. The fish will gorge themselves with worms picked up on the inundated meadows, until they are so full that the worms actually begin falling out of their mouths. I picked several up last autumn which had been stabbed, I suppose, by a heron. They were unharmed, save for a small round hole, as if made by a bullet; there was no other mark on them. But when taken up, the worms came out of their mouths by the score! Kingfishers are carefully preserved, in spite of their destructiveness, but one must draw the line at herons.

Waiting for wild duck coming into the "spring" on a frosty night is cold work, but very good fun. They breed here in fair numbers, and fly away in August. But when the ground becomes "scrumpety," as the natives say, with the first severe frost, back they come from the frozen meres to their old home; and if one can keep out of sight (and this is no easy matter in December) many a shot can be obtained in the withybeds by the river. Teal and widgeon may be shot occasionally in the same manner.

Sometimes, when you are upon the hills with Tom Peregrine, the keeper, trying to pick up a brace or two of partridges for the house, he will suddenly say, "*Quad down!*" then, throwing himself on to his hands and knees in breathless anxiety, he will begin whistling for "all he knows." You imitate him to the best of your ability, and soon, if you are lucky, an enormous flock of golden plover flash over you. Four barrels are fired almost instantaneously, and the deadly "twelve-bore" of your companion is seldom fired in vain.

Green plover, or lapwings, are numerous enough on the Cotswolds. They are wonderfully difficult to circumvent, nevertheless. You crouch down under a wall, while your men go ever so far round to drive them to you; but it is the rarest thing in the world to bag one. Their eggs are very difficult to find in the breeding season. It is the male bird that, like a terrified and anxious mother, flies round and round you with piteous cries; the female bird, when disturbed, flies straight away.

Pigeon-shooting with decoys is a very favourite amusement among the Cotswold farmers. They manage to bag an enormous quantity in a hard winter, sometimes getting over a hundred in a day. Wood-pigeons come in thousands to the stubble fields when the beech nuts have come to an end. Large flocks of them annually migrate to England from Northern Europe. Crouching in a hedge or under a wall, you may enjoy as pretty a day's sport as ever fell to the lot of mortal man. A few dead birds are placed on the stubble to attract the flocks, and a grand variety of flying shots may be obtained as the wood-pigeons fly over. The year 1897 was remarkable for this shooting. Between November 20th and 30th two of our farmers killed close on a thousand of these birds. Some of them doubtless were potted on the ground. Tom Peregrine remarked that "he never saw such a sight of dead pigeons. The cheese-room up at the farm was full of them." The vast flocks that blacken the skies for a few short weeks in November disappear as suddenly as they come. After November they are no more seen.

There would be many more partridges were it not for the rooks and magpies. Hedges wherein the birds can hide their nests are few and far between in the wall country, so the keen-eyed rook spies out many a nest in the spring of the year. For this reason and because they eat the corn, the farmers hate them. We cannot share their feelings. We should be sorry to see the old rookery in the garden diminished in the slightest degree. Jays and magpies are terribly numerous; they are rare egg-stealers. We have seen as many as twelve of the latter lately flying all together. Magpies are difficult to get at; they will sit perched upon the topmost twigs of the trees, but will invariably fly away before you get within shot.

It is interesting to rear a few pheasants annually. There is no bird which gives more delight, even if fairly tame; their beautiful colouring and cheerful crowing are always pleasant in the garden and woods around your house. If you feed them every day, they will come regularly up to the very door; and with them come the swans, waddling up from the water, looking very much out of their element. Sometimes, too, a moorhen will join the party; whilst two little wild ducks, the sole survivors of a brood of sixteen, which were attacked and killed by a stoat, will take food right out of the mouths of the good-natured old swans. Peacocks I would not care to have round the house; but there is nothing more in touch with English country life than the glorious red, green, and brown colouring of a "fine" cock pheasant strutting proudly across the lawn on his way to his roosting-place in the firs, contrasting as he does with the majestic form and snowy plumage of the stately swans, which glide about the silent Coln at the bottom of the garden—the incarnation of grace and symmetry. Truly some of the most common of animals are also the most beautiful.

Besides the rooks, there is another bird which the farmers love to wage incessant war upon. The other day I received the following message printed on the back of a postcard:—

"A meeting will be held at the Swan Hotel, Bibury, on Friday, November 13th, at 6.30 p.m., to arrange about starting a *Sparrow Club* for the district."

"What is a Sparrow Club?" I anxiously enquired the other day of a labouring man, a particular friend of mine, whom I happened to fall in with on his way to chapel. He answered that it was a club for killing sparrows when they get too numerous—paying boys a farthing a head for every bird they catch, and giving prizes for the greatest number killed. Boys may often be seen out at night, with long poles and nets attached to them, catching sparrows in the trees. But my friend tells me that the way he likes to catch them is to go into a barn at night with a lantern. "You must hold the lantern under your coat so as to half screen the light, and the birds will fly at the light and settle on your shoulders." He tells me you can pick them off your clothes by the dozen. I have never tried it, certainly, as, personally, I have no quarrel with the sparrows. I was disappointed that the "Sparrow Club," for which a great public meeting had to be convened, was not of a more exciting nature. One was led to believe by the importance of the printed postcard that some good old English custom was about to be revived.

A farmer has just brought me in a peregrine falcon that he shot this morning. He is of course very proud of the achievement. It is useless to argue with him on the question of preserving birds that are becoming scarce in England. He considers that a *rara avis* such as this, which is "here to-day and gone to-morrow," is a prize which does not often fall to the lot of the gunner; it must be bagged at all hazards. Nor is it easy to answer the argument which he seldom fails to put forth, that if he doesn't shoot it, somebody else will.

Talking of rare birds, I shall never forget seeing a wild swan come sailing up the Coln during a very hard frost two years ago. Two of us were out after wild duck, and it was a grand sight to watch this magnificent bird winging his way rapidly up stream at a height of about fifty yards. It is rare indeed to see them in these parts, though the vicar of Bibury tells me that seven wild swans were once seen on the Coln near that village; but this was some years ago. On the same authority I learn that a Solan goose, or gannet, has been known to visit this stream. Tom Peregrine shot one a few years back; also a puffin, a bird with a parrot-like beak and of the auk tribe. Wild geese frequently pass over us, following the course of the stream.

On a bright, warm day in October, such a day as we usually have a score or more of in the course of our much-abused English autumn, it is pleasant to take one's gun and, leaving behind the quiet, peaceful valley and the old-world houses of the Cotswold hamlet, to ascend the hill and seek the great, rolling downs, a couple of miles away from any sign of human habitation. You may get a shot at a partridge or a wood-pigeon as you go. Hares you might shoot, if you cared to, in every field. But on the other hand you will be equally well pleased if your gun is not fired off, for it is peace and quiet that you are really in search of,—the noise of a shot and the jar of a gun do not suit your present mood.

After walking for half an hour you come to a bit of high ground, where you have often stood before, and, resting your gun against a wall, you gaze at the view beyond.

"Quocunque adspicias, nihil est nisi gramen et aer."

Nothing particularly striking, perhaps, is visible to the eye, yet to my mind there is a charm about it which the pen is quite unable to describe. Below is a wide expanse of undulating downland, divided into fifty-acre fields by means of loose, uncemented walls of grey stone. The grass is green for the time of year, and scattered about are horses, cattle, and sheep, contentedly nibbling the short fine turf. In the midst of mile upon mile of rolling downs stands forth prominently one field of plough, of the richest brown hue; whilst six miles away a long belt of tall trees, half hidden by haze, marks the outline of Stowell Park. Save for one ivy-covered homestead, miles away on the right, nothing else is in sight.

It is past five o'clock, and the sun, which has been shining brightly all day, with that genial warmth which one only fully appreciates as the winter approaches, is beginning to descend. It is the lights and shades which play over this wide stretch of open country which makes the landscape look so beautiful. And when the wreaths of white, woolly clouds begin to glow round their furthermost edges like coals of fire on a frosty night, with all the promise of a brilliant sunset, this stretch of hill and plain wears an aspect which, once seen, you will never forget. It takes your thoughts away into the great unknown—the infinite,—that mysterious world which is ever around us, and which seems nearer when we are looking at a beautiful sunset or a beautiful view than at any other time in this life, save, for ought we know, during the last few moments of our earthly existence. And although no human habitation is anywhere to be seen, the air is full of the spirits of bygone generations and of bygone *races* of men. There are traces of humanity in all directions, wherever your eye may gaze, but they are the traces of a forgotten people.

Yonder semicircular ridge was once the rampart of an ancient British town; though, save in the tangled copse hard by, where the plough has never been at work, it is fast disappearing. Many a stone lying about the camp bears unmistakable marks of fire.

A glance of the eye westwards, and your thoughts are carried back to the Roman invasion; for scarce five miles off lies the ancient Roman villa of Chedworth. Then, again, tradition has it that a mile away from this spot, and close to the old manor house, skirmishes were fought in later days, at the time the Civil Wars were raging, when many a chivalrous cavalier and many a stern, unbending Puritan lay dead on yonder field, or, maybe, was carried into the old house to linger and to die in the very room in which you slept last night. Everywhere in England are battlefields; but they are, in the words of De Quincey, "battlefields that nature has long ago reconciled to herself with the sweet oblivion of flowers."

This very mound on which you are standing, is it not the burying-place of a race which dwelt on the Cotswolds full three thousand years ago? And were not human remains found here a few years back, when this, in common with many other barrows hard by, was opened, and an underground chamber discovered therein—the earthly resting-place of the bones of the unknown dead?

"The silence of deep eternities, of worlds from beyond the morning stars—does it not speak to thee? The unborn ages,—the old graves, with their long-mouldering dust,—the very tears that wetted it, now all dry,—do not these speak to thee what ear hath not heard?"

> "Solemn before us
> Veiled the dark Portal—
> Goal of all mortal.
> Stars silent rest o'er us,
> Graves under us silent."

Well has Carlyle translated the great German poet. And the old barrows that lie scattered over these wide-stretching downs are not dumb; they are continually speaking to us of those things "which ear hath not heard"; and at no time have they more to tell than at the close of a mild, peaceful day in October, when all else, save for the faint tinkling of the distant sheep-bells, is silent as death, and the sun, ere once more disappearing, is shedding a solemn glow over the deserted, mysterious uplands of the Cotswold Hills.

But the partridges are "calling" all around, and a covey actually passes over your head. Your sporting instincts begin to revive, and you take up your gun and proceed to stalk that covey, stealing round under a wall. Then you suddenly remember that the V.W.H. hounds meet in your village to-morrow, and you begin wondering whether they will once again find the great dog fox that several times last season led you over the wide, open country that now lies mapped out before you. *Your* fox, too, one of a litter you came upon two springs ago, in a little spinney not half a mile from where you are standing now, stub-bred and of the greyhound stamp, fleet of foot and lithe of limb. Each time the hounds had come to draw he was at home in the covert on the brow of the hill which shelters the old manor house you inhabit from the cold blast of winter. Here he loved to dwell, and hunt moorhens and dabchicks and water-rats all night long by the banks of silvery Coln. But on three occasions within six weeks, no sooner did the hounds enter the wood than a shrill scream proclaimed him away on the far side. You were mounted on a good horse, and were away as soon as the pack. And then for thirty minutes the "old customer" cantered away over those broad pastures, hounds and horses tearing after him on a breast-high scent, but never gaining an inch of ground. Two leagues were quickly traversed ere yonder distant belt of trees was reached, where the dry leaves lay rotting on the ground, and there was not an atom of scent. So he saved his life, and the tired, mud-bespattered sportsmen vow that there never was such a run seen before, so thrilling is the ecstasy of "pace" and so enchanting the stride of a well-bred horse.

'Tis a wild, deserted tract of country that stretches from Cirencester right away to the north of Warwickshire. For fifty miles you might gallop on across those undulating fields, and meet no human being on your way. We have ridden forty miles on end along the Fosseway, and, save in the curious half-forsaken old towns of Moreton-in-the-Marsh and Stow-on-the-Wold, we scarcely met a soul on the journey. What a marvellous work was that old Roman Fosseway! Raised high above the level of the adjoining fields, it runs literally "as straight as an arrow" through the heart of the grassy Midlands. And what a rare hunting country it passes through! We saw but one short piece of barbed wire in our journey of over forty miles. Now that farming is no longer remunerative, the whole country seems to be given up to hunting. Depend upon it, it is this sport alone that circulates money through this deserted land.

Time was when the uplands of Gloucestershire were almost entirely under the plough, when good scenting days seldom gladdened the heart of the hunting man, and when, in a ride over the Cotswold tableland, the excitement of a fast gallop on grass was an impossibility. Those were the days when land at thirty shillings an acre was eagerly sought after and the wheat crop amply repaid those who cultivated it. Now, alas! farms are to be had for the asking, rent free; but nobody will take them, and the country is rapidly going back to its original uncultivated state. The farmer, nevertheless, does not lose heart.

To lay down such light land into permanent pasture does not pay; it is therefore left to its own devices, with the result that in a short time weeds and moss and rough grasses spring up—less unprofitable than ploughed fields, and almost as favourable for hunting the fox as the fair pastures of the Vale of Aylesbury. However,

> "Nihil est ab omni
> Parte beatum."

There are other things to be done in this life besides riding across country in the wake of the flying pack, glorious and exhilarating though the pastime be; and the sooner these great wastes of unprolific land are once more transformed into wheat-growing plough, the better will it be for all of us.

So you stroll dreamily homewards, musing on these things, and wondering whether you will have another glorious gallop to-morrow. You will just go round by that spinney to see if the earth you gave orders to be stopped up is properly closed. But stop! What is that lying curled up under the wall not ten yards off? See, he stirs! he rises lazily and looks round! 'Tis the very fox! Long and lean and wiry is he, fine drawn and sleek as a trained racehorse, with a brush nearly two feet long! Brown as the ploughed field you were looking at just now, save for the tip of his brush, which is white as snow. He trots off along the wall, offering the easiest of broadside shots if you were villain enough to take advantage of it. He does not hurry; he stops and looks round after a bit, as much as to say, "I trust you." But when you steal cautiously towards him he once more lollops along. You follow, to see where he goes to when he has jumped over the high wall into the next field. But he does not jump over, but *on to* the wall, and there he sits looking at you until you are once more nearly up to him; then he disappears the other side, and you run up and peep over. He is nowhere to be seen! You look along the wall for a hole into which he could have popped, but in vain. You stoop down and try to track him by scent and the mark of his pad, but all to no purpose; and from that day to this you have never discovered what became of him.

CHAPTER VI.

A GALLOP OVER THE WALLS.

"Waken, lords and ladies gay,
To the greenwood haste away;
We can show you where he lies,
Fleet of foot and tall of size."

SIR WALTER SCOTT.

The next morning you are up betimes, for the hounds meet at the house at nine o'clock. You are not sorry on looking out of your window to see that a thick mist at present envelopes the country. With the ground in the dry state it is in, this mist, accompanied as it is by a heavy dew, is your only chance of a scent. How else could they hunt the jackal in India if it was not for this dew? Thus reflecting, you recall pleasant recollections of gallops over hard ground with the Bombay hounds, and comfort yourself with the thought that the ground here to-day cannot be as hard as that Indian soil. You are soon into your breeches and boots and down to breakfast. In the dining-room a large party is already assembled, for there are five men and two ladies turning out from the house, whilst one or two keen sportsmen have already put in an appearance from afar.

The hounds turn up punctual to the appointed time. How beautiful and majestic they look as they suddenly come into sight amid beech and ash and walnut, whilst the bright pageant advances leisurely and in order over the ancient ivy-covered bridge which spans the silent river, where the morning mist still hangs, and the grass shines white with silvery dew. In good condition they look, too—a credit to their huntsman, who evidently has not neglected giving them plenty of exercise on the roads during the summer. You greet the genial master; then in answer to his enquiry as to where you would like him to draw, you point to the hanging wood on the brow of the hill, and tell him that as you heard them barking there this very morning it is a certain find. No sooner are the words out of your mouth than a holloa breaks the silence of the early morn: the gardener has "viewed" a cub within a hundred yards of the house. Desperately bold are the cubs at this time of year, before they have been hunted. Their first experience of being "stopped out" for the night does not seem to have frightened them at all. They have been kicking up a rare shindy most of the night in the covert close to the house.

> "Alas I regardless of their doom,
> The little victims play."

By to-night they will have become sadder and wiser beings. Several people will be glad of this, the keeper included: for the fowls have suffered lately; there have also been one or two well-planned and carefully thought out sallies on the young pheasants—without much damage, however. Not long ago a bold young cub spent some time in breaking open the lid of one of the coops, in which were some late pheasants. He actually forced the wire netting from the roof of the coop, although it was firmly nailed to the woodwork. But he could not quite get his head in, for when the keeper arrived on the scene at five o'clock a.m., there he was, clawing and scratching at the birds. His efforts met with no success, however, for not a single bird was badly injured, though some damage might have been done if Master Reynard had not been interrupted at this critical moment. Young cubs are like puppies, very mischievous. There are plenty of rabbits about, and they are the food foxes like best; poultry and pheasants are pursued and killed out of pure love of mischief.

We must return to the hounds. Our huntsman wisely determines not to go to the holloa, for he prefers to let the young entry draw for their game. Besides which, if this cub has gone away, he is one of the right sort, and does not require schooling. For as we all know, one of the objects of cub-hunting is to teach the young foxes that if they don't leave the covert when the hounds are thrown in, they will get a rare dusting. So, the hounds having been taken to the "up-wind" end of the wood, the huntsman begins drawing steadily "down wind." Let them have every chance now; it will be quite early enough to begin drawing up wind when the leaf is off and Reynard has got a bit shy. Blood is an excellent thing for young hounds, nay, for all hounds, early in the season; but we don't want to chop any cubs before they know where they are or what it all means.

And soon the whole valley re-echoes with hound music, as the pack come crashing towards us through the thick underwood. We get a splendid view of the proceedings—for the covert is a long, narrow strip of about ten acres, running in the shape of a bow round the hill immediately above the place where we are stationed. There is another small wood of about the same size on the other side of the little valley. For this our fox makes, the hounds dashing close after him through the brook. Round and round they go, and it is evident that this cub (unlike several of his brethren who have taken their departure, viewed by the whole field, but *not* holloaed at) does not intend to face the open country. Scent is good in covert, perhaps because there are at present few of those dry leaves on the ground that spoil scent after the "fall of the leaf"; the result is, we kill a cub. This will be a lesson to the rest of the family when they return to-night and discover the fearful end that befalls foxes that "hang in covert." Another cub having gone to ground in a rabbit-hole, the keeper is given injunctions to have this hole, together with any other large ones he can find, stopped up, after allowing a day or two to pass, especially making sure, by the use of terriers and also by the tracks, that he does not stop any cubs in.

We now leave the home coverts and start away for a withybed about a mile up the river, where we are told there is a litter. Here, however, we do not find, though it is the likeliest place in the world for a fox. As the hounds dash into the withybed a whole string of wild ducks get up, circle round us, and then fly straight away up stream in the shape of the letter V—a sight unsurpassed if you happen to be a lover of nature.

Our next draw is an isolated artificial gorse of about six acres. If we find here, we must have a gallop, for there is no covert of any size within a four-mile radius; a fine open country lies all around; walls to jump and large fields of fifty acres apiece to gallop over. There is some light plough, but each year the plough gets scarcer, for the Cotswolds are rapidly being allowed to tumble back into grass or, rather, into *weeds*.

A great proportion of the stone-wall country hereabouts consists of downs divided into large enclosures; when the walls are low there is no reason why the pace should not be almost as good as it is in an unenclosed country. Happily to-day we seem to be in for a quick thing, for before the whip has had time to get to the end of the covert, hounds are away, without a sound, and we start off fully two hundred yards behind them.

The old fox, for a fiver! But there is no stopping them; so, knowing the country and the earth he is making for, you make tracks, as hard as your horse can pelt, in the direction in which the hounds are going, and very soon they turn to you, and you find yourself almost alongside of them. They are running "mute," with their noses several inches off the ground; it almost looks as if they had "got a view" of him. But this is not the case. Scent is "breast high." Two old hounds that you know well—Crusty and Governor—are leading, though you are glad that one or two you do not know (evidently some of this year's entry) are not far behind.

The country, which has so far been rather hilly, now opens out into a flat tableland. You fly on, thankful that you are on a thoroughbred, and that he is in good condition. It pays well to keep a horse "up" all the summer in this country, for some of the quickest things of the season take place in October. Scent is often good at this time of the year, because the fields are full of keep: there is plenty of rough grass about. Later on they will be pared down by sheep, and the frost will make them as bare as a turnpike road. Then again that abomination, a "carrying" plough, is not so likely to be met with in October; the white frosts are not severe enough. Later on they are a constant source of annoyance to a huntsman, and invariably cause a check.

But your horse, well bred and fit though he be, is doing all he can to live with the hounds. Fortunately, you know that he is too good to chance a wall, even when blown. At the pace hounds are going you have not much time to trot slowly at the walls in the orthodox fashion; you must take them as they come, high and low alike, at a fair pace, taking a pull a few strides before your mount takes off. Oh, how exhilarating is a gallop in this fine Cotswold air in the cool autumnal morning! and what a splendid view you get of hounds!

Here are no tall fences to hide them from your sight and to tempt a fox to run the hedgerows, no boggy woodlands where your horse flounders up to his girths in yellow clay, no ridge and furrow, and no deep ploughed fields.

What is the charm which belongs so exclusively to a fast and *straight* "run" over this wild, uncultivated region? It does not lie in the successful negotiation of Leicestershire "oxers," Aylesbury "doubles," or Warwickshire "stake-and-bound" fences, for there need be no obstacle greater than an occasional four-foot stone wall. Perhaps it lies partly in the fact that in a run over a level stone-wall country, where the enclosures are large and the turf sound, given a good fox and a "burning scent," hounds and horses travel at as great a pace as they attain in any country in England. Here, moreover, if anywhere, is to be found the "greatest happiness for the greatest number," the maximum of sport with the minimum of danger; the fine, free air of the high-lying Cotswold plains; the good fellowship engendered when all can ride abreast; the very muteness of the flying pack; the onslaught of a light brigade, or of "a flying squadron under the Admiral of the Red" sailing away over a sea of grass towards a region almost untrodden by man; the long sweeping stride of a well-bred horse; the unceasing twang of the horn to encourage flagging hounds beaten off by the pace and those which got left behind at the start; lastly, the *glorious uncertainty*! Can it last? Where will it all end? Shall we run "bang into him" in the open, or will he beat us in yonder cold scenting woodland standing boldly forth on the skyline miles ahead? All these things add a peculiar fascination to a fast run over this wild country.

Sooner or later there is a sudden check, a couple of sharp turns, and the spell is gone. Hounds may run back ever so well, to the very covert whence an hour ago they forced him. The pleasure of watching them work out a scent, growing rapidly colder, may indeed be left to us; but the glorious possibilities, which lasted as long as a gallant though invisible "quarry" was leading us *straight away* from home into unfamiliar regions, have passed away; the record run, which we thought had really commenced at last, far, far into the unknown land, into the country leading to nowhere, is not yet attained,—probably it never will be, for it existed in the human imagination alone during that thrilling thirty-minutes' burst, and was beyond the compass of foxes, horses, and hounds.

As a set off to this it must be admitted that fast runs do not take place every day on these hills. Perhaps there will not be more than half a dozen "clinkers" in a season with a "two-day-a-week" pack. For this reason, as regards all-round sport, the wall country cannot compare with a vale: a stranger might hunt there for three weeks in March, and at the end of that time take himself off in disappointment and disgust, declaring these fast-flying runs he had heard so much about to be an invention and a myth, and the wall country only fit for fools and funkers. For good scenting days in this hill country are few and far between, and a bad day in the wall district is the poorest fun imaginable. For this the field have generally themselves to thank, since they will not give the hounds a chance.

But there is a burning scent this morning, as there generally is when the dew is just going off. For twenty-five minutes hounds do not check once. The earth our fox has been making for is fortunately closed. This causes a moment's uncertainty among the hounds, but not a check, for they drive straight onwards, and it is evident that he is making for some earths five miles away in a neighbouring hunt's territory, which instinct tells him will be open.

There they go, old T.K. and J.A., and several ladies, past masters in the craft of crossing a country with the maximum of elegance and skill and the minimum of risk to their horses, themselves, or their friends. Though the hounds are travelling at their greatest possible pace, they ride alongside them, looking as cool as cucumbers (too cool, I think, for their own enjoyment; for the more excitable though less experienced rider probably enjoys himself more). Note how each wall, varying in height from three to four and a half feet, is taken at a steady pace by those well-schooled horses; even a five-foot wall, coped with sharp, jagged stones pointing straight upwards, does not turn them one hair's breadth from the line. And please note also that each has two hands on the reins, and no whip hand flung high in the air, or elbows thrust outwards, you gentlemen who are fond of painting pictures of hunting scenes for the press!

A good rider sitting at his ease on horseback,

"As if an angel dropped down from the clouds
To turn and wind a fiery Pegasus,
And witch the world with noble horsemanship,"

resembles a skilful musician seated at a piano or an organ. There is the same kind of communication between the man and the instrument, whereby the stricken chords respond to the lightest touch of the master, who guides as with a silken thread the keys that set the trembling strings in motion. For the rider's keys are curb and snaffle, and his hands, by means of the bridle, control the sensitive bars of his horse's mouth—the most harmonious, delicate organ yet discovered on earth, but too often, alas! thumped and banged on to such an awful extent by unsympathetic, heavy hands, as to become considerably out of tune, whereby discord occasionally reigns supreme instead of sweet melodious harmony.

Goodness gracious! what's up? Our horse, which has never refused before, has stopped dead at a wall. We stand up in the stirrups and peep over, and there below us is a narrow but deep quarry, a veritable death trap for the unwary sportsman. This is indeed a merciful escape; and how can we be too thankful that a horse—wise, sagacious animal that he is—has been endowed with an extraordinary instinct whereby he can *smell* danger, even though he cannot see it. Writing of this—one of the numerous escapes a merciful dispensation of Providence has granted us in the hunting field—we are reminded that no less than five good men and true have been killed suddenly with the V.W.H. hounds during the last eighteen years. The list commences with George Whyte Melville, prince of hunting men, who broke his neck in a ploughed field in 1878. And it is a very remarkable fact that Mr. Noel Smith was killed in 1896, on precisely the same day—viz., the first Thursday of December—as that on which Whyte Melville lost his life eighteen years before.

But soon after crossing a road, hounds suddenly check. After casting themselves beautifully forward right-and left-handed until they have completed a half circle, they throw up their heads and look round for the huntsman. By a sort of instinct, the result of previous observation, the foremost riders anticipated that check, and did not follow hounds over the road, though one or two later arrivals press forward rather too eagerly. The huntsman, who is not far off, seeing at a glance that there is no other cause for checking, as the hounds are in the middle of a large grass field, immediately decides that the fox has turned sharp down wind (he has been running up wind all the way), and casts his hounds left-handed and back towards the lane without much delay.

"And now," to quote from Mr. Madden's "Diary of Master William Silence," "may be seen the advantage of a good character honestly won." Crusty is busy "feathering" down the road, and as he is an absolutely reliable hound, the rest of the pack are not long in coming back to him, and soon, cheered by their huntsman, they are in full cry again.

Our fox has run the road for a quarter of a mile. This manoeuvre has probably saved his life, for it has given him time to get his breath back. In addition to this, the instant Reynard turned down wind the scent changed from a very good one to a most indifferent one. How often this happens in a run! And it is one of the fox-hunter's chief consolations that there is scarcely a day throughout the season on which a run is impossible, if only a fox will set his head resolutely *up wind*, just as in a ringing run there is a certain amount of consolation in the thought that a fox *must travel up wind part of the way*.

It is evident that, being beaten, Reynard has given up all idea of going for the earths three miles away. He is beginning, like all tired foxes, to twist and turn. There is no scent on the road; the hounds are therefore laid on in a grass field, and feather across it in an uncertain sort of way. This gives an opportunity to a sportsman who has just arrived by the road to proclaim that "as usual they are hunting hares." However, there is some pretty hunting done by the pack up a hedgerow and across a ploughed field; but with scent growing less and less, as is always the case with a tired, twisting fox, we do not get along very fast. Hares are jumping up in all directions, and a terrible nuisance they are on this sort of occasion! That hounds will stick to their fox, twist and turn though he may, in spite of hares, is a fact that is often proved in this country, when a lucky view has once more put them on good terms with the hunted fox, at a time when half the field have been crying "hare." But when a fox's scent has gradually diminished until it tends to vanishing point, it is useless to attempt to hunt him. This appears to be the case this morning, for the sun has scattered the mists, and has been shining the last ten minutes with tremendous vigour. We are glad when the master decides to give it up, for we hope to have some more runs with this old fox later on in the season. Hounds and horses have had enough for the time of year. So we turn our horses' heads to the cool breeze that is ever present on the Cotswolds, making the climate there one of the most delightful in the world in summer and autumn. And as we ride slowly homeward over the hill, past golden stubble fields, there is much that is picturesque to be seen on all sides: for some late barley is not yet gathered in; horses, drawing great yellow waggons, and old-fashioned Cotswold labourers are busy amongst the sheaves; and there is an air of activity and animation in the fields that is absent a month or two later. Bleak and desolate does this country sometimes look in winter, though when the sun shines it is fair enough. And suddenly, as we ride along, a lovely valley is seen below: old-world farmhouses and gabled cottages come into view, nestling amid stately elms and beech trees already touched by autumn's hand. As we gradually descend the hill, everything looks more beautiful than ever this morning; for we have had a gallop. For to-day at least we shall be in a thoroughly good temper. Whatever the morrow may bring forth, everything will appear to-day in the best possible light. Such an excellent tonic is a fast gallop over the walls for banishing dull care away.

CHAPTER VII.

A COTSWOLD TROUT STREAM.

"We may say of angling as Dr. Boteler said of strawberries: Doubtless God could have made a better berry, but doubtless God never did; and so, if I might be judge, God never did make a more calm, quiet, innocent recreation than angling.'" — *The Compleat Angler.*

Very few trout we have caught this season ('98) are pink-fleshed when cooked. Last year there were a good number. The reason probably is that they have not been feeding on the fresh-water shrimps or crustaceans, owing to the abundance of olive duns and other flies that have been on the water. Last winter, being so mild, was very favourable for the hatching out of fly in the spring. A hard winter doubtless commits sad havoc among the caddis and larvae at the bottom of the river; the trout, not being able to get much fly, are then compelled to fall back on the crustaceans. The food in these limestone rivers is so plentiful that the fish are able to pick and choose from a very varied bill of fare. This is the reason they are so difficult to catch. One is not able to increase the stock of trout to any great extent, thereby making them easier to catch, because the fish one introduces into the water are apt to crowd together in one or two places, with the result that they are far too plentiful in the shallows, where there is little food, and too scarce in the deeper water. Of the Loch Leven trout, turned in two years ago as yearlings, more than two-thirds inhabit the quick-running, gravelly reaches; in consequence, they have grown very little. The few that have stayed in the deeper water have done splendidly; they are now about three-quarters of a pound in weight. No fish, not even sea trout, fight so well as these bright, silvery "Loch Levens." They have cost us no end of casts and flies already this season, — not yet a month old. Experience proves, however, that ordinary *salmo fario*, or common brook trout, are the best for turning down; for the Loch Leven trout require deep water to grow to any size.

When a boy, I made a strange recovery of an eel that I had hooked and lost three weeks before. I was fishing with worms in a large deep hole in Surrey. My hook was a salmon fly with the feathers clipped off. I hooked what I believed to be an eel, but he broke the line through getting it entangled in a stick on the bottom. Three weeks afterwards, when fishing in the same fashion and in the same place, the line got fixed up on the bottom. I pulled hard and a stick came away. On that stick, strange to say, was entangled my old gut casting-line, and at the end of the line was an eel of two pounds' weight! On cutting him open, there, sure enough, was the identical clipped salmon fly; it had been inside that eel for three weeks without hurting him. This sounds like a regular angler's yarn, and nobody need believe it unless he likes; nevertheless, it is perfectly true. I had got "fixed up" in the same stick that had broken my line on the previous occasion.

That fish have very little sense of feeling is proved time after time. There is nothing unusual in catching a jack with several old hooks in his mouth. With trout, however, the occurrence is more rare. Last season my brother lost a fly and two yards of gut through a big trout breaking his tackle, but two minutes afterwards he caught the fish and recovered his fly and his tackle. We constantly catch fish during the may-fly time with broken tackle in their mouths.

Who does not recollect the rapturous excitement caused by the first fish caught in early youth? My first capture will ever remain firmly impressed on the tablet of the brain, for it was a red herring—"a common or garden," prime, thoroughly salted "red herring"! It came about in this way. At the age of nine I was taken by my father on a yachting expedition round the lovely islands of the west coast of Scotland. We were at anchor the first evening of the voyage in one of the beautiful harbours of the Hebrides, and, noticing the sailors fishing over the side of the boat, I begged to be allowed to hold the line. Somehow or other they managed to get a "red herring" on to the hook when my attention was diverted; so that when I hauled up a fish that in the darkness looked fairly silvery my excitement knew no bounds. After the sailors had taken it off the hook, and given it a knock on the head, I rushed down with it into the cabin, where my father and three others were dining. Throwing my fish down on to the table, I delightedly exclaimed, "Look what I have caught, father; isn't it a lovely fish?" I could not understand the roars of laughter which followed, as one of the party, with a horrified glance at my capture, shouted, "Take it away, take it away!" *Non redolet sed olet.* Oddly enough, although after this I caught any amount of real live fish, I never realised until months afterwards how miserably I had been taken in by the boat's crew on that eventful night.

Not long afterwards, whilst fishing with a worm just below the falls at Macomber, in the Highlands, I made what was for a small boy a remarkable catch of sea trout. I forget the exact number, but I know I had to take them back in sacks. They were "running" at the time, and it was very pretty to see them continually jumping up the seven-foot ladder out of the Spean into the Lochy. Underneath this ladder, where the water boiled and seethed in a thousand eddies, hundreds of trout lay ready to jump up the fall. Into this foaming torrent I threw my heavily leaded bait. No sooner was the worm in the water than it was seized by a fine sea trout. Some of them were nearly two pounds; and although I had a strong casting-line, they were often most difficult to land, for a series of small cataracts dashed down amongst huge rocks and slippery boulders, until, a hundred feet below, the calm, deep Macomber pool was reached. As the fish, when hooked, would often dash down this foaming torrent into the pool below, they gave a tremendous amount of play before they were landed. There was an element of danger about it, too, as a false step might have led to ugly complications amongst the rocks, over which the water came pouring down at the rate of ten miles an hour. A boy of twelve years old, as I was then, would not have stood a chance in that roaring torrent. A terrible accident happened here a few years afterwards. A party went from the house, where I always stayed, to fish at Macomber Falls. There were four ladies and two men. Whilst they were sitting eating their luncheon at this romantic spot, an argument arose as to whether a man falling into the seething pool below the fall would be drowned or not. The water was only about two feet deep; but the place was a miniature whirlpool, and, once started down the pent-in torrent, a man would be dashed along the rocky bed and carried far out into the deep Macomber pool beyond. A gentleman from Lincolnshire argued that in would be impossible for any one to be drowned in such shallow water. This was at lunch. Little did he imagine that within half an hour his theory would be put to the test. But so it was; for whilst he was standing on the rocks fishing, with a large overcoat on, he slipped and fell in. His fishing-line became entangled round his legs, and he was borne away at the mercy of the current. Unfortunately only ladies were present, his friend having gone down stream. Twice he clutched hold of the rocky bank opposite them, but it was too slippery, and his hold gave way. A man jumping across the chasm might possibly have saved him by risking his own life, for it was only fourteen feet wide; but it would have been madness for any of the ladies to have attempted it. So the poor fellow was drowned in two feet of water, before their eyes, and in spite of their brave endeavours to save him. He must have been stunned by repeated blows from the rocks, or else I think he would have baffled successfully with the torrent. The overcoat must have hampered him most dreadfully. It was a terrible affair, reminding one of the death of "young Romilly" in the Wharfe, of which Wordsworth tells in that beautiful poem, the "Force of Prayer." Bolton Abbey, as everybody knows, was built hard by, on the river bank, by the sorrowful mother, in honour of her boy.

> "That stately priory was reared;
>   And Wharf, as he moved along
> To matins, join'd a mournful voice,
>   Nor failed at evensong."

How many a beautiful spot in the British Isles has been endowed with a romance that will never entirely die away owing to some catastrophe of this kind! Macomber Falls are very beautiful indeed, but one cannot pass the place now without a shudder and a sigh.

It has been said that "the test of a river is its power to drown a man." There is doubtless a peculiar grandeur about the roaring torrent; but to me there is a still greater charm in the gentle flow of a south country trout stream, such as abound in Hampshire, Wiltshire, and in the Cotswolds. I do not think the Coln is capable of drowning a man, though one of the Peregrine family told me the other day that the only two men who ever bathed in our stream died soon afterwards from the shock of the intensely cold water! But then, it must be remembered that the old prejudice against "cold water" still lingers amongst the country folk of Gloucestershire; so that this story must always be taken *cum grano salis*.

"THE COLN NEAR BIBURY."

There are few trout streams to our mind more delightful from the angler's point of view than the Gloucestershire Coln. Rising a few miles from Cheltenham, it runs into the Thames near Lechlade, and affords some fifteen miles or more of excellent fishing. The scenery is of that quiet and homely type that belongs so exclusively to the chalk and limestone streams of the south of England.

From its source to the point at which it joins the Isis, the Coln flows continuously through a series of parks and small well-wooded demesnes, varied with picturesque Cotswold villages and rich water meadows. It swells out into fishable proportions just above Lord Eldon's Stowell property, steals gently past his beautiful woods at Chedworth and the Roman villa discovered a few years ago, then onward through the quaint old-world villages of Fossbridge to Winson and Coln-St-Dennis. Though not a hundred miles from

London, this part of Gloucestershire is one of the most primitive and old-fashioned districts in England. Until the new railway between Andover and Cheltenham was opened, four years ago, with a small station at Fosscross, there were many inhabitants of these old-world villages who had never seen a train or a railway. Only the other day, on asking a good lady, the wife of a farmer, whether she had ever been in London, I received the reply, "No, but I've been to Cheltenham." This in a tone of voice that meant me to understand that going to Cheltenham, a distance of about sixteen miles, was quite as important an episode in her life as a visit to London would have been.

On leaving Winson the Coln widens out considerably, and for the next two miles becomes the boundary between Mr. Wykeham-Musgrave's property of Barnsley and the manor of Ablington. It flows through the picturesque hamlet of Ablington, within a hundred yards of the old Elizabethan manor house, over an artificial fall in the garden, and passes onward on its secluded way through lovely woodland scenery, until it reaches the village of Bibury; here it runs for nearly half a mile parallel with the main street of the village, and then enters the grounds of Bibury Court. I know no prettier village in England than Bibury, and no snugger hostelry than the Swan. The landlady of this inn has a nice little stretch of water for the use of those who find their way to Bibury; and a pleasanter place wherein to spend a few quiet days could not be found. The garden and old court house of Bibury are sweetly pretty, the house, like Ablington, being three hundred years old; the stream passes within a few yards of it, over another waterfall of about ten feet, and soon reaches Williamstrip. Here, again, the scenery is typical of rural England in its most pleasing form; and the village of Coln-St.-Aldwyns is scarcely less fascinating than Bibury.

After leaving the stately pile of Hatherop Castle and Williamstrip Park on the left, the Coln flows silently onwards through the delightful demesne of Fairford Park. Here the stream has been broadened out into a lake of some depth and size, and holds some very large fish. Another mile and Fairford town is reached, another good specimen of the Cotswold village—for it is a large village rather than a town—with its lovely church, famous for its windows, its gabled cottages, and comfortable Bull Inn. There are several miles of fishing at the Bull, as many an Oxonian has discovered in times gone by, and we trust will again.

From what we have said, it will easily be gathered that this stream is unsurpassed for scenery of that quiet, homely type that Kingsley eulogises so enthusiastically in his "Chalk Stream Studies," and I am inclined to agree with him in his preference for it over the grander surroundings of mountain streams:

"Let the Londoner have his six weeks every year among crag and heather, and return with lungs expanded and muscles braced to his nine months' prison. The countryman, who needs no such change of air and scene, will prefer more homelike, though more homely, pleasures. Dearer to him than wild cataracts or Alpine glens are the still hidden streams which Bewick has immortalised in his vignettes and Creswick in his pictures. The long grassy shallow, paved with yellow gravel, where he wades up between low walls of fern-fringed rock, beneath nut and oak and alder, to the low bar over which the stream comes swirling and dimpling, as the water-ouzel flits piping before him, and the murmur of the ringdove comes soft and sleepy through the wood,—there, as he wades, he sees a hundred sights and hears a hundred tones which are hidden from the traveller on the dusty highway above."

But *chacun à son goût!* Let us now see what sort of sport may be had in the Coln. To begin with, it must be described as a "may-fly" stream. This means, of course, that there is a tremendous rise of fly early in June, with the inevitable slack time before and after the may-fly time.

But there is much pleasant angling to be had at other times. The season begins at the end of March, when a few small fish are rising, and may be caught with the March brown or the blue and olive duns. Few big fish are in condition until May, but much fun can be had with the smaller ones all through April. The half-pounders fight splendidly, and give one the idea, on being hooked, of pulling three times their real weight. The April fishing, at all events after the middle of the month, is very delightful in this river. One does not actually kill many fish, for a large number are caught and returned.

In May, when the larger fish begin to take up their places for the summer, one may expect good sport. This season, however, has been very disappointing; and, judging by the way the fish were feeding on the bottom for the first fortnight of the month, one is led to expect an early rise of the may-fly. Until the "fly is up," the April flies, especially the olive dun, are all that are necessary. For a couple of weeks before the "fly-fisher's carnival" sport is always uncertain.

If the wind is in a good quarter, sport may be had; but should it be east, the trout will not leave the caddis, with which the bed of the river is simply alive at this time. Of late years good sport has been obtained at the latter end of May with small flies. The may-fly generally comes up on the higher reaches about the last week in May, or about June 1st, though at Fairford, lower down, it is a week earlier. A good season means a steady rise of fly, lasting for nearly three weeks, but with no great amount of fly on any one day. A bad may-fly season means, as a rule, a regular "glut" of fly for three or four days, so that the fish are stuffed full almost to bursting point, and will not look at the natural fly afterwards, much less at your neatly "cocked" artificial one.

Large bags can, of course, be made on certain days in the may-fly season; but I do not know of any better than one hundred and six fish in three days, averaging one pound apiece.

Sport, however, is not estimated by the number of fish taken, and there is no better day's fun for the real fisherman than killing four or five brace of good fish when the trout are beginning to get tired of the fly, but are still to be caught by working hard for them. The "alder" will often do great execution at this time, and a small blue dun is sometimes very killing in the morning or evening.

After the "green-drake" has lived his short life and disappeared, there is a lull in the fishing, and the sportsman may with advantage take himself off to London to see the Oxford and Cambridge cricket match. All through July and August, when the water gets low and clear, the best and largest fish may be taken from an hour before sunset up to eleven o'clock at night by the red palmer. Although it savours somewhat of poaching, I confess to a weakness for evening and night fishing. The cool water meadows, the setting sun, with its golden glow on the water, add a peculiar charm to fishing at this time of day in the hot summer months. And then—the splash of your fish as you hook him! How magnified is the sound in the dim twilight, when you cannot see, but can only hear and feel your quarry! And what satisfaction to know that that great "logger-headed" two-pounder, that was devouring goodness knows how many yearlings and fry daily, is safe out of the water and in your basket!

On rainy days in these months good sport may be had with the wet fly; and in September a yellow dun, or a fly that imitates the wasp, will kill, if only you can keep out of sight, and place a well-dried fly right on the fish's nose.

The dry fly and up stream is of course the orthodox method of fishing in this as in other south-country chalk or limestone streams. No flogging the water indiscriminately all the way up, but marking your fish down, and stalking him, is the real game. For those who fish "wet" sport is not so good as it used to be, owing to the "schoolmaster being abroad" amongst trout as well as amongst men; but on certain windy days this method is the only one possible. There is a good deal of prejudice against the "chuck-and-chance-it" style among the advocates of the dry-fly method of fishing. That a man who fishes with a floating fly should be set down as a better sportsman than one who allows his fly to sink is, to my thinking, a narrow-minded argument, and one, moreover, that is not borne out by facts. True, in some clear chalk streams the fish can only be killed with the dry fly; and in such cases it is unsportsmanlike to thrash the water—in the first place, because there is no chance of catching fish, and in the second, in the interest of other anglers, because it is likely to make the fish shy. And therefore it is a somewhat selfish method of fishing.

But let those accomplished exponents of the art of fishing who are too fond of applying the epithet "poacher" to all those who do not fish in their own particular style remember that there are but few streams in England sluggish enough for dry-fly fishing; consequently many first-rate fishermen have never acquired the art. The dry-fly angler has no more right to consider himself superior as a sportsman to the advocate of the old-fashioned method than the county cricketer has to consider himself superior to the village player. In both cases time and practice have done their work; but the best fishermen and the most practised exponents of the game of cricket are very often inferior to their less distinguished brethren as *sportsmen*. At the same time, were I asked which of all our English sports requires the greatest amount of perseverance, the supremest delicacy of hand, the most assiduous practice, and the most perfect control of temper, in order that excellence may be attained, I would unhesitatingly answer, "Dry-fly fishing on a real chalk stream"; and I would sooner have one successful day under such conditions than catch fifty trout by flogging a Scotch burn.

In the Coln the fish run largest at Fairford, where the water has been deepened and broadened; and there three-pounders are not uncommon. Then at Hatherop and Williamstrip there are some big fish. Higher up the trout run up to two and a half pounds; and the average size of fish killed after May 1st is, roughly speaking, one pound. The higher reaches are very much easier to fish, for the following reason: at Bibury, and at intervals of about half a mile all the way down, the river is fed by copious springs of transparent water; the lower down you go, and the more springs that fall into the river, the more glassy does it become. The upper reaches of this river may be described as easy fishing. The water, when in good trim, is of a whey colour, though after June it becomes low and very clear. The flies I have mentioned are the only ones really necessary, and if the fish will not take them they will probably take nothing. They are, to sum up:

(1) March Brown.
(2) Olive Dun.
(3) Blue Dun.
(4) May-fly.
(5) Alder.
(6) Palmer.

"Wykeham's Fancy" and the "Grey Quill Gnat" are the only other flies that need be mentioned. The former has a great reputation on the river, but we ourselves have used it but little.

The food on the Coln is most abundant, and to this must be attributed the extraordinary size of the fish as compared with the depth and bulk of water. That one hundred and fifty brace of trout, averaging a pound in weight, are taken with rod and line each year on a stretch of water two miles in length, and varying in depth from two to three feet, with a few deep holes, the width of the water being not more than thirty feet for the most part, is sufficient proof that there is abundance of food in the river.

Where the water is shallow we have found great advantage accrue by putting in large stones and fir poles, to form ripples and also homes for the fish. By this means shallow reaches can be made to hold good fish, and the eddies and ripples make them easy to catch. The stones add to the picturesqueness of the stream, for they soon become coated with moss, and give the idea in some places of a rocky Scotch burn. A pleasant variety of fishing is thus obtained; for at one time you are throwing a dry fly on to the still and unruffled surface of the broader reaches, and a hundred yards lower down you may have to use a wet fly in the narrower and quicker parts, where the stones cause the water to "boil up" in all directions, and the eddies give a chance to those who are uninitiated into the mysteries of dry-fly angling.

The large fish prefer sluggish water, but in these artificial ripples fish may be caught on days on which the stream would be unfishable under ordinary circumstances. It would be invidious to make comparisons between the Coln and the Hampshire rivers—the Itchen and the Test,—these are larger rivers, with larger fish, and they require a better fisherman than those stretches of the Coin that we are dealing with, although the lower reaches of the latter stream are difficult enough for most people.

Otters used to be considered scarce on the River Coln, but two have lately been trapped in the parish of Bibury. With pike and coarse fish we are not troubled on the upper reaches, though lower down they exist in certain quantities. Of poachers I trust I may say the same. Rumour has sometimes whispered of nets kept in Bibury and elsewhere, and of midnight raids on the neighbouring preserves; but though I have walked down the bank on many a summer night, I have never once come upon anything suspicious, not even a night-line. The Gloucestershire native is an honest man. He may think, perhaps, that he has nothing to learn and cannot go wrong, but burglaries are practically unknown, and poaching is not commonly practised.

To sum up, the River Coln affords excellent sport amid surroundings seldom to be found in these days. The whole country reminds one of the days of Merrie England, so quaint and rural are the scenes. The houses and cottages are all built of the native stone, which can be obtained for the trouble of digging, so there is no danger of modern villas or the inroads of civilisation spoiling the face of the country. And moreover, these country people; being simple in their tastes, have never endeavoured to improve on the old style of building; the newer cottages, with their pointed gables, closely resemble the old Elizabethan houses. The new stone soon tones down, and every house has a pretty garden attached to it.

I have just returned from a stroll by the river, with my rod in hand, on the look-out for a rise. Not a fish was stirring. It is the middle of May, and this glorious valley is growing more and more glorious every day. An evening walk by the stream is delightful now, even though you may begin to wonder if all the fish have disappeared. The air is full of joyful sounds. The cuckoo, the corncrake, and the cock pheasant seem to be vieing with each other; but, alas! nightingales there are none. As I come round a bend, up get a mallard and a duck, and beautiful they look as they swing round me in the dazzling sunlight. A little further on I come upon a whole brood of nineteen little wild ducks. The old mothers are a good deal tamer now than they were in the shooting season. Many a time have they got up, just out of shot, when I was trying to wile away the time during the great frost with a little stalking. A kingfisher shoots past; but I have given up trying to find her nest. There is a brood of dabchicks, and, a little further on, another family of wild duck.

The spring flowers are just now in their flush of pride and glory. Clothing the banks, and reflected everywhere in the blue waters of the stream, are great clusters of marsh marigolds painting the meadows with their flaming gold; out of the decayed "stoles" of trees that fell by the water's edge years and years ago springs the "glowing violet"; here and there, as one throws a fly towards the opposite bank, a purple glow on the surface of the stream draws the attention to a glorious mass of violets on the mossy bank above; myriads of dainty cuckoo flowers,

> "With cowslips wan that hang the pensive head,
> And every flower that sad embroidery wears,"

are likewise to be seen. Farther away from the stream's bank, on the upland lawn and along the hedge towards the downs, the deep purple of the hyacinth and orchis, and the perfect blue of the little eyebright or germander speedwell, are visible even at a distance. In a week the lilac and sweet honeysuckle will fill the air with grateful redolence.

Ah! a may-fly. But I know this is only a false alarm. There are always a few stray ones about at this time; the fly will not be "up" for ten days at least. When it does come, the stream, so smooth and glassy now, will be "like a pot a-boiling," as the villagers say. You would not think it possible that a small brook could contain so many big fish as will show themselves when the fly is up.

In conclusion, we will quote once more from dear old Charles Kingsley, for what was true fifty years ago is true now—at all events, in this part of Gloucestershire; and may it ever remain so!

"Come, then, you who want pleasant fishing days without the waste of time and trouble and expense involved in two hundred miles of railway journey, and perhaps fifty more of highland road; come to pleasant country inns, where you can always get a good dinner; or, better still, to pleasant country houses, where you can always get good society—to rivers which always fish brimful, instead of being, as these mountain ones are, very like a turnpike road for three weeks, and then like bottled porter for three days—to streams on which you have strong south-west breezes for a week together on a clear fishing water, instead of having, as on these mountain ones, foul rain spate as long as the wind is south-west, and clearing water when the wind chops up to the north,—streams, in a word, where you may kill fish four days out of five from April to October, instead of having, as you will most probably in the mountain, just one day's sport in the whole of your month's holiday."

CHAPTER VIII.

WHEN THE MAY-FLY IS UP.

"Just in the dubious point where with the pool
Is mix'd the trembling stream, or where it boils
Around the stone, or from the hollow'd bank
Reverted plays in undulating flow,
There throw, nice judging, the delusive fly."

THOMSON'S *Seasons.*

When does the may-fly come, the gorgeous succulent may-fly, that we all love so well in the quiet valleys where the trout streams wend their silent ways?

It comes "of a Sunday," answers the keeper, who would fain see the prejudice against fishing "on the Sabbath" scattered to the four winds of heaven. He thinks it very contrary of the fly that it should invariably come up "strong" on the one day in the week on which the trout are usually allowed a rest.

"'Tis a most comical job, but it always comes up thickest of a Sunday," he frequently exclaims. Then, if you press him for further particulars, he grows eloquent on the subject, and tells you as follows: "We always reckons to kill the most fish on 'Durby day.' 'Tis a most singular thing, but the 'Durby day' is always the best."

Now, considering that Derby day is a movable feast, saving that it always comes on a Wednesday, there would appear to be no more logic in this statement than there is in the one about the fly coming up strong on a Sunday. However, so deep rooted is the theory that the Derby and the cream of the may-fly fishing are inseparably associated that we have come to talk of the biggest rise of the season as "the Derby day," whatever day of the week it may happen to be.

Thus Tom Peregrine, the keeper, when he sees the fly gradually coming up, will say: "I can see how it will be—next Friday will be

Durby day. You must 'meet' the fly that day; 'be sure and give it the meeting,' sir. We shall want six rods on the water on Friday." He is so desperately keen to kill fish that he would sooner have six rods and moderate sport for each fisherman than three rods and good sport all round. Wonderfully sanguine is this fellow's temperament:

> "A man he seems of cheerful yesterdays
>   And confident to-morrows."

It is always "just about a good day for fishing" before you start; and if you have a bad day, he consoles you with an account of an extraordinary day last week, or one you are to have next week. Sometimes it was last season that was so good; "or it will be a splendid season next year," for some reason or other only known to himself.

Three good anglers are quite sufficient for two miles of fishing on the best of days. Experience has taught us that "too many cooks spoil the broth" even in the may-fly season.

I shall never forget a most lamentable, though somewhat laughable, occurrence which took place five years ago. Foolishly responding to the entreaties of our enthusiastic friend the keeper, we actually did ask five people to fish one "Durby day." As luck would have it they all came; but unfortunately a neighbouring squire, who owns part of the water, but who seldom turns up to fish, also chose that day, and with him came his son. Seven was bad enough in all conscience, but imagine my feelings when a waggonette drove up, full of *undergraduates from Oxford*: my brother, who was one of the undergraduates, had brought them down on the chance, and without any warning. Of course they all wanted to fish, though for the most part they were quite innocent of the art of throwing a fly. Result: ten or a dozen fisherman, all in each other's way; every rising fish in the brook frightened out of its wits; and very little sport. The total catch for the day was only thirty trout, or exactly what three rods ought to have caught.

These were the sort of remarks one had to put up with: "I say, old chap, there's a d——d fellow in a mackintosh suit up stream; he's bagged my water"; or, "Who is that idiot who has been flogging away all the afternoon in one place? Does he think he's beating carpets, or is he an escaped lunatic from Hanwell?"

The whole thing was too absurd; it was like a fishing competition on the Thames at Twickenham.

Since this never-to-be-forgotten day I have come to the conclusion that to have too few anglers is better than too many; also, alas! that it is quite useless to ask your friends to come unless they are accomplished fishermen. It takes years of practice to learn the art of catching south-country trout in these days, when every fish knows as well as we do the difference between the real fly and the artificial. One might as well ask a lot of schoolboys to a big "shoot," as issue indiscriminate invitations to fish.

It is a prochronism to talk of the *May*-fly; for, as a matter of fact, the first ten days of *June* usually constitute the may-fly season. Of late years the rise has been earlier and more scanty than of yore. There are always several days, however, during the rise when all the biggest fish in the brook come out from their homes beneath the willows, take up a favourable place in mid stream, and quietly suck down fly after fly until they are absolutely stuffed. To have fished on one of these days in any well-stocked south-country brook is something to look back upon for many a long day. In a reach of water not exceeding one hundred yards in length there will be fish enough to occupy you throughout the day. You may catch seven or eight brace of trout, none of which are under a pound in weight, where you did not believe any large ones existed. The fact is, the larger fish of a trout stream are more like rats in their habits than anything else; they stow themselves away in holes in the bank and all sorts of inconceivable places, and are as invisible by day as the otter itself.

That man derives the greatest enjoyment from this annual carnival among the trout who has been tied to London all through May, sweltering in a stuffy office and longing for the country. Though his sympathies are bound up heart and soul in country pursuits, he has elected to "live laborious days" in the busy haunts of men. He does it, though he hates it; for he has sufficient insight to know that self-denial in some form or other is the inevitable destiny of mortal man: sooner or later it has to be undergone by all, whether we like it or not

> "Quanto quisque sibi plura negaverit
> Ab dis plura feret"

Horace never wrote anything truer than that, though we are not to suppose that the second line will necessarily come true in this life.

We will imagine that our friend is a briefless barrister, but a fine, all-round sportsman; a crack batsman, perhaps, at Eton and Oxford, or one of whom it might be said:

> "Give me the man to whom nought comes amiss,
> One horse or another, that country or this—
> Who through falls and bad starts undauntedly still
> Rides up to the motto, 'Be with them I will.'"

There may be good sportsmen enough enjoying life throughout the country villages of Merrie England, but in my humble opinion the *best* sportsmen must be sought in stifling offices in London, or serving "their country and their Queen" under the burning sun of a far country, or maybe in the reeking atmosphere of the East End, or as missionaries in that howling wilderness the inhospitable land of "the heathen Chinee."

Sitting in his dusty chambers, poring over grimy books and legal manuscripts, our "briefless" friend receives a telegram which he has been expecting rather anxiously the last few days. As brief as he is "briefless," it brings a flush to his cheek which has not been seen there since that great run with the hounds last Christmas holidays. "The fly is up; come at once." These are the magic words; and no time is lost in responding to the invitation, for, as prearranged, he is to start for Gloucestershire directly the wire arrives.

There is no need to rush off to Mr. Farlow and buy up his stock of may-flies; for though he does not tie his own flies, our angling friend has a goodly stock of them neatly arranged in rows of cork inside a black tin box; and, depend upon it, they are the *right* ones.

Many a fisherman goes through a lifetime without getting the right flies for the water on which he angles. It is ten to one that those in the shops are too light, both in the body and the wing; the may-flies usually sold are likewise much too big. About half life-size is quite big enough for the artificial fly, and as a general rule they cannot be too *dark*.

Some years ago we caught a live fly, and took it up to London for the shopman to copy. "At last," we said to ourselves, "we have got the right thing." But not a bit of it. The first cast on to the water showed us that the fly was utterly wrong. It was far too light. The fact is, the insect itself appears very much darker on the water than it does in the air. But the artificial fly shows ten times lighter as it floats on the stream than it does in the shop window.

Dark mottled grey for your wings, and a brown hackle, with a dark rather than a straw-coloured body, is the kind of fly we find most killing on the upper Coln. Of course it may be different on other streams, but I suspect there is a tendency to use too light a fly everywhere, save among those who have learnt by experience how to catch trout. As Sir Herbert Maxwell has proved by experiment, trout have no perception of colour except so far as the fly is light or dark. He found dark blue and red flies just as killing as the ordinary may-fly.

For the dry-fly fisherman equipment is half the battle. Show me the man who catches fish; ten to one his rod is well balanced and strong, his line heavy, though tapered, and his gut well selected and stained. The fly-book stamps the fisherman even more truly than the topboot stamps the fox-hunter. Nor does the accomplished expert with the dry fly disdain with fat of deer to grease his line, nor with paraffin to dress his fly and make it float. But he keeps the paraffin in a leather case by itself, so that his coat may not remain redolent for months. From top to toe he is a fisherman. His boots are thick, even though he does not require waders; on his knees are leather pads to ward off rheumatism; whilst on his head is a sober-coloured cap—not a white straw hat flashing in the sunlight, and scaring the timid trout to death.

Thus appears our sportsman of the Inner Temple not twelve hours after we saw him stewing in his London chambers. What a metamorphosis is this! Just as the may-fly, after two years of confinement as a wretched grub in the muddy bed of the stream, throws off its shackles, gives its wings a shake, and soars into the glorious June atmosphere, happy to be free, so does the poor caged bird rejoice, after grubbing for an indefinite period in a cramped cell, to leave darkness and dirt and gloom (though not, like the may-fly, for ever), and flee away on wings the mighty steam provides until he finds himself once again in the fresh green fields he loves so well. And truly he gets his reward. He has come into a new world— rather, I should say, a paradise; for he comes when meadows are green and trees are at their prime. Though the glory of the lilac has passed away, the buttercup still gilds the landscape; barley fields are bright with yellow charlock, and the soft, subdued glow of sainfoin gives colour to the breezy uplands as of acres of pink carnations. On one side a vast sheet of saffron, on the other a lake of rubies, ripples in the passing breeze, or breaks into rolling waves of light and shade as the fleecy clouds sweep across azure skies. He comes when roses, pink and white and red, are just beginning to hang their dainty heads in modest beauty on every cottage wall or cluster round the ancient porch; when from every lattice window in the hamlet (I wish I could say every *open* window) rows of red geraniums peep from their brown pots of terra-cotta, brightening the street without, and filling the cosy rooms with grateful, unaccustomed fragrance; when the scent of the sweet, short-lived honeysuckle pervades the atmosphere, and the faces of the handsome peasants are bronzed as those of dusky dwellers under Italian skies.

> No daintie flowre or herbe that grows on ground;
> No arborett with painted blossoms drest,
> And smelling sweete, but there it might be found,
> To bud out faire, and throwe her sweete smels al around.

E. SPENSER.

What a pleasant country is this in which to spend a holiday! How white are the limestone roads! how fresh and invigorating is the upland air! The old manor house is deserted, its occupants having gone to London. But a couple of bachelors can be happy in an empty house, without servants and modern luxuries, as long as the may-fly lasts. It is pleasant to feel that you can dine at any hour you please, and wear what you please. The good lady who cooks for you is merely the wife of one of the shepherds; but her cooking is fit for a king! What dinner could be better than a trout fresh from the brook, a leg of lamb from the farm, and a gooseberry tart from the kitchen garden? For vegetables you may have asparagus—of such excellence that you scarcely know which end to begin eating—and new potatoes.

For my part, I would sooner a thousand times live on homely fare in the country than be condemned to wade through long courses at London dinner parties, or, worse still, pay fabulous prices at "Willis's Rooms," the "Berkeley," or at White's Club.

What a comfort, too, to be without housemaids to tidy up your papers in the smoking-room and shut your windows in the evening! How healthful to sleep in a room in which the windows have been wide open night and day for months past!

Sport is usually to be depended upon in the may-fly time, as long as you are not late for the rise. Of late years the fly has "come up" so early and in such limited quantities that but few fishermen were on the water in time.

We are apt to grumble, declaring that the whole river has gone to the bad; that the fish are smaller and fewer in numbers than of yore, — but is this borne out by facts? The year 1896 was no doubt rather a failure as regards the may-fly; but as I glance over the pages of the game-book in which I record as far as possible every fish that is killed, I cannot help thinking that sport has been very wonderful, take it all round, during six out of seven seasons.

It is a lovely day during the last week in May. There has been no rain for more than a fortnight; the wind is north-east, and the sun shines brightly,—yet we walk down to the River Coln, anticipating a good day's sport among the trout: for, during the may-fly season, no matter how unpropitious the weather may appear, sport is more of a certainty on this stream than at any other time of year. Early in the season drought does not appear to have any effect on the springs; we might get no rain from the middle of April until half-way through June, and yet the water will keep up and remain a good colour all the time. But after June is "out," down goes the water, lower and lower every week; no amount of rain will then make any perceptible increase to the volume of the stream, and not until the nights begin to lengthen out and the autumnal gales have done their work will the water rise again to its normal height. If you ask Tom Peregrine why these things are so, he will only tell you that after a few gales the "springs be *frum*." The word "frum," the derivation of which is, Anglo-Saxon, "fram," or "from" = strong, flourishing, is the local expression for the bursting of the springs.

Our friend Tom Peregrine is full of these quaint expressions. When he sees a covey of partridges dusting themselves in the roads, he will tell you they are "bathering." A dog hunting through a wood is always said to be "breveting." "I don't like that dog of So-and-so's, he do 'brevet' so," is a favourite saying. The ground on a frosty morning "scrumps" or "feels scrumpety," as you walk across the fields; and the partridges when wild, are "teert." All these phrases are very happy, the sound of the words illustrating exactly the idea they are intended to convey. Besides ordinary Gloucestershire expressions, the keeper has a large variety that he has invented for himself.

When the river comes down clear, it is invariably described as like looking into a gin bottle, or "as clear as gin." A trout rising boldly at a fly is said to "'quap' up," or "boil up," or even "come at it like a dog." The word "mess" is used to imply disgust of any sort: "I see one boil up just above that mess of weed"; or, if you get a bit of weed on the hook, he will exclaim, "Bother! that mess of weed has put him down." Sometimes he remarks, "Tis these dreadful frostis that spiles everything. 'Tis enough to sterve anybody." When he sees a bad fisherman at work, he nods his head woefully and exclaims, "He might as well throw his 'at in!" Then again, if he is anxious that you should catch a particular trout, which cannot be persuaded to rise, he always says, "Terrify him, sir; keep on terrifying of him." This does not mean that you are to frighten the fish; on the contrary, he is urging you to stick to him till he gets tired of being harassed, and succumbs to temptation. All these quaint expressions make this sort of folk very amusing companions for a day's fishing.

It is eleven o'clock; let us walk down stream until we come to a bend in the river where the north-east wind is less unfavourable than it is in most parts. There is a short stretch of two hundred yards, where, as we fish up stream, the breeze will be almost at our backs, and there are fish enough to occupy us for an hour or so; afterwards, we shall have to "cut the wind" as best we can.

As we pass down stream the pale olive duns are hatching out in fair numbers, and a few fish are already on the move. What lovely, delicate things are these duns! and how "beautifully and wonderfully are they made"! If you catch one you will see that it is as delicate and transparent as it can possibly be. Not even the may-fly can compare with the dun. And what rare food for trout they supply! For more than six weeks, from April 1st, they hatch out by thousands every sunny day. The may-fly may be a total failure, but week after week in the early spring you may go down to the riverside with but one sort of fly, and if there are fish to be caught at all, the pale-winged olive dun will catch them; and in spite of the fact that there are a few may-flies on the water, it is with the little duns that we intend to start our fishing to-day. The trout have not yet got thoroughly accustomed to the green-drake, and the "Durby day" will not be here for a week. It is far better to leave them "to get reconciled" to the new fly (as the keeper would put it); they will "quap" up all the better in a few days if allowed, in angling phraseology, "to get well on to the fly."

On arriving at the spot at which we intend commencing operations, it is evident that the rise has begun. Happily, everything was in readiness. Our tapered gut cast has been wetted, and a tiny-eyed fly is at the end. The gut nearest the hook is as fine as gut can possibly be. Anything thicker would be detected, for a spring joins the river at this point and makes the water rather clear. Higher up we need not be so particular. There is a fish rising fifteen yards above us; so, crouching low and keeping back from the bank, we begin casting. A leather kneecap, borrowed from the harness-room, is strapped on to the knee, and is a good precaution against rheumatism. The first cast is two feet short of the rise, but with the next we hook a trout. He makes a tremendous rush, and runs the reel merrily. We manage to keep him out of the weeds and land him — a silvery "Loch Leven," about three-quarters of a pound, and in excellent condition. Only two years ago he was put into the stream with five hundred others as a yearling. The next two rising fish are too much for us, and we bungle them. One sees the line, owing to our throwing too far above him, and the other is frightened out of his life by a bit of weed or grass which gets hitched on to the barb of the hook, and lands bang on to his nose. These accidents will happen, so we do not swear, but pass on up stream, and soon a great brown tail appears for a second just above some rushes on the other side. Kneeling down again, we manage, after a few casts — luckily short of our fish — to drop the fly a foot above him. Down it sails, not "cocking" as nicely as could be wished, but in an exact line for his nose. There is a slight dimple, and we have got him. For two or three minutes we are at the mercy of our fish, for we dare not check him — the gut is too fine. But, lacking condition, he soon tires, and is landed. He is over a pound and a half, and rather lanky; but kill him we must, for by the size of his head we can see that he is an old fish, and as bad as a pike for eating fry. Two half-pounders are now landed in rapid succession, and returned to the water. Then we hook a veritable monster; but, alas! he makes a terrific rush down stream, and the gut breaks in the weeds. Of course he is put down as the biggest fish ever hooked in the water. As a matter of fact, two pounds would probably "see him." Putting on another olive dun, we are soon playing a handsome bright fish of a pound, with thick shoulders and a small head. And a lovely sight he is when we get him out of the water and knock him on the head.

We now come to a place where some big stones have been placed to make ripples and eddies, and the stream is more rapid. Glad of the chance of a rest from the effort of fishing "dry," which is tiring to the wrist and back, we get closer to the bank, and flog away for five minutes without success. Suddenly we hear a voice behind, and, looking round, see our mysterious keeper, who is always turning up unexpectedly, without one's being able to tell where he has sprung from. "The fish be all alive above the washpool. I never see such a sight in all my life!" he breathlessly exclaims.

"All right," we reply; "we'll be up there directly. But let's first of all try for the big one that lies just above that stone."

"There's one up! ... There's another up! The river's boiling," says our loquacious companion.

"That's the big fish," we reply, vigorously flogging the air to dry the fly; for when there is a big fish about, one always gives him as neatly a "cocked" fly as is possible.

"*Must* have him! Bang over him!" exclaims Tom Peregrine excitedly.

But there is no response from the fish.

"Keep *terrifying* of him, keep *terrifying* of him," whispers Tom; "he's bound to make a mistake sooner or later." So we try again, and at the same moment that the fly floats down over the monster's nose he moves a foot to the right and takes a live may-fly with a big roll and a flop.

"Well, I never! Try him with a may-fly, sir," says Peregrine.

Thinking this advice sound, we hastily put on the first may-fly of the season; and no sooner have we made our cast than, as Rudyard Kipling once said to the writer, there is a boil in the water "like the launch of a young yacht," a tremendous swirl, and we are fast into a famous trout. Directly he feels the insulting sting of the hook he rushes down stream at a terrific rate, so that the line, instead of being taut, dangles loosely on the water. We gather the line through the rings in breathless haste—there is no time to reel up—and once more get a tight strain on him. Fortunately there are no weeds here; the current is too rapid for them. Twice he jumps clean out of the water, his broad, silvery sides flashing in the sunlight. At length, after a five minutes' fight, during which our companion never stops talking, we land the best fish we have caught for four years. Nearly three pounds, he is as "fat as butter," as bright as a new shilling, with the pinkest of pink spots along his sides, and his broad back is mottled green. The head is small, indicating that he is not a "cannibal," but a real, good-conditioned, pink-fleshed trout. And it is rare in May to catch a big fish that has grown into condition.

We have now four trout in the basket. "A pretty dish of fish," as Peregrine ejaculates several times as we walk up stream towards the washpool. For thirty years he has been about this water, and has seen thousands of fish caught, yet he is as keen to-day as a boy with his first trout. As we pass through a wood we question him as to a small stone hut, which appeared to have fallen out of repair.

"Oh!" he replied, "that was built in the time of the Romans"; and then he went on to tell us how a *great* battle was fought in the wood, and how, about twenty years ago, they had found "a *great* skeleton of a man, nearly seven feet long"—a sure proof, he added, that the Romans had fought here.

As a matter of fact, there are several Roman villas in the neighbourhood, and there was also fighting hereabouts in the Civil Wars. But half the country folk look upon everything that happened more than a hundred years ago as having taken place in the time of the Romans; and Oliver Cromwell is to them as mythical a personage and belonging to an equally remote antiquity as Julius Caesar. The Welsh people are just the same. The other day we were shown a huge pair of rusty scissors whilst staying in Breconshire. The man who found them took them to the "big house" for the squire to keep as a curiosity, for, "no doubt," he said, "they once belonged to *some great king*"!

To our disgust, on reaching the upper water we found it as thick as pea-soup. Sheep-washing had been going on a mile or so above us. Never having had any sport under these conditions in past times, we had quite decided to give up fishing for the day; but Tom Peregrine, who is ever sanguine, swore he saw a fish rise. To our astonishment, on putting the fly over the spot, we hooked and landed a large trout Proceeding up stream, two more were quickly basketed. When the water comes down as thick as the Thames at London Bridge, after sheep washing, the big trout are often attracted out of their holes by the insects washed out of the wool; but they will seldom rise freely to the artificial fly on such occasions. To-day, oddly enough, they take any fly they can see in the thick water, and with a "coch-y-bondu" substituted for the may-fly, as being more easily seen in the discoloured water, any number of fish were to be caught. But there is little merit and, consequently, little satisfaction in pulling out big trout under these conditions, so that, having got seven fish, weighing nine pounds, in the basket, we are satisfied.

As a rule, it is only in the may-fly season that the biggest fish rise freely; an average weight of one pound per fish is usually considered first-rate in the Coln. On this day, however, although the may-fly was not yet properly up, the big fish, which generally feed at night, had been brought on the rise by the sheep-washing.

All the way home we are regaled with impossible stories of big fish taken in these waters, one of which, the keeper says, weighed five pounds, "all but a penny piece." As a matter of fact, this fish was taken out of a large spring close to the river; and it is very rarely that a three-pounder is caught in the Coln above Bibury, whilst anything over that weight is not caught once in a month of Sundays. Last January, however, a dead trout, weighing three pounds eight ounces, was found at Bibury Mill, and a few others about the same size have been taken during recent years. At Fairford, where the stream is bigger, a five-pounder was taken during the last may-fly.

We are pleased to find that our friend from London, who has been fishing the same water, has done splendidly; he has killed six brace of good trout, besides returning a large number to the water. With a glow of satisfaction he

> "Tells from what pool the noblest had been dragg'd;
> And where the very monarch of the brook,
> After long struggle, had escaped at last."

WORDSWORTH.

We laid our combined bag on the cool stone floor in the game larder;

> "And verily the silent creatures made
> A splendid sight, together thus exposed;
> Dead, but not sullied or deformed by death,
>   That seem'd to pity what he could not spare."

WORDSWORTH.

But the killing of trout is only a small part of the pleasure of being here when the may-fly is up. How pleasant to live almost entirely in the open air! after the day's fishing is over to rest awhile in the cool manor house hard by the stream, watching from the window of the oak-panelled little room the wonders of creation in the garden through which the river flows! Now, from the recesses of the overhanging boughs on the tiny island opposite, a moorhen swims forth, cackling and pecking at the water as she goes. She is followed by five little balls of black fur—her red-beaked progeny; they are fairly revelling in the evening sunlight, diving, playing with each other, and thoroughly enjoying life.

"A DISH OF FISH. CAUGHT BY THE VICAR OF FAIRFORD (WEIGHT 17 1/2 LBS.)"

Up on the bough of the old fir, bearing its heavy mantle of ivy from base to topmost twig, and not twenty yards from the window, a thrush sits and sings. You must watch him carefully ere you assure yourself that those sweet, trilling notes of peerless music come from that tiny throat. A rare lesson in voice production he will teach you. Deep breathing, headnotes clear as a bell and effortless, as only three or four singers in Europe can produce them, without the slightest sense of strain or throatiness—such are the songs of our most gifted denizens of the woods.

What a wondrous amount of life is visible on an evening such as this! Among the fast-growing nettles beyond the brook scores of rabbits are running to and fro, some sitting up on their haunches with ears pricked, some gamboling round the lichened trunk of the weeping ash tree.

Out of the water may-flies are rising and soaring upwards to circle round the topmost branches of the firs. Looking upwards, you may see hundreds of them dancing in unalloyed delight, enjoying their brief existence in this beautiful world.

Birds of many kinds, swallows and swifts, sparrows, fly-catchers, blackbirds, robins and wrens, all and sundry are busy chasing the poor green-drakes. As soon as the flies emerge from their husks and hover above the surface of the stream, many of them are snapped up. But the trout have "gone down,"—they are fairly gorged for the day; they will not trouble the fly any more to-night.

And then those glorious bicycle rides in the long summer evenings, when, scarcely had the sun gone down beyond the ridge of rolling uplands than the moon, almost at the full, and gorgeously serene, cast her soft, mysterious light upon a silent world. One such night two anglers, gliding softly through the ancient village of Bibury, dismounted from their machines and stood on the bridge which spans the River Coln. Below them the peaceful waters flowed silently onwards with all the smoothness of oil, save that ever and anon rays of silvery moonlight fell in streaks of radiant whiteness upon its glassy surface.

From beneath the bridge comes the sound of busy waters, a sound, as is often the case with running water, that you do not hear unless you listen for it carefully. Close by, too, at the famous spring, crystal waters are welling forth from the rock, pure and stainless as they were a thousand years ago. All else is silent in the village. The sky is flecked by myriads of tiny cloudlets, all separate from each other, and mostly of one shape and size; but just below the brilliant orb, which floats serene and proud above the line of mackerel sky, fantastic peaks of clouds, like far-off snow-capped heights of rugged Alps, are pointing upwards.

Suddenly there comes a change. A fairy circle of prismatic colour is gathering round the moon, beautifying the scene a thousandfold; an inner girdle of hazy emerald hue immediately surrounds the lurid orb, which is now seen as "in a glass darkly"; whilst encircling all is a narrow rim of red light, like the rosy hues of the setting sun that have scarcely died away in the west. The beauty of this lunar rainbow is enhanced by the framework of shapely ash trees through whose branches it is seen.

Along the river bank, nestling under the hanging wood, are rows of old stone cottages, with gables warped a little on one side. One light shines forth from the lattice window of the ancient mill; but in the cool thick-walled houses the honest peasants are slumbering in deep, peaceful sleep.

> "Ne'er saw I, never felt, a calm so deep.
>   The river glideth at his own sweet will:
> Dear God, the very houses seem asleep."

WORDSWORTH.

We are in the very heart of England. What a contrast to London at night, where many a poor fellow must be tossing restlessly in the stifling atmosphere!

As we return towards the old manor house the nightjar, or goatsucker, is droning loudly, and a nightingale—actually a nightingale!—is singing in the copse. These birds seldom visit us in the Cotswolds. In the deserted garden the scent of fresh-mown hay is filling the air, and

> "The moping owl doth to the moon complain
>   Of such as wander near her secret bower."

As we go we pluck some sprigs of fragrant honeysuckle and carry them indoors. And so to bed, passing on the broad oak staircase the weird picture of the man who built this rambling old house more than three hundred years ago.

There is a plain everyday phenomenon connected with pictures, and more especially photographs, which must have been noticed time after time by thousands of people; yet I never heard it mentioned in conversation or saw it in print. I allude to the extraordinary sympathy the features of a portrait are capable of assuming towards the expression of countenance of the man who is looking at it. There is something at times almost uncanny in it. Stand opposite a photograph of a friend when you are feeling sad, and the picture is sad. Laugh, and the mouth of your friend seems to curl into a smile, and his eyes twinkle merrily. Relapse into gloom and despondency, and the smile dies away from the picture. Often in youth, when about to carry out some design or other, I used to glance at my late father's portrait, and never failed to notice a look of approval or condemnation on the face which left its mark on the memory for a considerable time. The countenance of the grim old gentleman in the portrait on the stairs ("AETATIS SUAE 92. 1614 A.D.") wore a distinct air of satisfaction to-night as I passed by on my way to bed; he always looks pleased after there has been a good day with the hounds, and likewise in the summer when the may-fly is up.

CHAPTER IX.

BURFORD, A COTSWOLD TOWN.

Burford and Cirencester are two typical Cotswold towns; and perhaps the first-named is the most characteristic, as it is also the most remote and old-world of all places in this part of England. It was on a lovely day in June that we resolved to go and explore the ancient priory and glorious church of old Burford. A very slow train sets you down at Bampton, commonly called Bampton-in-the-Bush, though the forest which gave rise to the name has long since given place to open fields.

There are many other curious names of this type in Gloucestershire and the adjoining counties. Villages of the same name are often distinguished from each other by these quaint descriptions of their various situations. Thus:

> Moreton-in-the-Marsh distinguishes from More-ton-on-Lug.
> Bourton-on-the-Water distinguishes from Bourton-on-the-Hill.
> Stow-on-the-Wold distinguishes from Stowe-Nine-Churches.

Then we find

> Shipston-on-Stour and Shipton-under-Whichwood.
> Hinton-on-the-Green and Hinton-in-the-Hedges.
> Aston-under-Hill and Aston-under-Edge.

It may be noted in passing that the derivation of the word "Moreton-in-the-Marsh" has ever been the subject of much controversy. But the fact that the place is on the ancient trackway from Cirencester to the north, and also that four counties meet here, is sufficient reason for assigning Morton-hen-Mearc (=) "the place on the moor by the old boundary" as the probable meaning of the name.

We were fortunate enough to secure an outside seat on the rickety old "bus" which plies between Bampton and Burford, and were soon slowly traversing the white limestone road, stopping every now and then to set down a passenger or deposit a parcel at some clean-looking, stone-faced cottage in the straggling old villages.

It was indeed a glorious morning for an expedition into the Cotswolds. The six weeks' drought had just given place to cool, showery weather. A light wind from the west breathed the fragrance of countless wild flowers and sweet may blossom from the leafy hedges, and the scent of roses and honeysuckle was wafted from every cottage garden. After a month spent amid the languid air and depressing surroundings of London, one felt glad at heart to experience once again the grand, pure air and rural scenery of the Cotswold Hills.

What strikes one so forcibly about this part of England, after a sojourn in some smoky town, is its extraordinary cleanliness.

There is no such thing as *dirt* in a limestone country. The very mud off the roads in rainy weather is not dirt at all, sticky though it undoubtedly is. It consists almost entirely of lime, which, though it burns all the varnish off your carriage if allowed to remain on it for a few days, has nothing repulsive about its nature, like ordinary mud.

How pleasant, too, is the contrast between the quiet, peaceful country life and the restless din and never-ceasing commotion of the "busy haunts of men"! As we pass along through villages gay with flowers, we converse freely with the driver of the 'bus, chiefly about fishing. The great question which every one asks in this part of the world in the first week in June is whether the may-fly is up. The lovely green-drake generally appears on the Windrush about this time, and then for ten days nobody thinks or talks about anything else. Who that has ever witnessed a real may-fly "rise" on a chalk or limestone stream will deny that it is one of the most beautiful and interesting sights in all creation? Myriads of olive-coloured, transparent insects, almost as large as butterflies, rising out of the water, and floating on wings as light as gossamer, only to live but one short day; great trout, flopping and rolling in all directions, forgetful of all the wiles of which they are generally capable; and then, when the evening sun is declining, the female fly may be seen hovering over the water, and dropping her eggs time after time, until, having accomplished the only purpose for which she has existed in the winged state, she falls lifeless into the stream. But though these lovely insects live but twenty-four hours, and during that short period undergo a transformation from the *sub-imago* to the *imago* state, they exist as larvae in the bed of the river for quite two years from the time the eggs are dropped. The season of 1896 was one of the worst ever known on some may-fly rivers; probably the great frost two winters back was the cause of failure. The intense cold is supposed to have killed the larvae.

The Windrush trout are very large indeed; a five-pound fish is not at all uncommon. The driver of the 'bus talked of monsters of eight pounds having been taken near Burford, but we took this *cum grano salis.*

After a five-mile drive we suddenly see the picturesque old town below us. Like most of the villages of the country, it lies in one of the narrow valleys which intersect the hills, so that you do not get a view of the houses until you arrive at the edge of the depression in which they are built.

Having paid the modest shilling which represents the fare for the five miles, we start off for the priory. There was no difficulty in finding our way to it. In all the Cotswold villages and small towns the "big house" stands out conspicuously among the old cottages and barns and farmhouses, half hidden as it is by the dense foliage of giant elms and beeches and chestnuts and ash; nor is Burford Priory an exception to the rule, though its grounds are guarded by a wall of immense height on one side. And then once more we get the view we have seen so often on Cotswold; yet it never palls upon the senses, but thrills us with its own mysterious charm. Who can ever get tired of the picture presented by a gabled, mediaeval house set in a framework of stately trees, amid whose leafy branches the rooks are cawing and chattering round their ancestral nests, whilst down below the fertilising stream silently fulfils its never-ceasing task, flowing onwards everlastingly, caring nothing for the vicissitudes of our transitory life and the hopes and fears that sway the hearts of successive generations of men?

There the old house stands "silent in the shade"; there are the "nursery windows," but the "children's voices" no longer break the silence of the still summer day. Everywhere—in the hall, in the smoking-room, where the empty gun-cases still hang, and in "my lady's bower,"

"Sorrow and silence and sadness
Are hanging over all."

Until we arrived within a few yards of the front door we had almost forgotten that the place was a ruin; for though the house is but an empty shell, almost as hollow as a skull, the outer walls are absolutely complete and undamaged. At one end is the beautiful old chapel, built by "Speaker" Lenthall in the time of the Commonwealth. There is an air of sanctity about this lovely white freestone temple which no amount of neglect can eradicate. The roof, of fine stucco work, has fallen in; the elder shrubs grow freely through the crevices in the broken pavement under foot,—and yet you feel bound to remove your hat as you enter, for "you are standing on holy ground."

"EXUE CALCEOS, NAM TERRA EST SANCTA."

Over the entrance stands boldly forth this solemn inscription, whilst angels, wonderfully carved in white stone, watch and guard the sacred precincts. At the north end of the chapel stands intact the altar, and, strangely enough, the most perfectly preserved remnants of the whole building are two white stone tablets plainly setting forth the Ten Commandments. The sun, as we stood there, was pouring its rays through the graceful mullioned windows, lighting up the delicate carving,—work that is rendered more beautiful than ever by the "tender grace of a day that is dead,"—whilst outside in the deserted garden the birds were singing sweetly. The scene was sadly impressive; one felt as one does when standing by the grave of some old friend. As we passed out of the chapel we could not help reflecting on the hard-heartedness of men fifty years ago, who could allow this consecrated place, beautiful and fair as it still is, to fall gradually to the ground, nor attempt to put forth a helping hand to save it ere it crumbles into dust. How ungrateful it seems to those whose labour and hard, self-sacrificing toil erected it two hundred and fifty years ago! Those men of whom Ruskin wrote: "All else for which the builders sacrificed has passed away; all their living interests and aims and achievements. We know not for what they laboured, and we see no evidence of their reward. Victory, wealth, authority, happiness, all have departed, though bought by many a bitter sacrifice."

It should be mentioned, however, that Mr. R. Hurst is at the present time engaged in a laudable endeavour to restore this chapel to its original state. Inside the house the most noteworthy feature of interest is a remarkably fine ornamental ceiling. Good judges inform us that the ballroom ceiling at Burford Priory is one of the finest examples of old work of the kind anywhere to be seen. The room itself is a very large and well-proportioned one; the oak panels, which completely cover the walls, still bear the marks of the famous portraits that once adorned them. Charles I. and Henry Prince of Wales, by Cornelius Jansen; Queen Henrietta Maria, by Vandyke; Sir Thomas More and his family, by Holbein; Speaker Lenthall, the former owner of the house; and many other fine pictures hung here in former times. The staircase is a fine broad one, of oak.

But now let us leave the inside of the house, which *ought* to be so beautiful and bright, and *is* so desolate and bare, for it is of no great age, and let us call to mind the picture which Waller painted, engravings of which used to adorn so many Oxford rooms: "The Empty Saddle." For, standing in the neglected garden we may see the very terrace and the angle of the house which were drawn so beautifully by him. Then, as we stroll through the deserted grounds towards the peaceful Windrush, where the great trout are still sucking down the poor short-lived may-flies, let us try to recollect what manner of men used to walk in these peaceful gardens in the old, stirring times.

Little or nothing is known of the monastery which doubtless existed somewhere hereabouts prior to the dissolution in Henry VIII.'s reign.

Up to the Conquest the manor of Burford was held by Saxon noblemen. It is mentioned in Doomsday Book as belonging to Earl Aubrey; but the first notable man who held it was Hugh le Despencer. This man was one of Edward II.'s favourites, and was ultimately hung, by the queen's command, at the same time that Edward was committed to Kenilworth Castle. Burford remained with his descendants till the reign of Henry V., when it passed by marriage to a still more notable man, in the person of Richard Neville, Earl of Warwick, the "kingmaker." Space does not allow us to romance on the part that this great warrior played in the history of those times; Lord Lytton has done that for us in his splendid book, "The Last of the Barons." Suffice it to say that he left an undying fame to future generations, and fell in the Wars of the Roses when fighting at the battle of Barnet against the very man he had set on the throne. The almshouses he built for Burford are still to be seen hard by the grand old church.

"For who lived king, but I could dig his grave?
And who durst smile, when Warwick bent his brow?
Lo, now my glory's smear'd in dust and blood!
My parks, my walks, my manors that I had,
Even now forsake me; and of all my lands,
Is nothing left me, but my body's length!"

3 *King Henry VI.*, V. ii.

In the reign of Henry VIII. this manor, having lapsed to the Crown, was granted to Edmund Harman, the royal surgeon. Then in later days Sir John Fortescue, Chancellor of the Exchequer to Queen Elizabeth, got hold of it, and eventually sold it to Sir Lawrence Tanfield, a great judge in those times. The latter was buried "at twelve o'clock in the Night" in the church of Burford; and there is a very handsome aisle there and an immense monument to his memory. The Tanfield monument, though somewhat ugly and grotesque, is a wonderful example of alabaster work. The cost of erecting it and the labour bestowed must have been immense. It was this knight who built the great house of which the present ruins form part, and the date would probably be about 1600. But in 1808 nearly half the original building is supposed to have been pulled down, and what was allowed to remain, with the exception of the chapel, has been very much altered.

It was in the time of Lucius Carey's (second Lord Falkland) ownership of this manor that the place was in the zenith of its fame. This accomplished man, whose father had married Chief Justice

Tanfield's only daughter, succeeded his grandfather in the year 1625. He gathered together, either here or at Great Tew, a few miles away, half the literary celebrities of the day. Ben Jonson, Cowley, and Chillingworth all visited Falkland from time to time. Lucius Carey afterwards became the ill-fated King Charles's Secretary of State, an office which he conscientiously filled until his untimely death.

Falkland left little literary work behind him of any mark, yet of no other man of those times may it be said that so great a reputation for ability and character has been handed down to us. Novelists and authors delight in dwelling on his good qualities. Even in this jubilee year of 1897 the author of "Sir Kenelm Digby" has written a book about the Falklands. Whyte Melville, too, made him the hero of one of his novels, describing him as a man in whose outward appearance there were no indications of the intellectual superiority he enjoyed over his fellow men. Indeed, as with Arthur Hallam in our own times, so it was with Falkland in the mediaeval age. Neither left behind them any work of their own by which future generations could realise their abilities and almost godlike charm, yet each has earned a kind of immortality through being honoured and sung by the pens of the greatest writers of his respective age.

That great, though somewhat bombastic, historian, Lord Clarendon, tells us that Falkland was "a person of such prodigious parts of learning and knowledge, of that inimitable sweetness and delight in conversation, of so flowing and obliging a humanity and goodness to mankind, and of that primitive simplicity and integrity of life, that if there were no other brand upon this odious and accursed Civil War than that single loss, it must be most infamous and execrable to all posterity." From the same authority we learn that although he was ever anxious for peace, yet he was the bravest of the brave. At the battle of Newbury he put himself in the first rank of Lord Byron's regiment, when he met his end through a musket shot. "Thus," says Clarendon, "fell that incomparable young man, in the four-and-thirtieth year of his age, having so much despatched the true business of life that the eldest rarely attain to that immense knowledge, and the youngest enter not into the world with more innocency."

When it is remembered that Falkland was not a soldier at all, but a learned scholar, whose natural proclivities were literature and the arts of peace, his self-sacrifice and bravery cannot fail to call forth admiration for the man, and we cannot but regret his untimely end.

King Charles was several times at Burford, for it was the scene of much fighting in the Civil Wars.

"BURFORD PRIORY."

It was in the year 1636 that Speaker Lenthall purchased Burford Priory. He was a man of note in those troublous times, and even Cromwell seems to have respected him; for, although the latter came down to the House one day with a troop of musketeers, with the express intention of turning the gallant Speaker out of his chair, and effected his object amid the proverbial cries of "Make way for honester men!" yet we find that within twelve months the crafty old gentleman had once more got back again into the chair, and remained Speaker during the Protectorate of Richard Cromwell. He declared on his deathbed that, although, like Saul, he held the clothes of the murderers, yet that he never consented to the death of the king, but was deceived by Cromwell and his agents.

The priory remained in the Lenthall family up to the year 1821. At the present time it belongs to the Hurst family.

We have now briefly traced the history of the manor from the time of the Conquest, and, doubtless, all the men whose names occur have spent a good deal of time on this beautiful spot.

Alas that the garden should be but a wilderness! The carriage drive consists of rich green turf. In a summer-house in the grounds John Prior, Speaker Lenthall's faithful servant, was murdered in the year 1697. The Earl of Abercorn was accused of the murder, but was acquitted.

In addition to King Charles I., many other royal personages have visited this place. Queen Elizabeth once visited the town, and came with great pomp.

The Burgesses' Book has a note to the effect that in 1663 twenty-one pounds was paid for three saddles presented to Charles II. and his brother the Duke of York. Burford was celebrated for its saddles in those days. It was a great racing centre, and both here and at Bibury (ten miles off) flat racing was constantly attracting people from all parts. Bibury was a sort of Newmarket in old days. Charles II. was at Burford on three occasions at least.

It was in the year 1681 that the Newmarket spring meeting was transferred to Bibury. Parliament was then sitting at Oxford, some thirty miles away; so that the new rendezvous was more convenient than the old. Nell Gwynne accompanied the king to the course. For a hundred and fifty years the Bibury club held its meetings here. The oldest racing club in England, it still flourishes, and will in future hold its meetings near Salisbury.

In 1695 King William III. came to Burford in order to influence the votes in the forthcoming parliamentary election. Macaulay tells us that two of the famous saddles were presented to this monarch, and remarks that one of the Burford saddlers was the best in Europe. William III. slept that night at the priory. The famous "Nimrod," in his "Life of a Sportsman," gives us a picture, by Alken, of Bibury racecourse, and tells us how gay Burford was a hundred years ago:

"Those were Bibury's very best days. In addition to the presence of George IV., then Prince of Wales, who was received by Lord Sherborne for the race week at his seat in the neighbourhood, and who every day appeared on the course as a private gentleman, there was a galaxy of gentlemen jockeys, who alone rode at this meeting, which has never since been equalled. Amongst them were the Duke of Dorset, who always rode for the Prince; the late Mr. Delme-Radcliffe; the late Lords Charles Somerset and Milsington; Lord Delamere, Sir Tatton Sykes, and many other first-raters.

"I well remember the scenes at Burford and all the neighbouring towns after the races were over. That at Burford 'beggars' description; for, independently of the bustle occasioned by the accommodation necessary for the club who were domiciled in the town, the concourse of persons of all sorts and degrees was immense."

Old Mr. Peregrine told me the other day that during the race week the shopkeepers at Bibury village used to let their bedrooms to the visitors, and sleep on the shop board, while the rest of the family slept underneath the counter.

Ah well! *Tempora mutantur!* "Nimrod" and his "notables" are all gone.

> "The knights' bones are dust,
> And their good swords rust,
> Their souls are with the saints, I trust."

And whereas up to fifty years ago Burford was a rich country town, famous for the manufacture of paper, malt, and sailcloth—enriched, too, by the constant passage of numerous coaches stopping on their way from Oxford to Gloucester—it is now little more than a village—the quietest, the cleanest, and the quaintest place in Oxfordshire. Perhaps its citizens are to be envied rather than pitied:

> "bene est cui deus obtulit
> Parca, quod satis est, manu."

Let us go up to the top of the main street, and sit down on the ancient oak bench high up on the hill, whence we can look down on the old-world place and get a birdseye view of the quaint houses and the surrounding country. And now we may exclaim with Ossian, "A tale of the times of old! The deeds of days of other years!" For yonder, a mile away from the town, the kings of Mercia and Wessex fought a desperate battle in the year A.D. 685. Quite recently a tomb was found there containing a stone coffin weighing nearly a ton. The bones of the warrior who fought and died there were marvellously complete when disturbed in their resting-place—in fact, the skeleton was a perfect one.

"Whose fame is in that dark green tomb? Four stones with their heads of moss stand there. They mark the narrow house of death. Some chief of fame is here! Raise the songs of old! Awake their memory in the tomb." [4]

[4] Ossian.

Tradition has it that this was the body of a great Saxon chief, Aethelhum, the mighty standard-bearer of the Mercian King Ethelbald. It was in honour of this great warrior that the people of Burford carried a standard emblazoned with a golden dragon through the old streets on midsummer eve, annually, for nigh on a thousand years. We are told that it was only during last century that the custom died out.

How beautiful are some of the old houses in the broad and stately High Street!

The ancient building in the centre of the town is called the "Tolsey"; it must be more than four hundred years old. The name originated in the custom of paying tolls due to the lord of the manor in the building. There are some grand old iron chests here; one of these old boxes contains many interesting charters and deeds, some of them bearing the signatures of chancellors Morton, Stephen Gardiner, and Ellesmere. There are letters from Elizabeth, and an order from the Privy Council with Arlington's signature attached. "The stocks" used to stand on the north side of this building, but have lately been removed. Then the houses opposite the Tolsey are as beautiful as they possibly can be. They are fifteenth century, and have oak verge-boards round their gables, carved in very delicate tracery.

Another house has a wonderful cellar, filled with grandly carved stonework, like the aisle of a church; this crypt is probably more than five hundred years old. Perhaps this vaulted Gothic chamber is a remnant of the old monastery, the site of which is not known. Close by is an ancient building, now turned into an inn; and this also may have been part of the dwelling-place of the monks of Burford. From the vaulted cellar beneath the house, now occupied by Mr. Chandler, ran an underground passage, evidently connected with some other building.

How sweetly pretty is the house at the foot of the bridge, as seen from the High Street above! The following inscription stands out prominently on the front:—

"SYMON WYSDOM ALDERMAN
THE FYRST FOUNDER OR THE SCHOLE
IN BURFORD GAVE THE TENEMENES
IN A.D. 1577."

The old almshouses on the green by the church have an inscription to the effect that they were founded by Richard Earl of Warwick (the kingmaker), in the year 1457. They were practically rebuilt about seventy years ago; but remnants of beautiful Gothic architecture still remain in the old stone belfry, and here and there a piece of tracery has been preserved. In all parts of the town one suddenly alights upon beautiful bits of carved stone—an Early English gateway in one street, and lancet doorways to many a cottage in another. Oriel windows are also plentiful. Behind the almshouses is a cottage with massive buttresses, and everywhere broken pieces of quaint gargoyles, pinnacles, and other remnants of Gothic workmanship are to be seen lying about on the walls and in odd corners. A careful search would doubtless reveal many a fine piece of tracery in the cottages and buildings. At some period, however, vandalism has evidently been rampant. Happening to find our way into the back premises of an ancient inn, we noticed that the coals were heaped up against a wall of old oak panelling.

And now we come to the most beautiful piece of architecture in the place—the magnificent old church. It is grandly situated close to the banks of the Windrush, and is more like a cathedral than a village church. The front of the porch is worked with figures representing our Lord, St. Mary Magdalene, and St. John the Evangelist; but the heads were unfortunately destroyed in the Civil Wars. Inside the porch the rich fan-tracery, which rises from the pilasters on each side, is carved with consummate skill.

Space does not allow us to dwell on the grandeur of the massive Norman tower, the great doorway at the western entrance with its splendid moulding, the quaint low arch leading from nave to chancel, and the other specimens of Norman work to be seen in all parts of this magnificent edifice. Nor can we do justice to the glorious nave, with its roof of oak; nor the aisles and the chancel; nor the beautiful Leggare chapel, with its oak screen, carved in its upper part in fifteenth-century tracery, its faded frescoes and ancient altar tomb. The glass of the upper portion of the great west window and the window of St Thomas' chapel are indeed "labyrinths of twisted tracery and starry light" such as would delight the fastidious taste of Ruskin. Several pages might easily be written in describing the wonderful and grotesque example of alabaster work known as the Tanfield tomb. The only regret one feels on gazing at this grand old specimen of the toil of our simple ancestors is that it is seldom visited save by the natives of rural Burford, many of whom, alas! must realise but little the exceptional beauty and stateliness of the lovely old church with which they have been so familiar all their lives.

A few years ago Mr. Oman, Fellow of All Souls', Oxford, made a curious discovery. Whilst going through some documents that had been for many years in the hands of the last survivor of the ancient corporation, and being one of the few men in England in a position to identify the handwriting, he came across a deed or charter signed by "the great kingmaker" himself; it was in the form of a letter, and had reference to the gift of almshouses he made to Burford in 1457 A.D. The boldly written "R.I. Warrewyck" at the end is the only signature of the kingmaker's known to exist save the one at Belvoir. In this letter prayers are besought for the founder and the Countess

Anne his wife, whilst attached to it is a seal with the arms of Neville, Montacute, Despencer, and Beauchamp.

On the font in the church is a roughly chiselled name:

"ANTHONY SEDLEY. 1649. Prisner."

Not only prisoners, but even their *horses*, were shut up in these grand old churches during the Civil Wars. This Anthony Sedley must have been one of the three hundred and forty Levellers who were imprisoned here in 1649.

The register has the following entry:—

"1649. Three soldiers shot to death in Burford Churchyard, buried May 17th."

Burford was the scene of a good deal of fighting during the Civil Wars. On January 1st, 1642, in the dead of night, Sir John Byron's regiment had a sharp encounter with two hundred dragoons of the Parliamentary forces. A fierce struggle took place round the market cross, during which Sir John Byron was wounded in the face with a poleaxe. Cromwell's soldiers, however, were routed and driven out of the town.

In the parish register is the following entry :—

"1642. Robert Varney of Stowe, slain in Burford and buried January 1st.

"1642. Six soldiers slain in Burford, buried 2nd January.

"1642. William Junks slain with the shot of musket, buried January 10th.

"1642. A soldier hurt at Cirencester road was buried."

Many other entries of the same nature are to be seen in the parish register.

The old market cross of Burford has indeed seen some strange things. Mr. W.J. Monk, to whose "History of Burford" I am indebted for valuable information, tells us that the penance enjoined on various citizens of Burford for such crimes as buying a Bible in the year 1521 was as follows: —

"Everyone to go upon a market day thrice about the market of Burford, and then to stand up upon the highest steps of the cross there, a quarter of an hour, with a faggot of wood upon his shoulder.

"Everyone also to beare a faggot of wood before the procession on a certain Sunday at Burford from the Quire doore going out, to the quire doore going in, and once to bear a faggot at the burning of a heretic.

"Also none of them to hide their mark [+] upon their cheek (branded in)," etc., etc.

"In the event of refusal, they were to be given up to the civil authorities to be burnt."

CHAPTER X.

A STROLL THROUGH THE COTSWOLDS.

"In Gloucestershire
These high, wild hills and rough, uneven ways
Draw out our miles, and make them wearisome."

King Richard II.

It cannot be said that there are many pleasant walks and drives in the Cotswold country, because, as a rule, the roads run over the bleak tableland for miles and miles, and the landscape generally consists of ploughed fields divided by grey stone walls; the downs I have referred to at different times are only to be met with in certain districts. Once upon a time the whole of Cotswold was one vast sheep walk from beginning to end. It was about a hundred and fifty years ago that the idea of enclosing the land was started by the first Lord Bathurst. Early in the eighteenth century he converted a large tract of downland round Cirencester into arable fields; his example was soon followed by others, so that by the middle of last century the transformation of three hundred square miles of downs into wheat-growing ploughed fields had been accomplished. It is chiefly owing to the depression in agricultural produce that there are any downs now, for they merely exist because the tenants have found during the last twenty years that it does not pay to cultivate their farms, hence they let a large proportion go back to grass.

But there is one very pleasant walk in that part of the Cotswolds we know best, and this takes you up the valley of the Coln to the Roman villa at Chedworth.

The distance by road from Fairford to the Chedworth woods is about twelve miles; and at any time of the year, but more especially in the spring and autumn, it is a truly delightful pilgrimage.

And here it is worth our while to consider for a moment how tremendously the abolition of the stage coach has affected places like

143

Fairford, Burford, and other Cotswold towns and villages. It was through these old-world places, past these very walls and gables, that the mail coaches rattled day after day when they "went down with victory" conveying the news of Waterloo and Trafalgar into the heart of merry England. In his immortal essay on "The English Mail Coach," De Quincey has told us how between the years 1805 and 1815 it was worth paying down five years of life for an outside place on a coach "going down with victory." "On any night the spectacle was beautiful. The absolute perfection of all the appointments about the carriages and the harness, their strength, their brilliant cleanliness, their beautiful simplicity—but more than all, the royal magnificence of the horses—were what might first have fixed the attention. But the night before us is a night of victory: and behold! to the ordinary display what a heart-shaking addition! horses, men, carriages, all are dressed in laurels and flowers, oak leaves and ribbons." The brilliancy of the royal liveries, the thundering of the wheels, the tramp of those generous horses, the sounding of the coach horn in the calm evening air, and last, but not least, the intense enthusiasm of travellers and spectators alike, as amid such cries as "Salamanca for ever!" "Hurrah for Waterloo!" they cheered and cheered again, letting slip the dogs of victory throughout those old English villages,—all these things must have united the hearts of the classes and masses in one common bond, rendering such occasions memorable for ever in the hearts of the simple country folk. In small towns like Burford and Northleach, situated five or six miles from any railway station, the prosperity and happiness of the natives has suffered enormously by the decay of the stage coach; and even in smaller villages the cheering sound of the horn must have been very welcome, forming as it did a connecting link between these remote hamlets of Gloucestershire and the great metropolis a hundred miles away.

Fairford Church is known far and wide as containing the most beautiful painted glass of the early part of the sixteenth century to be found anywhere in England. The windows, twenty-eight in number, are usually attributed to Albert Dürer; but Mr. J.G. Joyce, who published a treatise on them some twenty years ago, together with certain other high authorities, considered them to be of English design and workmanship. They would doubtless have been

A Cotswold Village; or, Country Life and Pursuits in Gloucestershire

destroyed in the time of the Civil Wars by the Puritans had they not been taken down and hidden away by a member of the Oldysworth family, whose tomb is in the middle chancel.

John Tame, having purchased the manor of Fairford in 1498, immediately set about building the church. He died two years later, and his son completed the building, and also erected two other very fine churches in the neighbourhood—those at Rendcombe and Barnsley. He was a great benefactor to the Cotswold country. Leland tells us that the town of Fairford never flourished "before the cumming of the Tames into it."

You may see John Tame's effigy on his tomb, together with that of his wife, and underneath these pathetic lines:

"For thus, Love, pray for me.
I may not pray more, pray ye:
With a pater noster and an ave:
That my paynys relessyd be."

If I remember rightly his helmet and other parts of his armour still hang on the church wall. Leland describes Fairford as a "praty uplandish towne," meaning, I suppose, that it is situated on high ground. It is certainly a delightful old-fashioned place—a very good type of what the Cotswold towns are like. Chipping-Campden and Burford are, however, the two most typical Cotswold towns I know.

In the year 1850 a remarkable discovery was made in a field close to Fairford. No less than a hundred and fifty skeletons were unearthed, and with them a large number of very interesting Anglo-Saxon relics, some of them in good preservation. In many of the graves an iron knife was found lying by the skeleton; in others the bodies were decorated with bronze fibulae, richly gilt, and ornamented in front. Mr. W. Wylie, in his interesting account of these Anglo-Saxon graves, tells us that some of the bodies were as large as six feet six inches; whilst one or two warriors of seven feet were unearthed. All the skeletons were very perfect, even though no signs of any coffins were to be seen. Bronze bowls and various kinds of pottery, spearheads of several shapes, a large number of coloured beads, bosses of shields, knives, shears, and two remarkably fine swords were some of the relics found with the bodies. A glass vessel, coloured yellow by means of a chemical process in which iron was utilised, is considered by Mr. Wylie to be of Saxon manufacture, and not Venetian or Roman, as other authorities hold.

Whether this is merely an Anglo-Saxon burial-place, or whether the bodies are those of the warriors who fell in a great battle such as that fought in A.D. 577, when the Saxons overthrew the Britons and took from them the cities of Gloucester, Cirencester, and Bath, it is impossible to determine. The natives are firmly convinced that the skeletons represent the slain in a great battle fought near this spot; but this is only tradition. At all events, the words of prophecy attributed to the old Scotch bard Ossian have a very literal application with reference to this interesting relic of bygone times: "The stranger shall come and build there and remove the heaped-up earth. An half-worn sword shall rise before him. Bending above it, he will say, 'These are the arms of the chiefs of old, but their names are not in song.'" The "heaped-up" earth has long ago disappeared, for there are no "barrows" now to be seen. Cottages stand where the old burial mounds doubtless once existed, and all monumental evidences of those mighty men—the last, perhaps, of an ancient race—have long since been destroyed by the ruthless hand of time.

The manor of Fairford now belongs to the Barker family, to whom it came through the female line about a century ago.

We must now leave Fairford, and start on our pilgrimage to the Roman villa of Chedworth. At present we have not got very far, having lingered at our starting-point longer than we had intended. The first two miles are the least interesting of the whole journey; the Coln, broadened out for some distance to the size of a lake, is hidden from our view by the tall trees of Fairford Park. It was along this road that John Keble, the poet used to walk day by day to his cure at Coln-St.-Aldwyns. His home was at Fairford. Two eminent American artists have made their home in Fairford during recent years—Mr. Edwin Abbey and Mr. J. Sargent, both R.A's. Close by, too, at Kelmscott, dwelt William Morris, the poet.

On reaching Quenington we catch a glimpse of the river, whilst high up on the hill to our right stands the great pile of Hatherop Castle.

This place, the present owner of which is Sir Thomas Bazley, formerly belonged to the nunnery of Lacock. After the suppression of the monasteries it passed through various heiresses to the family of Ashley. It was practically rebuilt by William Spencer Ponsonby, first Lord de Mauley; his son, Mr. Ashley Ponsonby, sold it to Prince Duleep Singh, from whom it passed to the present owner. Sir Thomas Bazley has done much for the village which is fortunate enough to claim him as a resident; his estate is a model of what country estates ought to be, unprofitable though it must have proved as an investment.

As we pass on through the fair villages of Quenington and Coln-St.-Aldwyns we cannot help noticing the delightful character of the houses from a picturesque point of view; in both these hamlets there are the same clean-looking stone cottages and stone-tiled roofs. Here and there the newer cottages are roofed with ordinary slate; and this seems a pity. Nevertheless, there still remains much that is picturesque to be seen on all sides. Roses grow in every garden, clematis relieves with its rich purple shade the walls of many a cosy little dwelling-house, and the old white mills, with their latticed windows and pointed gables, are a feature of every tiny hamlet through which the river flows.

> "How gay the habitations that adorn
> This fertile valley! Not a house but seems
> To give assurance of content within,
> Embosom'd happiness, and placid love."

WORDSWORTH.

The beautiful gabled house close to the Norman church of Coln-St.-Aldwyns is the old original manor house. Inside it is an old oak staircase, besides other interesting relics of the Elizabethan age. For many years this has been a farmhouse, but it has recently been restored by its owner, Sir Michael Hicks-Beach, the present Chancellor of the Exchequer, who intends to make it his country abode. A piece of carved stone with four heads was discovered by the workmen engaged in the restoration, and is to be placed over the front door. It is doubtless a remnant of an old monastery, and dates back to Norman times.

Williamstrip House and Park lie on your right-hand side as you leave the village of "Coln" behind you. This place also belongs to Sir Michael Hicks-Beach; it has always seemed to us the *beau-ideal* of an English home. A medium-sized, comfortable square house of the time of George I., surrounded by some splendid old trees, in a park not too large, a couple of miles or so of excellent trout-fishing, very fair shooting, and good hunting would seem to be a combination of sporting advantages that few country places enjoy. Williamstrip came into the family of the present owner in 1784. The three parishes of Hatherop, Quenington, and Coln-St.-Aldwyns practically adjoin each other. Each has its beautiful church, the Norman doorways in that of Quenington being well worth a visit. Close to the church of Quenington are the remnants of an ancient monastery.

The "Knights Templar" of Quenington were famous in times gone by. There is a fine entrance gate and porch on the roadside, which no doubt led to the abbey.

There is little else left to remind us of these Knights Templar. Here and there are an old lancet window or a little piece of Gothic tracery on an ancient wall, an old worm-eaten roof of oak or a heap of ruined stones on a moat-surrounded close,—these are all the remnants to be found of the days of chivalry and the monks of old.

We have now two rather uneventful miles to traverse between Coln-St.-Aldwyns and Bibury, for we must once more leave the valley and set out across the bleak uplands. On the high ground we have the advantage of splendid bracing air at all events. The hills have a charm of their own on a fine day, more especially when the fields are full of golden corn and the old-fashioned Cotswold men are busy among the sheaves.

And very soon we get a view which we would gladly have walked twenty miles to see. Down below us and not more than half a mile away is the fine old Elizabethan house of Bibury, standing out from a background of magnificent trees. Close to the house is the grey Norman tower of the village church, which has stood there for mote than six centuries. Nestling round about are the old stone-roofed cottages, like those we have seen in the other villages we have passed through. A broad reach of the Coln and a grand waterfall enhance the quiet and peaceful beauty of the scene. But this description falls very short of conveying any adequate idea of the truly delightful effect which the old grey buildings set in a framework of wood and water present on a fine autumnal afternoon.

Never shall I forget seeing this old place from the hill above during one September sunset. There was a marvellous glow suffused over the western sky, infinitely beautiful while it lasted; and immediately below a silvery mist had risen from the surface of the broad trout stream, and was hanging over the old Norman tower of the church. Amid the rush of the waterfall could be heard the distant voices of children in the village street. Then on a sudden the church clock struck the hour of six, in deep, solemn tones. Against the russet-tinted woods in the background the old court house stood out grey and silent under the shadow of the church tower, preaching as good a sermon as any I ever heard.

> "An English home, grey twilight poured
>   On dewy pastures, dewy trees,
> Softer than sleep,—all things in order stored,
>   A haunt of ancient peace."

Bibury Court is a most beautiful old house. Some of it dates back to Henry VIII.'s time. The most remarkable characteristic of its interior is a very fine carved oak staircase. The greater part of this house was built in the year 1623 by Sir Thomas Sackville. It was long the seat of the Creswell family, before passing by purchase to the family of the present owner—Lord Sherborne. The fine old church has some Saxon work in it, whilst the doorways and many other portions are Norman. Its delightful simplicity and brightness is what pleases one most. On coming down into the village, one notices a little square on the left, not at all like those one sees in London, but very picturesque and clean looking. In the olden times were to be seen in many villages little courts of this kind; in the centre of them was usually a great tree, round which the old people would sit on summer evenings, while the children danced and played around. Gilbert

White speaks of one at Selborne, which he calls the "Plestor." The original name was "Pleystow," which means a play place. We have noticed them in many parts of the Cotswold country. Here, too, children are playing about under the shade of some delightful trees in the centre of the miniature square, whilst the variegated foliage sets off the gabled cottages which form three sides of it.

"BIBURY STREET."

I have often wondered, as I stood by these chestnut trees, whether there is any architecture more perfect in its simplicity and grace than that which lies around me here. Not a cottage is in sight that is not worthy of the painter's brush; not a gable or a chimney that would not be worthy of a place in the Royal Academy. The little square is bordered for six months of the year with the prettiest of flowers. Even as late as December you may see roses in bloom on the walls, and chrysanthemums of varied shade in every garden. Then, as we passed onwards,

> "On the stream's bank, and everywhere, appeared
>   Fair dwellings, single or in social knots;
> Some scattered o'er the level, others perch'd

On the hill-sides—a cheerful, quiet scene."

WORDSWORTH.

There is a Gothic quaintness about all the buildings in the Cotswolds, great and small alike, which is very charming. Bibury is indeed a pretty village. As you walk along the main street which runs parallel with the river, an angler is busy "swishing" his rod violently in the air to "dry" the fly, ere he essays to drop it over the nose of one of the speckled fario which abound; so be careful to step down off the path which runs alongside the stream, in case you should put the fish "down" and spoil the sport. And now on our left, beyond the green, may be seen a line of gabled cottages called "Arlington Row," a picture of which by G. Leslie was hung at the Royal Academy this year (1898).

A few hundred yards on you stop to inspect the spring which rises in the garden of the Swan Hotel. It has been said that two million gallons a day is the minimum amount of water poured out by this spring. It consists of the rain, which, falling on a large area of the hill country, gradually finds its way through the limestone rocks and eventually comes out here. It would be interesting to trace the course of some of these underground rivers; for a torrent of water such as this cannot flow down through the soft rock without in the course of thousands of years, producing caves and grottoes and underground galleries and all the wonders of the Mammoth Cave in Kentucky, with its stalactite pillars and fairy avenues and domes—though the Cotswold caves are naturally on a much smaller scale. At Torquay and on the Mendip Hills, as everybody knows, there are caves of wondrous beauty, carved by the water within the living rock.

Probably within a hundred yards of Bibury spring there are beautiful hidden caves, such as those funny little "palaeolithic" men lived in a few thousand years ago; but why there have not been more discoveries of this nature in this part of the Cotswolds it is difficult to say. There is a cave hereabouts, men say, but the entrance to it cannot now be found. There is likewise a Roman villa on the hill here which has not yet been dug out of its earthy bed. A hundred years ago a large number of Roman antiquities were discovered near this village.

We now leave Bibury behind us, and a mile on we pass through the hamlet of Ablington, which is very like Bibury on a smaller scale, with its ancient cottages, tithe barns and manor house; its springs of transparent water, its brook, and wealth of fine old trees. We have no time to linger in this hamlet to-day, though we would fain pause to admire the old house.

> "The pillar'd porch, elaborately embossed;
>   The low, wide windows with their mullions old;
> The cornice richly fretted of grey stone;
>   And that smooth slope from which the dwelling rose
> By beds and banks Arcadian of gay flowers,
>   And flowering shrubs, protected and adorned."

WORDSWORTH

After leaving Ablington we once more ascend the hill and make our way along an old, disused road, probably an ancient British track, in preference to keeping to the highway—in the first place because it is by far the shortest, and secondly because we intend to go somewhat out of our way to inspect two ancient barrows, the resting-place of the chiefs of old, of whom Ossian (or was it Macpherson?)[5] sang: "If fall I must in the field, raise high my grave. Grey stones and heaped-up earth shall mark me to future times. When the hunter shall sit by the mound and produce his food at noon, 'Some warrior rests here,' he will say; and my fame shall live in his praise."

[5] In spite of Dr. Johnson and other eminent critics, one cannot help believing in the genuineness of some of the poems attributed to Ossian. "The proof of the pudding is in the eating"; and those wonderful old songs are too wild and lifelike to have had their origin in the eighteenth century. Macpherson doubtless enlarged upon the originals, but he must have had a good foundation to work upon.

A very large barrow lies about a mile out of our track to the right hand; as it is somewhat different from the other barrows in the neighbourhood, we will briefly describe it. It is a "long barrow," with the two horns at one end that are usually associated with "long" barrows. In the middle of the curve between these ends stands a great stone about five feet square, not very unlike our own gravestones, though worn by the rains of thousands of years. The mound is surrounded by a double wall of masonry. At the north end, when it was opened forty years ago, a chamber was found containing human bones. It is supposed that this mound was the burying-place of a race which dwelt on Cotswold at least three thousand years ago. From the nature of the stone implements found, it is conjectured that the people who raised it were unacquainted with the use of metal.

Now we will have a look at another barrow a few fields away. This is a mound of a somewhat later age; for it was raised over the ashes of a body or bodies that had been cremated. It was probably the Celts who raised this barrow. The other day it was opened for a distinguished society of antiquaries to inspect; they found that in the centre were stones carefully laid, encircling a small chamber, whilst the outer portions were of ordinary rubble. Nothing but lime-dust and dirt was found in the chamber; but in the course of thousands of years most of these barrows have probably been opened a good many times by Cotswold natives in search of "golden coffins" and other treasures.

There is a small, round underground chamber within a short distance of these barrows, which the natives consider to be a shepherd's hut, put up about two centuries back, and before the country was enclosed, as a retreat to shelter the men who looked after the flocks. It has been declared, however, by those who have studied the question of burial mounds, that it was built in very early times, and contained bodies that had not been cremated. The antiquaries who came a short time back to view these remains describe it as "an underground chamber, circular in shape, and an excellent sample of dry walling. The roof is dome-shaped, and gradually projects inwards." I narrowly escaped taking this "society" for a band of poachers; for when out shooting the other day, somebody remarked, "Look at all those fellows climbing over the wall of the fox-covert."

Now the fox-covert is a very sacred institution in these parts; for it is a place of only four acres, standing isolated in the midst of a fine, open country—so that no human being is allowed to enter therein save to "stop the earth" the night before hunting. We rushed up in great haste, fully prepared for mortal combat with this gang of ruffians, until, when within a hundred yards, the thought crossed us that we had given leave to the Cotswold Naturalist Society to make a tour of inspection, and that one of the barrows was in our fox-covert.

Labouring friends of mine often bring me relics of the stone age which they have picked up whilst at work in the fields. Quite recently a shepherd brought me a knife blade and two flint arrowheads. He also tells me they have lately found a "himmige" up in old Mr. Peregrine's "barn-ground." Tom Peregrine possesses a bag of old coins of all dates and sizes, which he tells you with great pride have been an heirloom in his family for generations.

When we once more resume our pilgrimage along the track which leads to Chedworth we find ourselves in a country which is never explored by the tourist. Far removed from railways and the "busy haunts of men," it is not even mentioned in the guide-books. Our way lies along the edge of the hill for the next few miles, and we look down upon the picturesque valley of the Coln. Four villages, all very like those we have described, are passed in rapid succession. Winson, Coln Rogers, Coln-St.-Dennis, and Fossbridge all lie below us as we wend our way westwards. But although the architecture is of the same massive yet graceful style, and the old Norman churches still tower their grand old heads and cast their shadows over the cottages and farm buildings, there are no manor houses of note in any of these four villages, and no well-timbered demesnes; so that they are not so interesting as some of those we have passed through. In all, however, there dwell the good old honest labouring folk, toiling hard day by day at "the trivial round, the common task," just earning enough to scrape up a livelihood, but enjoying few of the amenities of life. The village parsons—good, pious men—share in the quiet, uneventful life of their flock. And who shall contemn their lot? As Horace tells us:

"Vivitur parvo bene, cui paternum
Splendet in mensa tenui salinum
Nec leves somnos timor aut cupido
Sordidus aufert."

"ARLINGTON ROW."

These four villages were all built two centuries or more ago, when the Cotswolds were the centre of much life and activity and the days of agricultural depression were not known. When we look down on their old, grey houses nestling among the great trees which thrive by the banks of the fertilising stream, we cannot but speculate on their future fate. Gradually the population diminishes, as work gets scarcer and scarcer. Unless there is an unexpected revival in prices through some measure of "protection" being granted by law, or the medium of a great European war, or some such far-reaching dispensation of Providence, terrible to think of for those who live to see it, but with all its possibilities of "good arising out of evil" for future generations, these old villages will contain scarcely a single inhabitant in a hundred year's time. This part of the Cotswold country will once more become a huge open plain, retaining only long rows of tumbled-down stone walls as evidences of its former enclosed state; no longer on Sundays will the notes of the beautiful bells call the toilers to prayer and thanksgiving, and all will be desolation. If only the capitalist or wealthy man of business would take up his abode in these places, all might be well. But, alas! the peace and quiet of such out-of-the-way spots, with all their fascinating contrast to the smoke and din of a manufacturing town, have little attraction for those who are unused to them. And yet there is much happiness and content in these rural villages. The lot of those who are able to get work is a thousand times more supportable than that of the toiling millions in our great cities. There is less drinking and less vice among these villagers than there is in any part of this world that we are acquainted with; consequently you find them cheerful, good-humoured, and, if they only knew it, happy. Grumble they must, or they would not be mortal. Ah! if they could but realise the blessings of the elixir of life—pure air, and fresh, clear, spring water, and sunshine—three inestimable privileges that they enjoy all the year round, and which are denied to so many of the inhabitants of this globe—there would be little grumbling in the Cotswolds.

> "From toil he wins his spirits light,
> From busy day the peaceful night;
> Rich from the very want of wealth
> In heaven's best treasures, peace and health."

GRAY.

"But these villages are so *dull*, and life is so monotonous there," is the constant complaint. But what part of this earth is there, may I ask, that is not dull to those who live there, unless we drive out dull care and *ennui* by that glorious antidote to gloom and despondency, a fully occupied mind? There are two chapters in Carlyle's "Past and Present" that ought to be printed in letters of gold, set in an ivory frame, and hung up in the sleeping apartment of every man, woman, and child on the face of this earth. They are called "Labour" and "Reward." In those few short pages is embodied the whole secret of content and happiness for the dwellers in quiet country villages and smoky towns alike. They contain the philosopher's stone, which makes men cheerful under all circumstances, but especially those who are poor and down-trodden. The secret is a very simple one; but if the educated classes are continually losing sight of it, how much easier is it for those who have only the bare necessaries of life and few of the comforts to become deadened to its influence! It lies first of all in the realisation of the fact that the object of life is not to get, still less to enjoy, riches and pleasure. It teaches for the thousandth time that the humblest and the highest of us alike are immortal souls imprisoned for threescore years and ten in a tenement of clay, preparing for a better and higher existence. It reverses the position of things on earth—placing the crown of kings on the head of the toiling labourer, and making "the last first and the first last." Its very essence lies in the dictum of the old monks, *"Laborare est orare"* ("Work is worship").

It was one of the chief characteristics of the Roman people in the time of their greatness that their most successful generals were content to return to the plough after their wars were over. Thus Pliny in his "Natural History" remarks as follows: "Then were the fields cultivated by the hands of the generals themselves, and the earth rejoiced, tilled as it was by a ploughshare crowned with laurels, he who guided the wheel being himself fresh from glorious victories." And no sooner did honest hand labour become despised than effeminacy crept in, and this once haughty nation was practically blotted out from the face of the earth.

Let the Cotswold labourer realise that to work on the land, ploughing and reaping, summer and winter, seedtime and harvest, come weal, come woe, is no mean destiny for an honest man; there is scope for the display of a noble and generous spirit in the beautiful green fields as well as in the smoky atmosphere of the east end of London, in a Birmingham factory, or a Warrington forge.

"What is the meaning of nobleness?" asks Carlyle. "In a valiant suffering for others did nobleness ever lie. Every noble crown is, and on earth will for ever be, a crown of thorns. All true work is sacred. In all true work, were it but true hand labour, there is something of divineness. Sweat of the brow; and up from that to sweat of the brain, sweat of the heart; up to that 'agony of bloody sweat' which all men have called divine. Oh, brother, if this is not worship, then, I say, the more pity for worship: for this is the noblest thing yet discovered under God's sky. Who art thou that complainest of thy life of toil? Complain not. Look up, my wearied brother; see thy fellow workmen there in God's eternity surviving those, they alone surviving; peopling, they alone, the unmeasured solitudes of Time.

To thee Heaven, though severe, is not unkind. Heaven is kind, as a noble mother; as that Spartan mother, saying, while she gave her son his shield, 'With it, my son, or upon it, thou, too, shalt return home in honour—to thy far distant home in honour—doubt it not—if in the battle thou keep thy shield!' Thou in the eternities and deepest death kingdoms art not an alien; thou everywhere art a denizen. Complain not; the very Spartans did not complain."

Would that the toiling labourer in the Cotswolds and in our great smoky cities might keep these words continually before him, so that he might grasp, not merely the secret of content and happiness in this life, but the golden key to the immeasurable blessings of "the sure and certain hope" of that life which is to come! Then shall he hear the words:

> "King, thou wast called Conqueror;
> In every battle thou bearest the prize."

Conqueror will he be in life's battle if he follow in the footsteps of the Spartan of old or of Wordsworth's "Happy Warrior":

> "Who, doomed to go in company with pain,
> And fear, and bloodshed—miserable train!—
> Turns his necessity to glorious gain."

Finally, the countryman who feels discontented with his lot—and there are few indeed who do not occasionally pine for a change of employment—should go on a railway journey through "the black country" at night, and mark the fierce light that reddens the murky skies as the factory fires send forth their livid flames and clouds of sooty smoke. He should watch the swarms of long-suffering human beings going to and fro and in and out like busy bees around their hive, toiling, ever toiling, round about the blazing fires. He should spend an hour in the streets of Birmingham, where, as I passed through one fine September morning recently on my way to Ireland, the atmosphere was darkened and the human lungs stifled by a thick yellow fog. Or he should go down to the engine-room of a mighty liner, when it is doing its twenty knots across the seas, and then think of his own life in the happy hamlets and the fresh, green fields of our English country.

Coming once more down the hill into the valley of the Coln, we must cross the old Roman road known as the Fossway, follow the course of the stream, and, about a mile beyond the snug little village of Fossbridge, we reach the great woods of Chedworth.

These coverts form part of the property of Lord Eldon. His house of Stowell stands well up on the hill. It is a grey, square building of some size, placed so as to catch all the sun and the breezes too, — very much more healthy and bright than most of the old houses we have passed, which were built much too low down in the valley, where the winter sunbeams seldom penetrate and the river mists rise damp and cold at night. As we walk along the drive which leads through the woods to the Roman villa, any amount of rabbits and pheasants are to be seen. And here take place annually some of those big shoots which ignorant people are so fond of condemning as unsportsmanlike, simply because they have not the remotest idea what they are talking about. Why it should be cruel to kill a thousand head in a day instead of two hundred on five separate days, one fails to understand. As a matter of fact, the bigger the "shoot" the less cruelty takes place, because bad shots are not likely to be present on these occasions, whilst in small "shoots" they are the rule rather than the exception. Instead of birds and ground game being wounded time after time, at big *battues* they are killed stone dead by some well-known and acknowledged good shot. To see a real workman knocking down rocketer after rocketer at a height which would be considered impossible by half the men who go but shooting is to witness an exhibition of skill and correct timing which can only be attained by the most assiduous practice and the quickest of eyes. No, it is the pottering hedgerow shooter, generally on his neighbour's boundary, who is often unsportsmanlike. We know one or two who would have no hesitation in shooting at a covey of partridges on the ground, when they were within shot of the boundary hedge; and if they wounded three or four and picked them up, they would carry them home fluttering and gasping, because they are too heartless to think of putting the wretched creatures out of their sufferings.

The extensive Roman remains discovered some years ago in the heart of this forest doubtless formed the country house of some Roman squire. They are well away from the river bank, and about three parts of the way up the sloping hillside. The house faced as nearly as possible south-east. In this point, as in many others, the Romans showed their superiority of intellect over our ancestors of Elizabethan and other days. Nowadays we begin to realise that houses should be built on high ground, and that the aspect that gives most sun in winter is south-east. The old Romans realised this fifteen hundred years ago. In other words, our ancestors in the dark ages were infinitely behind the Romans in intellect, and we are just reaching their standard of common sense. The characteristics of the interior of these old dwellings are simplicity combined with refinement and good taste. And it is worthy of remark that the men who are ahead of the thought and feeling of the present day are crying out for more simplicity in our homes and furniture, as well as for more refinement and real architectural merit. No useless luxuries and nick-nacks, but plenty of public baths, and mosaic pavements laboriously put together by hard hand labour, — these are the points that Ruskin and the Romans liked in common.

With this grandly timbered valley spread beneath them, no more suitable spot on which to build a house could anywhere be found. And though the Romans who inhabited this villa could not from its windows see the sun go down in the purple west, emblematic of that which was shortly to set over Rome, they could see the glorious dawn of a new day—boding forth the dawn that was already brightening over England, even as "The old order changeth, yielding place to new";—and they could see the splendours of the moon rising in the eastern sky.

The principal apartment in this Roman country house measures about thirty feet by twenty; it was probably divided into two parts, forming the dining-room and drawing-room as well. The tessellated pavements are wonderfully preserved, though not quite so perfect as a few others that have been found in England. With all their beautiful colouring they are merely formed of different shades of local stone, together with a little terra-cotta. Perhaps these pavements, with their rich mellow tints of red sandstone, and their shades of white, yellow, brown, and grey, afforded by different varieties of limestone, are examples of the most perfect kind of work which the labours of mankind, combined with the softening influences of time, are able to produce. In one corner the design is that of a man with a rabbit in his hand; and no doubt there were lots of rabbits in these woods in those days, as well as deer and other wild animals long since extinct.

In these woods of Chedworth the rose bay willow herbs grow taller and finer than is their wont elsewhere. In every direction they spring up in hundreds, painting the woodlands with a wondrously rich purple glow. Here, too, the bracken thrives, and many a fine old oak tree spreads its branches, revelling in the clay soil. On the limestone of the Cotswolds oaks are seldom seen; but wherever a vein of clay is found, there will be the oaks and the bracken. Every forest tree thrives hereabouts; and in the open spaces that occur at intervals in the forest there grow such masses of wild flowers as are nowhere else to be seen in the Cotswold district. White spiraea, or meadow-sweet, crowds into every nook and corner of open ground, raising its graceful stems in almost tropical luxuriance by the brook-side. Campanula and the blue geranium or meadow crane's-bill, with flowers of perfect blue, grow everywhere amid the white blossoms of the spiraea. St John's wort, with its star-shaped golden flowers, white and red campion, and a host of others, are larger and more beautiful on the rich loam than they are on the stony hills. Even the lily-of-the-valley thrives here.

In the bathroom may be seen an excellent example of the hypocaust—an ingenious contrivance, by means of which the rooms were heated with hot air, which passed along beneath the floors.

In the museum are portions of the skulls of men and of oxen, the antlers of red deer, oyster shells, knives, spear-heads, arrow-heads, bits of locks with keys, and excellent horseshoes, not to speak of such things as bronze spurs, spoons, part of a Roman weighing-machine, and a splendid pair of compasses. There are pieces of earthenware with potter's marks on them, and red tiles bearing unmistakable marks of fingering, as well as footprints of dogs and goats; these impressions must have been made when the tiles were in a soft state.

But the most interesting relics are three freestone slabs, on which are inscribed the Greek letters [Greek: chi] and [Greek: rho]. It was Mr. Lysons who first noticed this evidence of ancient faith, and he is naturally of the opinion that the sacred inscription proves that the builder was a Christian. Another stone in this collection has the word "PRASIATA" roughly chiselled on it.

There was a British king, by name Prasutagus, said to have been a Christian, and possibly it was this man who built the old house in the midst of the Chedworth woods. A mile beyond this interesting relic of Roman times is the manor house of Cassey Compton, built by Sir Richard Howe about the middle of the seventeenth century. It stands on the banks of the Coln, and in olden times was approached by a drawbridge and surrounded by a moat. The farmer by whom it is inhabited tells me that, judging by the fish-ponds situated close by, he imagines it was once a monastery. This was undoubtedly the case, for we find in Fozbrooke that the Archbishop of York had license to "embattle his house" here in the reign of Edward I.

A mosaic pavement, discovered here about 1811, was placed in the British Museum.

It is very sad to come upon these remote manor houses in all parts of the Cotswold district, and to find that their ancient glory is departed, even though their walls are as good as they were two hundred years ago, when the old squires lived their jovial lives, and those halls echoed the mirth and merriment which characterised the life of "the good old English gentleman, all of the olden time."

Other fine old houses in this immediate district which have not been mentioned are Ampney Park, a Jacobean house containing an oak-panelled apartment, with magnificently carved ceiling and fine stone fireplace; Barnsley and Sherborne, partly built by Inigo Jones; Missarden, Duntisborne Abbots, Kemble, and Barrington. Rendcombe is a modern house of some size, built rather with a view to internal comfort than external grace and symmetry.

CHAPTER XI.

COTSWOLD PASTIMES.

It is not surprising that in those countries which abound in sunshine and fresh, health-giving air, the inhabitants will invariably be found to be not only keen sportsmen, but also accomplished experts in all the games and pastimes for which England has long been famous. Given good health and plenty of work mankind cannot help being cheerful and sociably inclined; for this reason we have christened the district of which we write the "Merrie Cotswolds." From time immemorial the country people have delighted in sports and manly exercises. On the north wall of the nave in Cirencester Church is a representation of the ancient custom of Whitsun ale. The Whitsuntide sports were always a great speciality on Cotswold, and continue to the present day, though in a somewhat modified form.

The custom portrayed in the church of Cirencester was as follows:—

The villagers would assemble together in one of the beautiful old barns which are so plentiful in every hamlet. Two of them, a boy and a girl, were then chosen out and appointed Lord and Lady of the Yule. These are depicted on the church wall; and round about them, dressed in their proper garb, are pages and jesters, standard-bearer, purse-bearer, mace-bearer, and a numerous company of dancers.

The reason that a representation of this very secular custom is seen in the church probably arises from the fact that the Church ales were feasts instituted for the purpose of raising money for the repair of the church. The churchwardens would receive presents of malt from the farmers and squires around; they sold the beer they brewed from it to the villagers, who were obliged to attend or else pay a fine.

The church house—a building still to be seen in many villages—was usually the scene of the festivities.

The "Diary of Master William Silence" tells us that the quiet little hamlets presented an unusually gay appearance on these memorable occasions. "The village green was covered with booths. There were attractions of various kinds. The churchwardens had taken advantage of the unusual concourse of strangers as the occasion of a Church ale. Great barrels of ale, the product of malt contributed by the parishioners according to their several abilities, were set abroach in the north aisle of the church, and their contents sold to the public. This was an ordinary way of providing for church expenses, against which earnest reformers inveighed, but as yet in vain so far as Shallow was concerned. The church stood conveniently near the village green, and the brisk trade which was carried on all day was not interrupted by the progress of divine service." The parson's discourse, however, appears to have suffered some interruption by reason of the numbers who crowded into the aisles to patronise the churchwardens' excellent ale.

In the reign of James I. one, Robert Dover, revived the old Olympic games on Cotswold. Dover's Hill, near Weston-under-Edge, was called after him.

These sports included horse-racing, coursing, cock-fighting, and such games as quoits, football, skittles, wrestling, dancing, jumping in sacks, and all the athletic exercises.

The "Annalia Dubrensia" contain many verses about these sports by the hand of Michael Drayton, Ben Jonson, and others.

> "On Cotteswold Hills there meets
> A greater troop of gallants than Rome's streets
> E'er saw in Pompey's triumphs: beauties, too,
> More than Diana's beavie of nymphs could show
> On their great hunting days."

That hunting was practised here in these days is evident, for Thomas Randall, of Cambridge, writes in the same volume:

> "Such royal pastimes Cotteswold mountains fill,
> When gentle swains visit Anglonicus hill,
> When with such packs of hounds they hunting go
> As Cyrus never woon'd his bugle to."

Fozbrooke tells us that the Whitsuntide sports are the *floralia* of the Romans. They are still a great institution in all parts of the Cotswolds, though Church ales, like cock-fighting and other barbaric amusements, have happily long since died out.

Golf and archery are popular pastimes in the merry Cotswolds. It is somewhat remarkable that this district has produced in recent years the amateur lady champions of England in each of these fascinating pastimes, Lady Margaret Scott, of Stowell, being *facile princeps* among lady golfers, whilst Mrs. Christopher Bowly, of Siddington, even now holds the same position in relation to the ancient practice of archery.

The ancient art of falconry is still practised in these parts. Thirty years ago, when Duleep Singh lived at Hatherop, hawking on the downs was one of his chief amusements. But the only hawking club hereabouts that we know of is at Swindon, in Wiltshire.

Coursing is as popular as ever among the Cotswold farmers. These hills have always been noted for the sport. Drayton tells us that the prize at the coursing meetings held on the Cotswolds in his day was a silver-studded collar. Shakespeare, in his *Merry Wives of Windsor* alludes to the coursing on "Cotsall." There is an excellent club at Cirencester. The hares in this district are remarkably big and strong-running. The whole district lends itself particularly to this sport, owing to the large fields and fine stretches of open downs.

CRICKET.

In an agricultural district such as the Cotswolds it is inevitable that the game of cricket should be somewhat neglected. Men who work day after day in the open air, and to whom a half-holiday is a very rare experience, naturally seek their recreations in less energetic fashion than the noble game of cricket demands of its votaries. The class who derive most benefit from this game spring as a rule from towns and manufacturing centres and those whose work and interests confine them indoors the greater part of their time. Among the Cotswold farmers, however, a great deal of interest is shown; the scores of county matches are eagerly pursued in the daily papers; and if there is a big match on at Cheltenham or any other neighbouring town, a large number invariably go to see it. There is some difficulty in finding suitable sites for your ground in these parts, for the hill turf is very stony and shallow; it is not always easy to find a flat piece of ground handy to the villages. A cricket ground is useless to the villagers if it is perched up on the hill half a mile away. It must be at their doors; and even then, though they may occasionally play, they will never by any chance trouble to roll it. We made a ground in the valley of the Coln some years ago, and went to some expense in the way of levelling, filling up gravel pits, and removing obstructions like cowsheds; but unless we had looked after it ourselves and made preparations for a match, it would have soon gone back to its original rough state again. And yet two of the young Peregrines in the village are wonderfully good cricketers, and as "keen as mustard" about it; though when it comes to rolling and mowing the ground they are not quite as keen. They will throw you over for a match in the most unceremonious way if, when the day comes, they don't feel inclined to play. We have often tried to persuade these two young fellows to become professional cricketers, there being such a poor prospect in the farming line; but they have not the slightest ambition to play for the county, though they are quite good enough; so they "waste their sweetness on the desert air."

Old Mr. Peregrine, a man of nearly eighty years of age, is splendid fun when he is watching his boys play cricket. He goes mad with excitement; and if you take them off bowling, however much the batsmen appear to relish their attack, he won't forgive you for the rest of the day.

His eldest son, Tom—our old friend the keeper—generally stands umpire; he is not so useful to his side as village umpires usually are, because he hasn't got the moral courage to give his side "in" when he knows perfectly well they are "out." The other day, however, he made a slight error; for, on being appealed to for the most palpable piece of "stumping" ever seen in the cricket field, the ball bouncing back on to the wicket from the wicket-keeper's pads while the batsman was two yards out of his ground, he said, "Not out; it hit the wicket-keeper's pads." He imagined he was being asked whether the batsman had been bowled, and it never occurred to him that you could be "stumped out" in this way. Altogether, Cotswold cricket is great fun.

The district is full of memories of the prehistoric age, and in certain parts of the country *prehistoric* cricket is still indulged in. Never shall I forget going over to Edgeworth with the Winson Cricket XI. to play a *grand* match at that seat of Roman antiquities. The carrier drove us over in his pair-horse brake—a rickety old machine, with a pony of fourteen hands and a lanky, ragged-hipped old mare over sixteen hands high in the shafts together. A most useful man in the field was the honest carrier, whether at point or at any other place where the ball comes sharp and quick; for, to quote Shakespeare,

> "he was a man
> Of an unbounded stomach."

The rest of our team included the jovial miller; two of the village carpenter's sons—excellent folk; the village curate, who captained the side, and stood six feet five inches without his cricket shoes; one or two farmers; a footman, and a somewhat fat and apoplectic butler.

The colours mostly worn by the Winson cricketers are black, red, and gold—a Zingaric band inverted (black on top); their motto I believe to be "Tired, though united."

As the ground stands about eight hundred feet above sea level, all of us, but especially the fat butler, found considerable difficulty in getting to the top of the hill, after the brake had set us down at the village public. But once arrived, a magnificent view was to be had, extending thirty miles and more across the wolds to the White Horse Hill in Berkshire. However, we had not come to admire the view so much as to play the game of cricket. We therefore proceeded to look for the pitch. It was known to be in the field in which we stood, because a large red flag floated at one end and proclaimed that somewhere hereabouts was the scene of combat. It was the fat butler, I think, who, after sailing about in a sea of waving buttercups like a veritable Christopher Columbus, first discovered the stumps among the mowing grass.

Evident preparations had been made either that morning or the previous night for a grand match; a large number of sods of turf had been taken up and hastily replaced on that portion of the wicket where the ball is supposed to pitch when it leaves the bowler's hand. There had been no rain for a month, but just where the stumps were stuck a bucket or two of water had been dashed hastily on to the arid soil; while, to crown all, a chain or rib roller—a ghastly instrument used by agriculturists for scrunching up the lumps and bumps on the ploughed fields, and pulverising the soil—had been used with such effect that the surface of the pitch to the depth of about an inch had been reduced to dust.

In spite of this we all enjoyed ourselves immensely. Delightful old-fashioned people, both farmers and labourers, were playing against us; quaint (I use the word in its true sense) and simple folk, who looked as if they had been dug up with the other Saxon and Roman antiquities for which Edgeworth is so famous.

I was quite certain that the man who bowled me out was a direct descendant of Julius Caesar. He delivered the ball underhand at a rapid rate. It came twisting along, now to the right, now to the left; seemed to disappear beneath the surface of the soil, then suddenly came in sight again, shooting past the block. Eventually they told me it removed the left bail, and struck the wicket-keeper a fearful blow on the chest. It was generally agreed that such a ball had never been bowled before. "'Twas a *pretty* ball!" as Tom Peregrine pronounced it, standing umpire in an enormous wideawake hat and a white coat reaching down to his knees, and smoking a bad cigar. "A very pretty ball," said my fellow batsman at the other wicket "A d—d pretty ball," I reiterated *sotto voce*, as I beat a retreat towards the flag in the corner of the field, which served as a pavilion.

When I went on to bowl left-handed "donkey-drops," Tom Peregrine (my own servant, if you please) was very nearly no-balling me. "For," said he, "I 'ate that drabby-handed business; it looks so awkid. Muddling work, I calls it." But I am anticipating.

As I prepared myself for the fray, and carefully donned a pair of well-stuffed pads and an enormously thick woollen jersey for protection, not so much against the cold as against the "flying ball," it flashed across me that I was about to personify the immortal Dumkins of Pickwick fame; whilst in my companion, the stout butler, it was impossible not to detect the complacent features and rounded form of Mr. Podder. Up to a certain point the analogy was complete. Let the Winson Invincibles equal the All Muggleton C.C., while the Edgeworth Daisy Cutters shall be represented by Dingley Dell; then sing us, thou divine author of Pickwick, the glories of that never-to-be-forgotten day.

"All Muggleton had the first innings, and the interest became intense when Mr. Dumkins and Mr. Podder—two of the most renowned members of that distinguished club—walked bat in hand to their respective wickets. Mr. Luffy, the highest ornament of Dingley Dell, was pitched to bowl against the redoubtable Dumkins, and Mr. Struggles was selected to do the same kind office for the hitherto unconquered Podder...The umpires were stationed behind the wickets [Tom Peregrine had been suborned for Winson, and proved the most useful man on the side], the scorers were prepared to notch the runs. A breathless silence ensued. Mr. Luffy retired a few paces behind the wicket of the passive Podder, and applied the ball to his right eye for several seconds. Dumkins [the author] confidently awaited its coming with his eyes fixed on the motions of Mr. Luffy. 'Play!' suddenly cried the bowler. The ball flew from his hand straight and swift towards the centre stump of the wicket. The wary Dumkins was on the alert; it fell upon the tip of his bat...."

Here, with deep sorrow, let it be stated that the writer failed to evince the admirable skill displayed by his worthy prototype; the Dumkins of grim reality was unable to compete with the Dumkins of fiction. Instead of "sending the ball far away over the heads of the scouts; who just stooped low enough to let it fly over them," I caught it just as it pitched on a rabbit-hole, and sent it straight up into the air like a soaring rocket. "Right, right, I have it!" yelled bowler and wicket-keeper simultaneously. "Run two, Podder; they'll never catch it!" shouted Dumkins with all his might. "Catch it in your 'at, Bill!" screamed the Edgeworth eleven. Never was such confusion! I was already starting for the second run, whilst my stout fellow batsman was halfway through the first, when the ball came down like a meteor, and, narrowly shaving the luckless "Podder's" head, hit the ground with a loud thud about five yards distant from the outstretched hands of the anxious bowler, who collided with his ally, the wicket-keeper, in the middle of the pitch. Half stunned by the shock, and disappointed at his want of success in his attempt to "judge" the catch, the bowler had yet presence of mind enough to seize the ball and hurl it madly at the stumps. But the wicket-keeper being still *hors de combat*, it flew away towards the spectators, and buried itself among the mowing grass. "Come six, Podder!" I shouted, amid cries of "Keep on running!" "Run it out!" etc., from spectators and scouts alike. And run we did, for the umpire forgot to call "lost ball," and we should have been running still but for the ingenuity of one of our opponents; for, whilst all were busily engaged in searching among the grass, a red-faced yokel stole up unawares, with an innocent expression on his face, raced poor "Podder" down the pitch, produced the ball from his trouser pocket, and knocked off the bails in the nick of time. "Out," says Peregrine, amid a roar of laughter from the whole field; and Mr. "Podder" had to go.

Now came the question how many runs should be scored, for I had passed my fellow batsman in the race, having completed seven runs to his five. Eventually it was decided to split the difference and call it a sixer; the suggestion of a member of our side that seven should be scored to me and five to Mr. "Podder" (making twelve in all) being rejected after careful consideration.

Thus, from the first ball bowled in this historic match there arose the whole of the remarkable events recorded above. Therein is shown the complete performances with the bat of two renowned cricketers; for, alas I in once more trying to play up to the form of Dumkins, I was bowled "slick" the very next ball, "as hath been said or sung."

There was much good-natured chaff flying about during the match, but no fighting and squabbling, save when a boundary hit was made, when the batsman always shouted "Three runs," and the bowler "No, only one." The scores were not high; but I remember that we won by three runs, that the carpenter's son got a black eye, that we had tea in an old manor house turned into an inn, and drove home in the glow of a glorious sunset, not entirely displeased with our first experience of "prehistoric" cricket.

Some of the pleasantest matches we have ever taken part in have been those at Bourton-on-the-Water. Owing to the very soft wicket which he found on arriving, this place was once christened by a well-known cricketer *Bourton-on-the-Bog*. Indeed, it is often a case of Bourton-*under*-the-Water; but, in spite of a soft pitch, there is great keenness and plenty of good-tempered rivalry about these matches. Bourton is a truly delightful village. The Windrush, like the Coln at Bibury, runs for some distance alongside of the village street.

The M.C.C., or "premier club"—as the sporting press delight to call the famous institution at Lord's—generally get thoroughly well beaten by the local club. For so small a place they certainly put a wonderfully strong team into the field; on their own native "bog" they are fairly invincible, though we fancy on the hard-baked clay at Lord's their bowlers would lose a little of their cunning.

In the luncheon tent at Bourton there are usually more wasps than are ever seen gathered together in one place; they come in thousands from their nests in the banks of the Windrush.

If you are playing a match there, it is advisable to tuck your trousers into your socks when you sit down to luncheon. This, together with the fact that the tent has been known to blow down in the middle of luncheon, makes these matches very lively and amusing. What more lively scene could be imagined than a large tent with twenty-two cricketers and a few hundred wasps hard at work eating and drinking; then, on the tent suddenly collapsing, the said cricketers and the said wasps, mixed up with chairs, tables, ham, beef, salad-dressing, and apple tart, and the various ingredients of a cricket lunch, all struggling on the floor, and striving in vain to find their way out as best they can? Fortunately, on the only occasion that the tent blew down when we were present, it was not a good wasp year.

Besides the matches at Bourton, there is plenty of cricket at Cirencester, Northleach, and other centres in the Cotswolds. The "hunt" matches are great institutions, even though hunting people as a rule do not care for cricket, and invariably drop a catch. A good sportsman and excellent fellow has lately presented a cup to be competed for by the village clubs of this district. This, no doubt, will give a great impetus to the game amongst all classes; our village club has already been revived in order to compete. Our only fear with regard to the cup competition is that when you get two elevens on to a ground, and two umpires, none of whom know the rules (for cricket laws are the most "misunderstandable" things in creation), the final tie will degenerate into a free fight.

Be this as it may, anything that can make the greatest pastime of this country popular in the "merrie Cotswolds" is a step in the right direction. It is pleasing to watch boys and men hard at work practising on summer evenings. The rougher the ground the more they like it. Scorning pads and gloves, they "go in" to bat, and make Herculean efforts to hit the ball. And this, with fast bowling and the bumpy nature of the pitch, is a very difficult thing to do. They play on, long after sunset, — the darker it gets, and the more dangerous to life and limb the game becomes, the happier they are. We are bound to admit that when we play with them, a good pitch is generally prepared. It would be bad policy to endeavour to compete in the game they play, as we should merely expose ourselves to ridicule, and one's reputation as the man who has been known "to play in the papers," as they are accustomed to call big county matches, would very soon be entirely lost.

I was much amused a few years ago, on arriving home after playing for Somersetshire in some cricket matches, when Tom Peregrine made up to me with "a face like a benediction," and asked if I was the gentleman who had been playing "in the papers."

While on the subject of cricket, for some time past we have made experiments of all sorts of cricket grounds, and have come to the conclusion that the following is the best recipe to prepare a pitch on a dry and bumpy ground. A week before your match get a wheelbarrow full of clay, and put it into a water-cart, or any receptacle for holding water. Having mixed your clay with water, keep pouring the mixture on to your pitch, taking care that the stones and gravel which sink to the bottom do not fall out. When you have emptied your water-cart, get some more clay and water, and continue pouring it on to the ground until you have covered a patch about twenty-two yards long and three yards wide, always remembering not to empty out the sediment at the bottom of the water-cart, for this will spoil all. Then, setting to work with your roller, roll the clay and water into the ground. Never mind if it picks up on to the roller: a little more water will soon put that to rights. After an hour's rolling you will have a level and true cricket pitch, requiring but two or three days' sun to make it hard and true as asphalt. You may think you have killed the grass; but if you water your pitch in the absence of rain the day after you have played on it, the grass will not die. It is chiefly in Australia that cricket grounds are treated in this way; they are dressed with mud off the harbours, and rolled simultaneously. Such grounds are wonderfully true and durable.

If the pitch is naturally a clay one, it might be sufficient to use water only, and roll at the same time; but for renovating a worn clay pitch, a little strong loamy soil, washed in with water and rolled down will fill up all the "chinks" and holes. It will make an old pitch as good as new.

The reason that nine out of ten village grounds are bad and bumpy is that they are not rolled soon enough after rain or after being watered. Roll and water them simultaneously, and they will be much improved.

Another excellent plan is to soak the ground with clay and water, and leave it alone for a week or ten days before rolling. Permanent benefit will be done to the soil by this method. For golf greens and lawn-tennis courts situated on light soil, loam is an indispensable dressing. Any loamy substance will vastly improve the texture of a light soil and the quality of the herbage. Yet it is most difficult to convince people of this fact. We have known cases in which hundreds of pounds have been expended on cricket grounds and golf greens when an application of clay top-dressing would have put the whole thing to rights at the cost of a few shillings. One committee had artificial wells made on every "putting green" of their golf course, in order to have water handy for keeping the turf cool and green. What better receptacle for water could they have found than a top-dressing of half an inch of loam or clay, retaining as it does every drop of moisture that falls in the shape of dew or rain, instead of allowing it to percolate through like a sieve, as is the case with an ordinary sandy soil? Yet this clay dressing, while retaining water, becomes hard, firm, and as level as a billiard table on the timely application of the roller.

Those who look after cricket grounds and the like have seldom any acquaintance with the constitution of soils; they are apt to treat all, whether sand, light loam, strong loam, heavy clay, or even peat, in exactly the same way, instead of recollecting that, as in agriculture, a judicious combination will alone give us that *ideal loam* which produces the best turf, and the best soil for every purpose. I am quite convinced that our farmers do not realise how much worthless light land may be improved by a dressing of clay or loam. Such dressings are expensive without a doubt, but the amelioration of the soil is so marked that in favourable localities the process ought to pay in the long run.

Turning to cricket in general, perhaps the modern game, as played on a good wicket, is in every respect, save one, perfection. If only something could be done to curtail the length of matches, and rid us of that awful nuisance the poking, time-wasting batsman, there would be little improvement possible.

"All the world's a stage," and even at cricket the analogy holds good. Thus Shakespeare:

> "As in a theatre the eyes of men,
> After a well-graced actor leaves the stage,
> Are idly bent on him that enters next,
> Thinking his prattle to be tedious."

So also one may say of some dull and lifeless cricketer who, after the famous Gloucestershire hitter has made things merry for spectators and scouts alike, "enters next":

> "As in a cricket field the eyes of men,
> After a well-*Graced* player leaves the *sticks*,
> Are idly bent on him that enters next,
> Thinking his *batting* to be tedious."

On the other hand, if we sow the wild oats of cricket—in other words, if we risk everything for the fleeting satisfaction of a blind "slog"—we shall be bowled, stumped, or caught out for a moral certainty. It is only a matter of time.

Perhaps the addition of another stump might help towards the very desirable end of shortening the length of matches, and thus enable more amateurs to take part in them. I cannot agree with those who lament the improved state of our best English cricket grounds; if only the batsmen play a free game and do not waste time, the game is far more entertaining for players and spectators alike, when a true wicket is provided. The heroes of old,

> "When Bird and Beldham, Budd, and such as they, —
> Lord Frederick, too, once England's chief and flower, —
> Astonished all who came to see them play,"

those "scorners of the ground" and of pads and gloves doubtless displayed more *pluck* on their rough, bumpy grounds than is now called forth in facing the attack of Kortright, Mold, or Richardson. But on the other hand, on rough grounds much is left to chance and *luck*; cricket, as played on a billiard-table wicket certainly favours the batsman, but it admits of a brilliancy and finish in the matter of style that are impossible on the old-fashioned wicket. Whilst the modern bowler has learnt extraordinary accuracy of pitch, the batsman has perfected the art of "timing" the ball. And what a subtle, delicate art is correct "timing"!—the skilful embodiment of thought in action, depending for success on that absolute sympathy of hand and eye which only assiduous practice, confidence, and a good digestion can give. And on uncertain, treacherous ground confident play is never seen. A ball cannot be "cut" or driven with any real brilliancy of style when there is a likelihood of its abruptly "shooting" or bumping. No; if we would leave as little as possible to chance, our grounds cannot be too good. Even from a purely selfish point of view, apart from the welfare of our side, the pleasure derived from a good

175

"innings" on a first-rate cricket ground is as great as that bestowed by any other physical amusement.

Perhaps one ought not to think of comparing the sport of fox-hunting, with its extraordinary variety of incident and surroundings, the study of a lifetime, to the game of cricket. At the same time, for actual all-round enjoyment, and for economy, the game holds its own against all amusements.

Bromley-Davenport has said that given a *good* country and a *good* fox, *and* a burning scent, the man on a *good* horse with a good *start*, for twenty or thirty minutes absorbs as much happiness into his mental and physical organisation as human nature is capable of containing at one time. This is very true. But how seldom the five necessary conditions are forthcoming simultaneously the keen hunting man has learnt from bitter experience. You will be lucky if the real good thing comes off once for every ten days you hunt. In cricket a man is dependent on his own quickness of hand and eye; in hunting there is that vital contingency of the well-filled purse. "'Tis money that makes the mare to go."

Then what a grand school is cricket for some of the most useful lessons of life! Its extraordinary fluctuations are bound to teach us sooner or later

> "Rebus angustis animosus atque
> Fortis appare."

The *rebus angustis* are often painfully impressed on the memory by a long sequence of "duck's eggs"; and how difficult is the *animosus atque fortis appare* when we return to the pavilion with a "pair of spectacles" to our credit!

Then, again, cricketers are taught to preserve a mind

> "Ab insolenti temperatam
> Laetitiâ."

We must not permit the *laetitiâ insolenti* to creep in when we have made a big score. How often do we see young cricketers over-elated under these circumstances, and suffering afterwards from temporary over-confidence and consequent carelessness!

But we must have no more Horace, lest our readers exclaim, with Jack Cade, "Away with him! away with him! he speaks *Latin*!"

Hope, energy, perseverance, and courage,—all these qualities are learnt in our grand English game. There is always hope for the struggling cricketer. In no other pursuit are energy and perseverance so absolutely sure of bearing fruit, if we only stick to it long enough.

The fact is that cricket, like many other things, is but the image and prototype of life in general. And the same qualities that, earnestly cultivated in spite of repeated failure and disappointment, make good cricketers lead ultimately to success in all the walks of life. In spite of the improvement in grounds, cricket is still an excellent school for teaching physical courage. Many grounds are somewhat rough and bumpy to field on, beautifully smooth though they look from the pavilion. We have only to stand "mid-off" or "point" on a cold day at the beginning of May whilst a hard-hitting batsman, well set on a true wicket, is driving or cutting ball after ball against our hands and shins, to realise what a capital school for courage the game is!

How exacting is the critic in this matter of fielding! and how delightfully simple the bowling looks from that admirably safe vantage-ground, the pavilion! Just as to a man comfortably stationed in the grand-stand at Aintree nothing looks easier than the way in which the best horses in the world flit over the five-foot fences, leaving them behind with scarcely an effort, their riders sitting quietly in the saddle all the while, so does the pavilion critic pride himself on the way he would have "cut" that short one instead of merely stopping it, or blocked that simple ball that went straight on and bowled the wicket. Everything that is well and gracefully performed appears easy to the looker-on. But that ease and grace, whether in the racehorse or in the man, has only been acquired by months and years of training and practice.

It is seldom that the spectator is able to form a true and unbiassed opinion as to the varied contingencies which lead to victory or defeat in cricket. The actual players and the umpires are perhaps alone qualified to judge to what extent the fluctuations of the game are affected by the vagaries of weather and ground. For this reason it is well to take newspaper criticism *cum grano salis*.

What is the cause of the extraordinary fluctuations of form which all cricketers, from the greatest to the least, are more or less subject to? It cannot be set down altogether to luck, for a run of bad luck, such as all men have at times experienced, is often compatible with being in the very best form. A man who is playing very well at the net often gets out directly he goes in to bat in a match, whilst many a good player, who tells you "he has not had a bat in his hand this season," in his very first innings for the year makes a big score. In subsequent innings's, oddly enough, he feels the want of net practice. *Confidence* would seem to be the *sine quâ non* for the successful batsman. Nothing succeeds like success; and once fairly started on a sequence of big scores, the cricketer goes on day by day piling up runs and *vires acquirit eundo*.

Perhaps "being in form" does not depend so much on the state of the digestion as on the state of the *mind*. Anxiety or excitement, fostered by over-keenness, usually results in a blank score-sheet. Some men, like horses, are totally unable to do themselves credit on great occasions. They go off their feed, and are utterly out of sorts in consequence. On the other hand, sheer force of will has often enabled men to make a big score. Many a good batsman can recall occasions on which he made a mental resolve on the morning of a match to make a century, and did it.

How curious it is that really good players, from staleness or some unknown cause, occasionally become absolutely useless for a time! Every fresh failure seems to bring more and more nervousness, until, from sheer lack of confidence, their case becomes hopeless, and a child could bowl them out. Ah well! we must not grumble at the ups and downs of the finest game in creation: "every dog will have his day" sooner or later; of that we may be sure.

And not the least of the advantages of cricket is the large number of friends made on the tented field. For this reason the jolliest cricket is undoubtedly that which is played by the various wandering clubs.

Whether you are fighting under the banner of the brotherhood whose motto is "United though untied," [6] or under the flag of the "Red, Black, and Gold," [7] or with any other of the many excellent clubs that abound nowadays, you will have an enjoyable game, whether you make fifty runs or a duck's egg.

[6] The Free Foresters.

[7] The I Zingari.

County cricket is nowadays a little over done. Two three-day matches a week throughout the summer don't leave much time for other pursuits. A liberal education at a good public school and university seems to be thrown away if it is to be followed by five or six days a week at cricket all through the summer year after year. Most of our best amateurs realise this, and, knowing that if they go in for county cricket at all they must play regularly, they give it up, and are content to take a back seat. They do wisely, for let us always remember that cricket is a game and not a business.

On the other hand, much good results from the presence in county cricket of a leavening of gentle; for they prevent the further development of professionalism. It is doubtless owing to the "piping times of peace" England has enjoyed during the past fifty years that cricket has developed to such an abnormal extent. The British public are essentially hero worshippers, and especially do they worship men who show manliness and pluck; and those feelings of respect and admiration that it is to be hoped in more stirring times would be reserved for a Nelson or a Wellington have been recently lavished on our Graces, our Stoddarts, our Ranjitsinhjis, and our Steels.

As long as war is absent, and we "live at home at ease," so long will our sports and pastimes flourish and increase. And long may they flourish, more especially those in which the quality of courage is essential for success! It will be a bad day for England when success in our sports and pastimes no longer depends on the exercise of pluck and manliness; when hunting gives place to bicycling, and cricket to golf; when, in fact, the wholesome element of *danger* is removed from our recreation and pursuits. Should, in the near future, the long-talked-of invasion of this country by a combination of European powers become an accomplished fact, Englishmen may perchance be glad, as the cannon balls and musket shots are whizzing round their heads, that on the mimic battlefields of cricket, football, polo, and fox-hunting they learnt two of the most useful lessons of life—coolness and courage.

CHAPTER XII.

THE COTSWOLDS THREE HUNDRED YEARS AGO.

Nowadays, thanks in a great measure to Mr. Madden's book, the "Diary of Master William Silence," it is beginning to dawn on us that the Cotswolds are more or less connected with the great poet of Stratford-on-Avon.

Mr. Blunt, in his "Cotswold Dialect," gives no less than fifty-eight passages from the works of Shakespeare, in which words and phrases peculiar to the district are made use of. Up to the reign of Queen Anne this vast open tract of downland formed a happy hunting ground for the inhabitants of all the surrounding counties. Warwickshire, Oxfordshire, and Wiltshire, as well as Gloucestershire folk repaired to the wolds for hunting, coursing, hawking, and other amusements; and in olden times, even more than to-day, Cotswold was, as Burton described it, "a type of what is most commodious for hawking, hunting, wood, waters, and all manner of pleasures." There never was a district so well adapted for stag-hunting. Nowadays the Cotswold district falls short in one desideratum, and that a most essential one, of being a first-rate hunting country. The large extent of ploughed land and the extreme dryness and poverty of the soil cause it on four days out of five to carry a most indifferent scent. But to-day we pursue the fox; in Shakespeare's time the stag was the quarry. And, as hunting men are well aware, the scent given off by a stag is not only ravishing to hounds, but it actually increases as the quarry tires, whilst that from a fox "grows small by degrees and beautifully less."

As with hunting, so also with coursing and hawking; the Cotswolds were the grand centre of Elizabethan sport. Here it was that Shakespeare marked the falcon "waiting on and towering in her pride of place." Here he saw the fallow greyhounds competing for the silver-studded collar.

What an interest and a dignity does a district such as this draw from even the slenderest association with the splendid name of William Shakespeare! For my part I freely confess that scenery, however grand and sublime, appeals but little to the imagination unless it be hallowed by association or blended in the thoughts with the recollection of those we have either loved or admired. Thus in India, in Natal and Cape Colony, in glorious Ceylon, I could admire those wonderful purple mountains and that tropical luxuriance of fertility and verdure; but I could not *feel* them. The boundless wolds of Africa, reminding one so much of Gloucestershire, yet far grander and far finer than anything of the kind in England, were to me a dreary wilderness. Passing through the fine broken hill country of Natal was like visiting chaos, a waste, inhospitable land,

> "Where no one comes
> Or hath come since the making of the world."

How well I remember the first sight of the wolds of South Africa! It was the hour of uncertain light that comes before the dawn; and as our railway train wound its tortuous course like a snake up the awful heights that would ultimately end in Majuba Hill—to which ill-fated spot I was bound—the billowy waves of rolling down seemed gradually to change to an immensely rough ocean running mountains high, and the mimosa trees dotting the plain for hundreds of miles appeared like armies of the souls of all the black men that ever lived on earth since the world began. There were passes and chasms like the portals of far-off, inaccessible Paradise,

> "With dreadful faces thronged and fiery arms."

And then the scene changed. The hills rose like graves of white men and barrows to the long-forgotten dead. Great oblong barrows, round Celtic barrows, and stately sarcophagi. Monumental effigies in alabaster, granite and porphyry; grim Gothic castles dating back to the foundation of the world, and grim Gothic cathedrals with long-drawn aisles, where the "great organ of Eternity" kept thundering ceaselessly. For the lightning and the thunder are powers to be reckoned with in those awful realms of chaos. And then the scene changed again. There suddenly uprose weird shapes of giants and leviathans, huge mammoths and whole regiments of fantastic monsters that looked like clouds and yet were mountains; and there were fortresses and towers of silence, with vultures hovering over them, and cliffs and crags and jutting promontories that looked like mountains, but were really clouds: for the black clouds and the frowning hills were so much alike that, save when the lightning shone, you could not say where the sky ended and the land began. But there was one gleam of hope in this weird and dismal scene, for on the farthest verge of the horizon there appeared, as it were, a lake—such a lake as saw the passing of Arthur, vanishing in mystery and silently floating away upon a barge towards the east. It was a lake of beryl, whose far-off golden shores were set with rubies and sardonyx, and beyond these, again, were the more distant waters of the silver sea; and as when Sir Bedivere

> "... saw,
> Straining his eyes beneath an arch of hand,
> Or thought he saw, the speck that bare the King,
> Down that long water opening on the deep
> Somewhere far off, pass on and on, and go
> From less to less and vanish into light.
> And the new sun rose bringing the new year,—"

so over the plains of Africa rose the mighty Alchemist and great revealer of truth, the scatterer of dreary darkness and secret night, turning those shadowy hills to purple and those mystic waters in the eastern sky to gold.

How different are our feelings when we traverse, either in reality or in fancy, such parts of the earth as are deeply blended in our hearts and minds with old familiar associations! Whilst wandering through the Lake District of England, how are we reminded of Wordsworth and the "Excursion"! How can we visit Devonshire and the West Country without summoning up pleasant thoughts of Charles Kingsley and Amyas Leigh; of the men of Bideford, Sir Richard Grenville, Kt., and "The little Revenge"? How vividly do the Trossachs recall "The Lady of the Lake" and Walter Scott! How with Edinburgh do we connect the sad story of Mary, the ill-fated queen! At Killarney, or standing amid the Gothic tracery of Tintern, how do we think on Alfred Tennyson and "the days that are no more"! These are only a few of the places in the British Isles that by universal consent are hallowed by tender associations. Of those spots in England which are dear to our hearts for personal reasons, there are of course hundreds. Every man has his own peculiar prejudices in this respect. To some London is the most sacred spot on earth. And who shall deny that with all her faults London is not a vastly interesting place? Is not every street hallowed by its associations with some great name or some great event in English history? Which of us can stand amid the Gothic tracery and the crumbling cloisters of Westminster, or under the shadow of the old grey towers of Whitehall, without recalling heart-stirring scenes and "paths of glory that lead but to the grave"? Who can stand unmoved on any of the famous bridges that span the silent river? Dr. Johnson, who acted up to Pope's well-known motto,

"The proper study of mankind is man,"

thought Fleet Street the most interesting place on the face of the earth; and perhaps he was right. Let us hear what he has to say about this halo of old association: "To abstract the mind from all local emotion would be impossible if it were endeavoured; and would be foolish if it were possible. Whatever withdraws us from the power of our senses; whatever makes the past, the distant, or the future predominate over the present, advances us in the dignity of thinking beings. Far from me and from my friends be such frigid philosophy as may conduct us indifferent and unmoved over any ground which has been dignified by wisdom, bravery, or virtue."

This, then, is the difference between the plains of Africa and the hills and valleys of England. The one is at present a vast inhospitable chaos, the other a land in which there is scarcely an acre that has not been dignified by wisdom, bravery, or virtue. Such are the signs by which we are to distinguish Cosmos from Chaos.

How far into the Cotswold Hills the halo of Stratford-on-Avon's glory may be said to extend it is not easy to determine. Let us allow at all events that the *reflection* from the arc reaches across the whole extent of the wolds as far as Dursley. For here on the western edge of the Cotswolds it is probable that Shakespeare spent that portion of his life which has always been involved in obscurity—the interval between his removal from Warwickshire and his arrival in London.

On a fine autumnal evening in the year 1592 a horseman, mounted on a little ambling nag, neared the Cotswold village of Bibury. Both man and steed showed unmistakable signs of weariness. The horse especially, though of that wiry kind known as the Irish hobby, hard as iron, and accustomed to long journeys, evinced by that sober and even dejected expression of countenance so well known to hunting men, that he had been ridden both far and fast. The saddle too, as well as the legs, chest, and flanks of the nag, appeared wet and mud-stained, as if some brook had been swum or some deep and muddy river forded, whilst the left shoulder and knee of the rider bore marks which told tales of a fall. The personal appearance of the man was not such as to excite the interest of the casual passer-by; for his dress, though extremly neat, was that worn by clerks and other townsfolk of the day; yet a keen observer might have noticed that the features were those of a man of uncommon character, in whom, as Carlyle would have said, a germ of irrepressible force had been implanted.

It had indeed been a glorious day. The hounds, after meeting close to Moreton-in-the-Marsh, in Warwickshire, had found a great hart in the forest near Seizincote, and had hunted him "at force" over the deep undrained vale up on to the Cotswold Hills, away past Stow-on-the-Wold and Bourton-on-the-Water, towards the great woods of Chedworth. But the stag, after crossing the Windrush close to Mr. Dutton's house at Sherborne, had failed to make his point, and had "taken soil" in a deep pool of the river Coln, near the little village of Coln-St-Dennis, where eventually the mort had sounded. Such a run had not been seen for many a long day; for it measured no less than fourteen miles "as the crow flies," and about five-and-twenty as the hounds ran. The time occupied had been close on seven hours. There had of course been several checks; but so strong had been the scent of this hart that, in spite of two "lets" of some twenty minutes' duration, the pack had been able to hunt their quarry to the bitter end. Only two men had seen the end. The pride and chivalry of Warwickshire, mounted on their high-priced Flanders mares, their Galway nags, and their splendid Barbaries, had been hopelessly thrown out of the chase; and besides the huntsman, on his plain-bred little English horse, the only remnant of the field was our friend with his tough and wiry Irish hobby.

It is five o'clock, and the sun as it disappears beyond a high ridge of the wolds, is tinging the grey walls of an ancient Gothic fane with a rosy glow. This our sportsman does not fail to notice; but in spite of his keen appreciation of the beauties of nature, the question uppermost in his mind, as he jogs along the rough, uneven road or track which leads to Bibury, is where to spend the night. The thought of returning home at that late hour does not enter his head; for the stag having gone away in exactly the opposite direction to that from which the Warwickshire man had set out early in the morning, there are no less than three-and-thirty long and weary miles between the hunter and his home. In the days of good Queen Bess, however, hospitality was proverbially free, and any decently set up Englishman was tolerably sure of a welcome at any of the country houses which were then, as now, scattered at long intervals over this wild, uncultivated district. And as he rides round a bend in the valley, a fair manor house comes into view, pleasantly placed in a sheltered spot hard by the River Coln. It was built in the style which had just come into vogue—the Elizabethan form of architecture; and in honour of the reigning monarch its front presented the appearance of the letter E. The windows, instead of being made of horn, were of glass; and tall stone chimneys (a modern luxury but lately invented) carried away the smoke from the chambers within.

It so happened that at the moment the stranger was passing, the owner of the house—a squire of some sixty years of age, but hale and hearty—was standing in front of his porch taking the evening air. This fact the horseman did not fail to notice, and with a ready eye to the main chance, which showed its possessor to be a man of no ordinary apprehension, he glanced approvingly at the groined porch, the richly carved pinnacles above it, and at the quaint belfry beyond, exclaiming with great enthusiasm:

"'Fore God, you have a goodly dwelling and a rich here. I do envy thee thine house, sir."

"BILBURY COURT."

"Barren, barren, barren; beggars all, beggars all," [8] was the reply, to which, after a pause, the squire added, "Marry, good air."

[8] *2 Henry IV*, V. iii.

"Ah, 'tis a good air up on these wolds," replied the sportsman. "But I am a stranger here in Gloucestershire; these high wild hills and rough, uneven ways draw out our miles and make them wearisome.[9] How far is it to Stratford?"

[9] *King Richard II.*, II. iii.

"Marry, 'tis nigh on forty mile, I warrant. Thou'll not see Stratford to-night, sir; thy horse is wappered[10] out, and that I plainly see."

[10] *Wappered* = tired. A Cotswold word.

To him replied the stranger wearily:

> Where is the horse that doth untread again
> His tedious measures with the unbated fire
> That he did pace them first? All things that are,
> Are with more spirit chased than enjoyed.[11]

[11] *Merchant of Venice*, II. vi.

"Hast been with the hounds to-day?" enquired the honest squire.

"Ah, sir, and that I have," was the reply; "and never have I seen such sport before. For seven long hours they made the welkin ring, and ran like swallows o'er the plain." [12]

[12] *Titus Andronicus*, II. ii.

"Please to step in; we be just a-settin' down to supper—a cold capon and a venison pasty. I'll tell my serving man to take thy nag to yonder yard, and make him comfortable for the night."

"Thanks, sir, I'll take him round myself, and give the honest beast a drench of barley broth,[13] and afterwards, to cheer him up a bit, a handful or two of dried peas." [14]

[13] *Henry V.*, III. v.

[14] *Midsummer Night's Dream*, IV. i.

Whilst the hunter was seeing to his nag, the squire thus addressed his serving man:

"Some pigeons, Davy, a couple of short-legged hens, a joint of mutton, and any pretty tiny kickshaws, tell William cook." [15]

[15] 2 *Henry IV.*, V. i.

DAVY: "Doth the hunter stay all night, sir?"

SQUIRE: "Yes, Davy. I will use him well; good sportsmen are ever welcome on Cotswold."

The wants of the Irish hobby having been thoroughly attended to, and the game little fellow having recovered in some measure his natural gaiety of spirits, the squire ushered the stranger into a long low hall, hung with pikes and guns and bows, and relics of the chase as well as of the wars. The stone floor was strewed with clean rushes, and lying about on tables were trashes, collars, and whips for hounds, as well as hoods, perches, jesses, and bells for hawks; whilst a variety of odds and ends, such as crossbows and jumping-poles, were scattered about the apartment. An enormous wood fire blazed at one end of the hall, and in the inglenook sat a girl of some twenty summers.

"My daughter, sir," exclaimed the squire; "as good a girl as ever lived to make a cheese, brew good beer, preserve all sorts of wines, and cook a capon with a chaudron! Marry! I forgot to ask thee thy name?"

"Oh, my name is Shakespeare—William Shakespeare, sir. I come from Stratford-on-the-Avon, up to'rds Warwick."

"Shakespy, Shakespy; a' don't know that name. Dost bear arms, sir?"

"I am entitled to them—a spear on a bend sable, and a falcon for my crest; but we have not yet applied to the heralds for the confirmation. And you, sir?"

"He writes himself *armigero* in any bill, warrant, quittance, or obligation," here put in Davy the serving man.

"Ah, that I do! and have done any time these three hundred years."

"All his successors gone before him hath done it; and all his ancestors that come after him may," added Davy, with pride.

"To be sure, to be sure," said the squire. "Well, welcome to Cotswold, Master Shakespeare; good sportsmen are ever welcome on Cotswold. But tell me, how didst thou get thy downfall?"

"The first was at the mound into the tyning by Master Blackett's house at Iccomb; old Dobbin breasted it, and the stones did rattle round mine ears like a house a-coming down. We made a shard[16] that let the rest of 'em through. It was the only wall that came in the way of the chase to-day. The second downfall was at the brook by Bourton-Windrush, I think they call it. Dobbin being a bit short of wind, and quilting sadly, stuck fast in the mire, and tumbled on to his nose in scrambling out. Marry, sir, but 'twas a famous chase; the like of it I never saw before. 'Twas grand at first to see the hart unharboured—a stag with all his rights, 'brow, bay, and trey.'"

[16] A Cotswold word = breach.

"Thou shouldst know, our hounds at Warwick are a noted pack,

> So flew'd, so sanded, and their beads are hung
> With ears that sweep away the morning dew;
> Crook-knee'd, and dew-lapp'd like Thessalian bulls;
> Slow in pursuit, but matched in mouth like bells,
> Each under each. A cry more tuneable
> Was never holla'd to, nor cheer'd with horn.'" [17]

[17] *Midsummer Night's Dream*, IV. i.

Then he told how, after leaving behind the deep undrained grass country round Moreton-in-the-Marsh, they rose the hills by Stow and came across the moor. How the riders who spurred their horses up the steep uprising ascent were soon left behind. For

> "To climb steep hills
> Requires slow pace at first; anger is like
> A full hot horse, who, being allowed his way,
> Self mettle tires him."

He told how, after an hour's steady running over the wolds, a "let" [18] occurred, and "the hot scent-snuffing hounds are driven to doubt";[19] how Mountain, Fury, Tyrant, and Ringwood, who had been leading the rest of the pack, strove in vain for a considerable time to pick out the cold scent, until suddenly the cheery sound of the old huntsman's voice was heard crying:

[18] *Two Noble Kinsmen*, III. v.

[19] *Venus and Adonis*, 692.

"Fury! Fury! There, Tyrant, there! Hark! Hark!" [20]

and the whole pack went "yoppeting" off as happy as the hunt was long. He told how Belman fairly surpassed himself, and "twice to-day picked out the dullest scent";[21] and how little Dobbin, the Irish hobby, went cantering on "as true as truest horse, that yet would never tire." [22] He told how, after running from scent to view, they came down into the woodlands of the valley of the Coln, and awoke the echoes with their "gallant chiding."

[20] *Tempest*, IV, i.

[21] *Taming of the Shrew*, Introduction.

[22] *Midsummer Night's Dream*, III. i.

> "... besides the groves,
> The skies, the fountains, every region near
> Seem'd all one mutual cry: I never heard
> So musical a discord, such sweet thunder." [23]

[23] *Midsummer Night's Dream*, IV.

And how the noble animal took soil in the Coln,

> "Under an oak whose antique root peeps out
> Upon the brook that brawls along this wood:
> To the which place our poor sequester'd stag
> Did come to languish; and indeed, my lord,
> The wretched animal heaved forth such groans
> That their discharge did stretch his leathern coat
> Almost to bursting, and the big round tears
> Coursed one another down his innocent nose
> In piteous chase.
>
> Left and abandon'd of his velvet friends,
> "Tis right,' quoth he: 'thus misery doth part
> The flux of company': anon a careless herd,
> Full of the pasture, jumps along by him,
> And never stays to greet him. 'Ah,' quoth Jaques,
> 'Sweep on, you fat and greasy citizens;
> 'Tis just the fashion: wherefore do you look
> Upon that poor and broken bankrupt there?'" [24]

[24] *As You Like It*, II. i.

And finally he told how the gallant beast died a soldier's death, fighting to the bitter end.

"Marry, 'twas a right good chase, and bravely must thy steed have borne thee. But thou wast too venturesome, Master Shakespeare," exclaimed the squire, "a-trying to jump that mound into the tyning by Master Blackett's house."

"Tell me, I prithee," answered Shakespeare, anxious to turn the conversation from his own share in the day's proceedings, "whose dog won the silver-studded collar this year in the coursing matches on Cotswold?" [25]

[25] *Merry Wives of Windsor.*

"Our Bill Peregrine, here, at the farm, carried it off. A prettier bit of coursing I never did see!"

"Ah! that was the country fellow that turned up when we sounded the mort by Col-Dene. He seemed to spring up out of the ground. He is a snapper up of unconsidered trifles, I'll be bound. The fellow claimed the hide: he said the skin was the keeper's fee." [26]

[26] 3 *Henry VI*, III. i.

"That 'ould be he. I warrant he lent a hand in taking assay and breaking up the deer. Tis just what he enjoys."

"Ah! I marked him disembowelling the poor dead beast in right good will, with hands besmeared with blood." [27]

[27] *Henry IV.*, V. iv.

Then they fell to talking of other things; and the honest old squire began to brag about his London days, and how he was once of Clement's Inn.

"There was I, and little John Doit of Staffordshire, and black George Barnes, and Francis Pickbone, and Will Squele, a Cotswold man; you had not four such swinge-bucklers in all the Inns o' Court again." [28]

[28] *Henry IV.*, III. ii.

But the old man was far too interested in his own doings to ask if his guest had ever been in London. It is the prerogative of age to take for granted that all younger men are of no account, and even as children, "to be seen and not heard."

"To-morrow," said the squire, "at break of day, we be a-going a-birding, to try some young falcons Bill Peregrine has lately trained. Wilt join us, Master Shakespeare?"

"Ah, that I will, sir! I know a hawk from a handsaw, or my name's not William Shakespeare."

By this time the cold capon and the venison pasty, as well as the "little tiny kickshaws," together with a gallon of "good sherris-sack," had been considerably reduced by the united efforts of the squire, the famished hunter, and those below the salt. During the meal such scraps of conversation as this might have been heard:

"Will you please to take a bit of bacon, Master Shakespeare?"

"Not any, I thank you," replied the poet.

"What, no bacon!" put in the serving man from behind, in a voice of surprise bordering on disappointment.

"No bacon for me, I thank you; *I never take bacon,*" repeated Shakespeare, with some emphasis.

Then the master of the house would occasionally address a remark to his serving man about the farm, such as, "How a good yoke of bullocks at Ciren Fair?" or, "How a score of ewes now?" meaning how much are they worth. Once the serving man took the initiative, asking, "Shall we sow the headlands with wheat?" receiving the reply, "With red wheat, Davy." [29]

[29] 2 *Henry IV*, V. i.

Then there was some discussion concerning the stopping of William's (Peregrine's?) wages, "About the sack he lost the other day at Hinckley Fair."

SHAKESPEARE: "This Davy serves you for good uses; he is your serving man and your husbandman."

SQUIRE: "A good varlet, a good varlet, a very good varlet.... By the mass, I have drunk too much sack at supper! A good varlet." [30]

[30] 2 *Henry IV*, V. iii.

These were the squire's last words that night. He soon slept peacefully, as was his wont after his evening meal; whereupon the poet, with his accustomed gallantry, commenced making love in right good earnest to the fair daughter of the house.

The Cotswold girls, like the Irish, have always been famous for their beauty. Even amongst the peasants you may nowadays see the most beautiful and graceful women in the world, though their attire is usually of a plain and unbecoming character, and but ill adapted to set off the features and form of the wearer. The squire's daughter, whom we will call Jessica, was no exception to the rule. She was a handsome brunette—indeed, the squire called her a "black ousel." Shakespeare fell in love with her at once, and, forgetting all about the family at Stratford, he plunged into the most desperate flirtation. The girl, with that natural perception of the divine in man common to her sex, could not help feeling a strange admiration for this unexpected, though not unwelcome, guest. There was something about his countenance which exercised a peculiar charm and fascination. The thoughtful brow, the keen hazel eye, and the gentle bearing of the man were what at first attracted attention. But it was his manner and speech, half serious and half mirthful, which made such an impression on her mind; and perhaps she felt that, "to the face whose beauty is the harmony between that which speaks from within and the form through which it speaks, power is added by all that causes the outer man to bear more deeply the impress of the inner."

The surroundings, too, were as romantic as they possibly could be. A pair of rush candles were shedding their dim light through the long low oak-panelled apartment; they were the only lights that were burning, and even these flickered ominously at times, as if threatening to go out and leave the place in total darkness. A full moon, however, was casting her silvery beams through the great lattice casement, and in one of the upper panes of this window were richly emblazoned the arms of which the squire was so proud.

It was a glorious evening. Opening the window, William Shakespeare looked out upon the peaceful garden. The moon was shedding a pale light upon the woods and the stream, "decking with liquid pearl the bladed grass." A hundred yards away the silent Coln was gliding slowly onwards towards the sea. Owls were breathing heavily in the hanging wood, and a pair of otters were hunting in the pool.

As the two sat by the open window, the poet's own life and its prospects formed the principal topic of conversation. After years of toil in London his fortunes were beginning at length to improve. He was manager of a theatre, and was at length earning a moderate competency. He had already saved a little money, and hoped soon to buy a house at Stratford. He looked forward some day to returning to his native place and living a country life. At present he was enjoying a short holiday, the first for over a year.

As they sat and talked over these matters, a minstrel began to play in one of the cottages of the village; the sound of the harp added another charm to the peaceful surroundings, and filled the poet's mind with a strange delight.

"I am never merry when I hear sweet music," said Jessica.

Whereupon her companion replied:

> "' ... soft stillness and the night
> Become the touches of sweet harmony.
> Sit, Jessica. Look how the floor of heaven
> Is thick inlaid with patines of bright gold:
> There's not the smallest orb which thou behold'st
> But in his motion like an angel sings,
> Still quiring to the young-eyed cherubins;
> Such harmony is in immortal souls;
> But whilst this muddy vesture of decay
> Doth grossly close it in, we cannot hear it.'" [31]

[31] *Merchant of Venice*, V. i.

Sweet is the sound of soft melodious music on a moonlight night; sweet the faint sigh of the breeze among the elms, and the light upon the silent stream; but sweeter far is music on a moonlight night, sweeter the faint sigh of the breeze, and the light upon the silent stream, when hope, renewed after years of sorrow and sadness, flatters once again the aims and objects of youth, gilding the landscape of life with wondrous alchemy, shedding rays of happy sunshine on the vague, mysterious yearnings of the soul of man towards the hidden destinies of the boundless future.

It was not long, however, before Shakespeare bade the fair Jessica good-night and retired to his sleeping apartment; for a run of such uncommon excellence as he had enjoyed that day was calculated to produce the tired, though not unpleasant, sensation which even now sends the hunting man sleepy, though happy, to bed.

So, lulled by the strains of the minstrel's harp did William Shakespeare seek his couch and sleep the sleep of the just But even while the body was wrapped in slumber, the highly wrought, powerful mind, though yet unconscious of its awful destiny, was hard at work, "moving about in worlds not realised." Yonder on the turret of that grey Gothic castle, whose pinnacles point ever upwards to the skies, they stand and wait, a glorious throng; and as they stand they wave him onwards. Dante, Homer, Virgil, Chaucer, Plutarch, Montaigne, and many another hero of old is waiting there. See the sharp-pointed features of the Italian bard, and Homer no longer blind! The two are holding animated converse, and ever beckoning him on. And a voice seemed to speak out loud and clear amid the solemn silence of eternity:

> "Heaven doth with us as we with torches do,
> Not light them for themselves; for if our virtues
> Did not go forth of us, 'twere all alike
> As if we had them not. Spirits are not finely touch'd
> But to fine issues." [32]

[32] *Measure for Measure*, I. i.

196

Can he linger? Away with blank misgivings, fears, and doubts! He will climb the rugged, steep ascent, and follow even unto the end.

The following morning a little before sunrise saw a party of five assembled for a hawking expedition on the downs. Besides the squire and William Shakespeare, the parson had turned up, whilst Bill Peregrine (ancestor of all the Peregrines, including, no doubt, the famous Peregrine Pickle) brought one of his brothers from the farm to "help him out" with the hawks. It was somewhat of a peculiar dawn—one of those dull grey mornings which often bodes a fine day. The bard was much interested in the glowing eastern sky, and as the sun began to appear he turned to William Peregrine and enthusiastically exclaimed:

> "'.... what envious streaks
> Do lace the severing clouds in yonder east:
> Night's candles are burnt out, and jocund day
> Stands tiptoe on the misty mountain tops.'" [33]

[33] *Romeo and Juliet*, III. v.

"To be sure, to be sure, it do look a bit comical, don't it?" answered the yeoman, with a cackle; and then, turning to his brother, he said, "Ain't 'e ever seen the sun rise before?"

"Please, squire, who be the gent from Warwickshire?" says Peregrine, *sotto voce*; "I cannot tell what the dickens his name is!"

"Oh! 'is name's Shakespy, William Shakespy. A good un at his books, I'll be bound. Get the hawks, Bill; the sun be up. A' must be off to Stratford shortly," answered the squire, glancing at the poet.

Whereupon the yeoman opened the door of a long covered shed commonly called the "mews," and shortly appeared again with four hooded hawks—two falcons, and two males or tiercel-gentles—placed on a wooden frame or cadge. These he handed to a stout yokel to carry, and the whole party sallied forth towards the downs. The squire and the parson were mounted on their palfreys, the rest of the party being on foot.

It was not long before William Peregrine started an interesting conversation with the stranger somewhat after this manner:

"Did you 'ave a pretty good day's spart yesterday, Master Quakespear?"

"Ah, that we had! I never saw such a day's sport in all my life!"

"I thought ye did. I could see the 'art was tired smartish. I qeum along by the bruk, and give un the meeting. When I sees un I says, 'I can see you've 'ad a smartish doing, old boy.' Then the 'ounds qeum yoppeting along as nice as could be. Then I sees you and the 'untsman lolloping along arter the dogs, and soon arter I 'urd the trumpets goin'; and so says I, 'It's a *case*,' and I qeums up and skins un. 'E did skin beautiful to be sure! I never see a better job in all my life—never!"

"'Twas a fine hart," replied Shakespeare, "and no dull and muddy-mettled rascal!" [34]

[34] *Hamlet*, II. ii.

"I be fond of a bit of spart like that," continued Peregrine; "but I never could away with books and larning. Muddling work, I calls it, messing over books. Do you care for that kind of stuff, Master Quakespear?"

"I dabble in it when I am away from the country," was the reply.

Then the Warwickshire man began soliloquising again, somewhat after this manner:

"'In his brain
He hath strange places crammed with observation,
The which he vents in mangled forms.'" [35]

[35] *As you Like It* vii.

"Drat the fellow!" whispered Peregrine, turning to the parson, who happened to be riding alongside "I don't like un, 'e's so unkit."

PARSON: "What makes him talk so, William?"

PEREGRINE (*touching his forehead*): "It's a case; I'll be bound it's a case. 'E's unkit."

"Would you mind saying that again, sir," said the bard, producing a notebook.

Peregrine goes into a fit of giggling, so Shakespeare writes down from memory; whereupon the yeoman makes up to the squire, and says, "Hist, squire, we must 'ave a care; 'e's takin' notes 'o anything we says. 'Tis my belief 'e's got to do with that 'ere case of Tom Barton's they're makin' such a fuss and do about at Coln. We shall all be 'ung for a set o' sheep-stealing ruffians."

"Thee be quite right, William," put in the parson "I thought a' looked a bit suspicious. If I was you, squire, I'd clap the baggage into Northleach gaol, and exercise the justice of the peace agin un for an idle varmint."

"Yet a milder mannered man I never saw," said the squire.

PARSON: "Mild-mannered fiddlestick!" Then, raising his voice so that the stranger should get the full benefit, he added, "He's as mild a mannered man as ever scuttled ship or cut a throat!"

Shakespeare hurriedly draws out notebook, and smilingly writes down the parson's words; then, in perfect good humour, he says:

"You must excuse me, gentlemen, but I have somewhat of a passion for writing down such sayings as suit my humour, lest I forget what good company I keep."

SQUIRE (*excitedly*): "Let go the hawk, Tom; there's a great lanky heron risin' at the withybed yonder."

And here it is necessary to say something about the methods and language of falconry as practised by our forefathers.

Shakespeare tells us to choose "a falcon or tercel for flying at the brook, and a hawk for the bush." In other words, we are to select the nobler species, the long-winged peregrine falcon, the male of which was called a tiercel-gentle, for flying at the heron or the mallard; and a short-winged hawk, such as the goshawk or sparrow-hawk, for blackbirds and other hedgerow birds. For as Mr. Madden explains, not only does the true falcon, be she peregrine, gerfalcon, merlin, or hobby, differ in size and structure of wing and beak from the short-winged hawks, but she also differs in her method of hunting and seizing her prey.

The falcons are "hawks of the tower and lure." They tower aloft and swoop down on partridge, rabbit, or heron, finally returning to the lure; and be it noted that the lure is a sham bird, with a "train" of food to entice the falcons back to their master.

The short-winged hawks, on the other hand, are birds of the fist or the bush. Instead of "towering" and "stooping," they lurch after their prey in wandering flight, finally returning to their master's fist.

In *Macbeth* we find allusion to the "falcon towering in her pride of place"; and indeed there is no prettier sport on a still day than a flight at the partridge or the heron with the noble peregrine falcon or her mate the tiercel-gentle.

At the honest squire's word of command, a male peregrine is forthwith despatched, and, soaring upwards into the air, he is almost lost to sight in the clouds, though the faint tinkling of the bells attached to his feet may yet be heard; then, stooping from the skies, the tiercel-gentle descends from the heavens and strikes his long-beaked adversary. Down, down they come, fighting and struggling in the air, until, exhausted by the unequal combat, the heron gradually falls to the ground, and receives from the falconer his final *coup de grâce*. Sometimes a pair of hawks are thrown off against a heron.

Now comes a flight at the partridge. First of all the spaniel is despatched to search the fields for a covey of birds. The desired quarry being found, he "points" to them, and this time the female peregrine or true falcon is sent on her way. Away she soars upwards, "waiting on and towering in her pride of place." Then the birds, lying like stones beneath her savage ken, are flushed by the dog, and the cruel peregrine, after selecting her bird, with her characteristic "swoop" brings it to the ground. If she is unsuccessful in her first attempt, she will tower again, and renew the attack. The riders have to gallop as fast as their nags can go, if they would keep in with the sport, for as often as not a mile or more of ground has to be covered in a long flight, ere the falcon "souses" [36] her prey. After the flight, a well-trained falcon will invariably return to the lure with its "train" of food.

[36] *King John.* V. ii.

As Mr. Madden has proved, the whole of Shakespeare's works teem with allusions to the art of falconry.

> "HENRY: But what a point, my lord, your falcon made,
> And what a pitch she flew above the rest!
> To see how God in all His creatures works!
> Yea, man and birds are fain of climbing high.
>
> SUFFOLK: No marvel, an it like your majesty,
> My lord protector's hawks do tower so well;
> They know their master loves to be aloft
> And bears his thoughts above his falcon's pitch.
>
> GLOUCESTER: My lord, 'tis but a base ignoble mind
> That mounts no higher than a bird can soar." [37]

[37] 2 *Henry VI.*, II. i.

But it was not the death of the poor partridge that appealed to the poet's mind so much as the pride and cunning of the mighty peregrine, and the beauty and stillness of the autumnal morning. He loved to hear the faint tinkling of the falcon's bells, the homely cry of the plover, and the sweet carol of the lark; but more than all he felt the mystery of the downs, wondering by what power and when those old seas were converted into a sea of grass.

But whilst the hawking party was moving slowly across the wolds to try fresh ground an event occurred which had the effect of bringing the morning's sport, as far as hawks were concerned, to an abrupt conclusion. This was nothing more nor less than the sight of a great Cotswold fox of the greyhound breed making his way towards a copse on the squire's demesne. The quick eye of the Peregrine family was the first to view him, and forthwith both Bill and his brother screamed in unison: "What's that sneaking across Smoke Acre yonder? 'Tis a fox—a great, lanky, thieving, villainous fox, darned if it ain't!"

"Where?" said parson and squire excitedly.

"There," said Peregrine, "over agin Smoke Acre."

"By jabbers, so it be!" said the parson. "Now look thee here, Joe Peregrine, go thee to the sexton and tell 'un to ring the church bells for the folks to come for a fox; and be sure and tell the churchwardens."

"Ah!" said the poet, almost as excited as the rest of the party,

> "'And do not stand on quillets how to slay him:
> Be it by gins, by snares, by subtlety,
> Sleeping or waking, 'tis no matter how,
> So he be dead.'" [38]

[38] *2 Henry VI.*, III. i.

Thus abruptly ended this hawking expedition on the Cotswolds; for the whole party made off to the manor house to fetch guns, spades, pickaxes, and dogs, as was the custom in those days, when a "lanky, villainous fox" was viewed.

As for Shakespeare, after bidding adieu to the old squire, and thanking him for his hospitality, he mounted his game little Irish hobby and steered his course due northward for Stow-on-the-Wold. His track lay along the old Fossway, a road infested in those days by murderous highwaymen; yet, unarmed and unattended, unknown and unappreciated, did that mighty man of genius set cheerfully out on his long and solitary way.

CHAPTER XIII.

CIRENCESTER.

The ancient town of Cirencester—the Caerceri of the early Britons, the Corinium of the Romans, and the Saxon Cyrencerne—has been a place of importance on the Cotswolds from time immemorial. The abbreviations Cisetre and Cysseter were in use as long ago as the fifteenth century, though some of the natives are now in the habit of calling it Ciren. The correct modern abbreviation is Ciceter.

The place is so rich in Roman antiquities that we must perforce devote a few lines to their consideration. A whole book would not be sufficient to do full justice to them.

No less than four important Roman roads meet within a short distance of Cirencester; and very fine and broad ones they are, generally running as straight as the proverbial arrow.

1. The Irmin Way, between Cricklade and Gloucester, *viâ* Cirencester.

2. Acman Street connects Cirencester with Bath.

3. Icknield Street, running to Oxford.

4. The Fossway, extending far into the north of England. This magnificent road may be said to connect Exeter in the south with Lincoln in the north. It is raised several feet above the natural level of the country, and in many places there still remain traces of the ancient ditch which was dug on either side of its course.

In the year 1849 two very fine tessellated pavements were unearthed in Dyer Street, and removed to a museum which Lord Bathurst built purposely for their reception and preservation. Another fine specimen of this kind of work may be seen in its original position at a house called the "Barton" in the park. It is a representation of Orpheus and his lute; and the various animals which he is said to have charmed are wonderfully worked in the coloured pavements.

Even as far back as three hundred years ago these beautiful relics were being discovered in this town; for Leland in his "Itinerary," mentions the finding of some tesserae; unfortunately but few have been preserved.

There are two inscribed stones in this collection which deserve special mention, as they are marvellously well preserved, considering the fact that they are probably eighteen hundred years old. They are about six feet in height and about half that breadth; on each is carved the figure of a mounted soldier, spear in hand. On the ground lies his prostrate foe, pierced by his adversary's spear. Underneath one of these carvings are inscribed the following words:—

DANNICVS. EQES. AIAE.
INDIAN. TVR. ALBANI.
STIP. XVI. CIVES. RAVR.
CVR. FVLVIVS. NATALIS. IT.
FVLIVS. BITVCVS. EX. TESTAME.
H S E.

The meaning of the above words is as follows:—

"Dannicus, a horseman of Indus's Cavalry, of the squadron of Albanus. He had seen sixteen years' service. A citizen of Rauricum. Fulvius Natalis and Fulvius Bitucus have caused this monument to be made in accordance with his will. He is buried here."

The other stone has a somewhat similar inscription.

The Romans, who did not use wallpapers, were in the habit of colouring their plaster with various pigments. Some very interesting specimens of wall-painting are preserved at Cirencester, and may be seen in the museum. The most remarkable example of the kind is a piece of coloured plaster, with the following square scratched on its surface:—

ROTAS
OPERA
TENET

AREPO
SATOR

It will be noticed that these five words, the meaning of which is, "Arepo, the sower, guides the wheels at work," form a kind of puzzle; they may be read in eight different directions.

A large variety of sepulchral urns have been found at Cirencester. When dug up they usually contain little besides the ashes of the dead, though a few coins are sometimes included. There is a very perfect specimen of a glass urn—a large green bottle, square, wide-mouthed, and absolutely intact—in this collection. It was found, wrapped in lead and enclosed in a hollow stone, somewhere near the town about the year 1758.

A fine specimen of a stone coffin is likewise to be seen. When discovered at Latton it was found to contain an iron axe, a dish of black ware of the kind frequently discovered at Upchurch in Kent, a juglike-handled vase of a light red colour, and some human bones.

The various kinds of pottery in the Corinium Museum are interesting on account of the potters' marks found on them. There must be considerably over a hundred different marks in this collection, chiefly of the following kind:—

Putri M. (Manû Putri), by the hand of Putrus.

Mara. F. (Formâ Marci), from the mould of Marcus.

Olini Off. (Officinâ Olini), from the workshop of Olinus.

The museum contains many good specimens of iron and bronze implements, as well as coins and stonework, and is well worthy of the attention bestowed on it, not only by antiquaries, but by the public at large.

At a place called the Querns, a short distance from the town, is a very interesting old amphitheatre called the Bull-ring. This is an ellipse of about sixty yards long by forty-five wide; it is surrounded by mounds twenty feet high. Originally the scene of the combats of Roman gladiators, in mediaeval times it was probably used for the pastime of bull-baiting, a barbarous amusement which has happily long since died out.

Amphitheatres of the same type are to be seen at Dorchester, Old Sarum, Silchester, and other Roman stations.

Mr. Wilfred Cripps, C.B., the head of a family that has been seated at Cirencester for many hundreds of years, has an interesting private collection of Roman antiquities which have been found in the neighbourhood from time to time. He has quite recently discovered the remnants of the Basilica or Roman law-courts.

Turning to the place as it now stands, one is struck on entering the town by the breadth and clean appearance of the main street, known as the market-place. The shops are almost as good as those to be found in the principal thoroughfares of London.

I have spoken before of the magnificent old church. There is, perhaps, no sacred building, except St. Mary Redcliffe at Bristol and Beverley Minster, that we know of in England which for perfect proportion and symmetry can vie with the imposing grandeur of this pile, as seen from the Cricklade-street end of Cirencester market-place.

"MARKET-PLACE, CIRENCESTER."

The south porch is a very beautiful and ornamental piece of architecture. The work is of fifteenth-century design, the interior of the porch consisting of delicately wrought fan-tracery groining. The carving outside is most picturesque, there being many handsome niches and six fine oriel windows. The whole of the *façade* is crowned with very large pierced battlements and crocketed pinnacles. Over this porch is one of those grand old sixteenth-century halls such as were built in former times in front of the churches. It is called the "Parvise," a word derived from the same source as Paradise, which in the language of architecture means a cloistered court adjoining a church. Many of these beautiful old apartments existed at one time in England, but were pulled down by religious enthusiasts because they were considered to be out of place when attached to the church and used for secular purposes. This is now known as the town hall, and contrasts very favourably with the hideous erections built in modern times in some of our English towns for this purpose.

The church of Cirencester contains a large amount of beautiful Perpendicular work.

In the grand old tower are twelve bells of excellent tone. The Early English stonework in the chancel and chapels is very curious, a fine arch opening from the nave to the tower. There is, in fact, a great deal to be seen on all sides which would delight the lover of architecture.

Some ancient brasses of great interest and beautiful design in various parts of this church claim attention; the earliest of them is as old as 1360; a pulpit cloth of blue velvet, made from the cape of one Ralph Parsons in 1478 and presented by him, is still preserved.

Cirencester House stands but a stone's throw from the railway station, but is hidden from sight by a high wall and a gigantic yew hedge. Behind it and on all sides, save one, the park—one of the largest in England—stretches away for miles. So beautiful and rural are the surroundings that the visitor to the house can hardly realise that the place is not far removed from the busy haunts of men.

The Cirencester estate was purchased by Sir Benjamin Bathurst rather more than two hundred years ago. This family has done good service to their king and country for many centuries. We read the other day that no less than *six* of Sir Benjamin's brothers died fighting for the king in the Civil Wars. Nor have they been less conspicuous in serving their country in times of peace.

The park, which was designed to a great extent by the first earl, with the assistance of Pope, has been entirely thrown open to the people of Cirencester; and "the future and as yet visionary beauties of the noble scenes, openings, and avenues" which that great poet used to delight in dwelling upon have become accomplished facts. The "ten rides"—lengthy avenues of fine trees radiating in all directions from a central point in the middle of the park—are a picturesque feature of the landscape.

The lover of horses and riding finds here a paradise of grassy glades, where he can gallop for miles on end, and tire the most obstinate of "pullers."

Picnic parties, horse shows, cricket matches, and the chase of the fox all find a place in this romantic demesne in their proper seasons. The enthusiast for woodland hunting, or the man who hates the sight of a fence of any description, may hunt the fox here day after day and never leave the recesses of the park.

The antiquary will find much to delight him. Here is the ancient high cross, erected in the fourteenth century, which once stood in front of the old Ram Inn. The pedestal is hewn from a single block of stone, and beautifully wrought with Gothic arcades and panelled quatrefoils; this and the shaft are the sole relics of the old cross. We may go into raptures over the ivy-covered ruin known as Alfred's Hall, fitted up as it is with black oak and rusty armour and all the pompous simplicity of the old baronial halls of England. Antiquaries of a certain order are easily deceived; and this delightful old ruin, though but two hundred years old, has been so skilfully put together as to represent an ancient British castle. That celebrated, though indelicate divine, Dean Swift, was, like Alexander Pope, deeply interested in the designing of this park.

As long ago as 1733 Alfred's Hall was a snare and delusion to antiquaries. In that year Swift received a letter stating that "My Lord

Bathurst has greatly improved the Wood-House, which you may remember was a cottage, not a bit better than an Irish cabin. It is now a venerable castle, and has been taken by an antiquary for one of King Arthur's."

The kennels of the V.W.H. hounds are in the park. Here the lover of hounds can spend hours discussing the merits of "Songster" and "Rosebud," or the latest and most promising additions to the families of "Brocklesby Acrobat" or "Cotteswold Flier."

In this house are some very interesting portraits. Full-length pictures of the members of the Cabal Ministry adorn the dining-room—all fine examples of Lely's brush; then there is a very large representation of the Duke of Wellington at Waterloo mounted on his favourite charger "Copenhagen" by Lawrence; two "Romneys," one "Sir Joshua," and several "Knellers."

Turning to the Abbey, the seat for the last three hundred and thirty years of the Master family, we find another instance of a large country house standing practically in a town. The house is situated immediately behind the church and within a stone's throw of the market-place. But on the side away from the town the view from this house extends over a large extent of rural scenery. The site of the mitred Abbey of Saint Mary is somewhere hereabouts, but in the time of the suppression of the monasteries every stone of the old abbey was pulled down and carried away; so that the twelfth-century gateway and some remnants of pillars are the sole traces that remain. This gateway, which is a very fine one, is still used as a lodge entrance. Queen Elizabeth granted this estate to Richard Master in 1564. When King Charles was at Cirencester in the time of the Rebellion he twice stayed at this house. In 1642 the townspeople of Cirencester rose in a body, and tried to prevent the lord lieutenant of the county, Lord Chandos, from carrying out the King's Commission of Array. For a time they gained their ends, but in the following year there was a sharp encounter between Prince Rupert's force and the people of Cirencester, resulting in the total defeat of the latter. Three hundred of them were killed, and over a thousand taken prisoners. They were confined in the church, and eventually taken to Oxford, where, upon their submitting humbly to the king, he pardoned them, and they were released. This is one account. It is only fair to state that another account is less complimentary to Charles.

When Charles II. escaped from Worcester he put up at an old hostelry in Cirencester called the Sun. King James and, still later, Queen Anne paid visits to this town.

Altogether the town of Cirencester is a very fascinating old place. The lot of its inhabitants is indeed cast in pleasant places. The grand bracing air of the Cotswold Hills is a tonic which drives dull care away from these Gloucestershire people; and when it is remembered that they enjoy the freedom of Lord Bathurst's beautiful park, that the neighbourhood is, in spite of agricultural depression, well off in this world's goods, it is not surprising that the pallid cheeks and drooping figures to be met with in most of our towns are conspicuous by their absence here. The Cotswold farmers may be making no profit in these days of low prices and competition, but against this must be set the fact that their fathers and grandfathers made considerable fortunes in farming three decades ago, and for this we must be thankful.

The merry capital of the Cotswolds abounds in good cheer and good fellowship all the year round; and one has only to pay a visit to the market-place on a Monday to meet the best of fellows and the most genial sportsmen anywhere to be found amongst the farming community of England.

One of the old institutions which still remain in the Cotswolds is the annual "mop," or hiring fair. At Cirencester these take place twice in October. Every labouring man in the district hurries into the town, where all sorts of entertainments are held in the market-place, including "whirly-go-rounds," discordant music, and the usual "shows" which go to make up a country fair. "Hiring" used to be the great feature of these fairs. In the days before local newspapers were invented every sort of servant, from a farm bailiff to a maid-of-all-work, was hired for the year at the annual mop. The word "mop" is derived from an old custom which ordained that the maid-servants who came to find situations should bring their badge of office with them to the fair. They came with their brooms and mops, just as a carter would tie a piece of whipcord to his coat, and a shepherd's hat would be decorated with a tuft of wool. Time was when the labouring man was never happy unless he changed his abode from year to year. He would get tired of one master and one village, and be off to Cirencester mop, where he was pretty sure to get a fresh job. But nowadays the Cotswold men are beginning to realise that "Two removes are as bad as a fire." The best of them stay for years in the same village. This is very much more satisfactory for all concerned. Deeply rooted though the love of change appears to be in the hearts of nine-tenths of the human race, the restless spirit seldom enjoys real peace and quiet; and the discontent and poverty of the labouring class in times gone by may safely be attributed to their never-ceasing changes and removal of their belongings to other parts of the country.

Now that these old fairs no longer answer the purpose for which they existed for hundreds of years, they will doubtless gradually die out. And they have their drawbacks. An occasion of this kind is always associated with a good deal of drunkenness; the old market-place of Cirencester for a few days in each autumn becomes a regular pandemonium. It is marvellous how quickly all traces of the great show are swept away and the place once more settles down to the normal condition of an old-fashioned though well-to-do country town.

There are many old houses in Cirencester of more than average interest, but there is nothing as far as we know that needs special description. The Fleece Hotel is one of the largest and most beautiful of the mediaeval buildings. It should be noted that some of the new buildings in this town, such as that which contains the post office, have been erected in the best possible taste. With the exception of some of the work which Mr. Bodley has done at Oxford in recent years, notably the new buildings at Magdalen College, we have never seen modern architecture of greater excellence than these Cirencester houses. They are as picturesque as houses containing shops possibly can be.

HUNTING FROM CICETER.

But it is as a hunting centre that Ciceter is best known to the world at large, and in this respect it is almost unique. The "Melton of the west," it contains a large number of hunting residents who are not mere "birds of passage," but men who live the best part of the year in or near the town. The country round about, from a hunting point of view, is good enough for most people. Five days a week can be enjoyed, over a variety of hill and vale, all of which is "rideable"; nor can there be any question but that the sport obtainable compares favourably with that enjoyed in the more grassy Midlands. Not that there is much plough round about Cirencester nowadays; agricultural depression has diminished the amount of arable in recent years. The best grass country round about, however, with the exception of the Crudwell and Oaksey district, rides decidedly deep. The enclosures are small and the fences rough and straggling.

A clever, bold horse, with plenty of jumping power in his quarters and hocks, is essential. It may safely be said that a man who can command hounds in the Braydon and Swindon district will find the "shires" comparatively plain sailing. The wall country of the Cotswold tableland is exactly the reverse of the vale. The pace there is often tremendous, but the obstacles are not formidable enough to those accustomed to walls to keep the eager field from pressing the pack, save on those rare occasions when, on a burning scent, the hounds manage to get a start of horses; and then they will never be caught. Well-bred horses are almost invariably ridden in this wall country; if in hard condition, and there are no steep hills to be crossed, they can go as fast and stay almost as long as hounds, for the going is good, and they are always galloping on the top of the ground.

At the time of writing, there are over two hundred hunters stabled in the little town of Cirencester, to say nothing of those kept at the numerous hunting boxes around. More than this need not be said to show the undoubted popularity of the place as a hunting centre. And a very sporting lot the people are. Brought up to the sport from the cradle, the Gloucestershire natives, squires, farmers, all sorts and conditions of men, ride as straight as a die.

From what has been said it will be readily gathered that the attraction of the place as a hunting centre lies in the variety of country it commands. Not only is a different stamp of country to be met with each day of the week, but on one and the same day you may be riding over banks, small flying fences, and sound grass, or deep ploughs and pasture divided by hairy bullfinches, or, again, over light plough and stone walls; and to this fact may be attributed the exceptional number of good performers over a country that this district turns out. Both men and horses have always appeared to us to reach a very high standard of cleverness.

To Leicestershire, Northants, Warwick, and the Vale of Aylesbury belongs by undisputed right the credit of the finest grass country in hunting England. But for Ireland and the rougher shires I claim the honour of showing not only the straightest foxes, but also the best sportsmen and the boldest riders. The reason seems to me to be this: in Leicestershire you find the field composed largely of smart London men; and after a certain age a man "goes to hounds" in inverse ratio to the pace at which he travels as a man about town. The latter (with a few brilliant exceptions to prove the rule) is not so quick and determined when he sees a nasty piece of timber or an awkward hairy fence as his reputation at the clubs would lead you to expect; whilst the rougher countryman, be he yeoman or squire, farmer or peer, endowed with nerves of iron, is able to cross a country with a confidence and a dash that are denied to the average dandy, with his big stud, immaculate "leathers," and expensive cigars. In Gloucestershire many an honest yeoman goes out twice a week and endeavours to drown for a while all thoughts of hard times and low prices, content for the day if the fates have left him a sound horse and the consolation of a gallop over the grass. Let it here be said that there are no grooms in the world who better understand conditioning hunters than those of Leicestershire. Nowhere can you see horses better bred or fitter to go; and he who rides a-hunting on *fat* horses must himself be *fat*.

The V.W.H. hounds, on Mr. Hoare's retirement in 1886, were divided into two packs. Mr. T. Butt Miller hunts three days a week on the eastern side, with Cricklade as his centre; whilst Lord Bathurst has sufficient ground for two days on the west, where the country flanks with the Duke of Beaufort's domain on the south and the Cotswold hounds on the north. Mr. Miller retains the original pack, and a very fine one it is. Lord Bathurst likewise, by dint of sparing no pains, and by bringing in the best blood obtainable from Belvoir, Brocklesby, and other kennels, has gradually brought his pack to a high state of excellence.

Turning to the week's programme for a man hunting five or six days a week from Cirencester, Monday is the day for the duke's hounds. Here you may be riding over some of the best of the grass, where light flying fences grow on the top of low banks, or else it will be a stone-wall country of mixed grass and light plough. In either case the country is very rideable, and sport usually excellent. The Badminton hounds and Lord Worcester's skill as a huntsman are too well known to require any description here.

On Tuesday Lord Bathurst's hounds are always within seven miles of the town, and the country is a very open one, but one that requires plenty of wet to carry scent. Though on certain days there is but little scent, in favourable seasons during recent years wonderful sport has been shown in this country. In the season of 1895-6 especially, a fine gallop came off regularly every Tuesday from October to the end of February. In '97, on the other hand, little was done. There is far more grass than there used to be, owing to so much of the land having gone out of cultivation. The plough rides lighter than grass does in nine counties out of ten, the coverts are small, and the pace often tremendous. Every country has its drawback, and in this case it lies partly in bad scent and partly in the fences being too easy. Men who know the walls with which the Cotswold tableland is almost entirely enclosed, ride far too close to hounds: thus, the pack and the huntsman not being allowed a chance, sport is often spoiled. Occasionally, when a real scent is forthcoming, the hounds can run right away from the field; but as a rule they are shamefully over-ridden. The fact is that in the hunting field, as elsewhere, John Wolcot's epigram, written a hundred years ago, exactly hits the nail on the head:

> "What rage for fame attends both great and small!
> Better be d—d than mentioned not at all."

We all want to ride in the front rank, and are, or ought to be, d—d accordingly by the long-suffering M.F.H.

On Wednesdays the Cotswold hounds are always within easy reach of Cirencester. There are few better packs than the Cotswold. Started forty years ago with part of the V.W.H. pack which Lord Gifford was giving up, the Cotswold hounds have received strains of the best blood of the Brocklesby, Badminton, Belvoir, and Berkeley kennels. They have therefore both speed and stamina as well as good noses. Their huntsman, Charles Travess, has no superior as far as we know; the result is that for dash and drive these hounds are unequalled. Notwithstanding the severe pace at which they are able to run, owing to the absence of high hedges and other impediments—for most of the country is enclosed with stone walls—they hunt marvellously well together and do not tail; they are wonderfully musical, too,—more so than any other pack.

Here it is worth our while to analyse briefly the qualities which combine to make this huntsman so deservedly popular with all who follow the Cotswold hounds. We venture to say that he pleases all and sundry, "thrusters," hound-men, and *liver-men* alike, because he invariably has a double object in view—he hunts his fox and he humours his field. And firstly he hunts his fox in the best possible method, having regard to the scenting capabilities of the Cotswold Hills.

He is quick as lightning, yet he is never in a hurry—that is to say, in a *"bad* hurry." When the hounds "throw up" or "check," like all other good huntsmen he gives them plenty of time. He stands still and he *makes his field stand still;* then may be seen that magnificent proof of canine brain-power, the fan-shaped forward movement of a well-drafted, old-established pack of foxhounds, making good by two distinct casts—right-and left-handed—the ground that lies in front of them and on each side. Should they fail to hit off the line, the advantage of a brilliant huntsman immediately asserts itself. Partly by certain set rules and partly by a knowledge of the country and the run of foxes, but more than all by that *daring* genius which was the making of Shakespeare and the great men of all time, he takes his hounds admirably in hand, aided by two quiet, unassuming whippers-in, and in four cases out of five brings them either at the first or second cast to the very hedgerow where five minutes before Reynard took his sneaking, solitary way. It may be "forward," or it may be down wind, right or left-handed, but it is at all events the *right* way; thus, owing to this happy knack of making the proper cast at a large percentage of checks this man establishes his reputation as a first-class huntsman.

Should the day be propitious, a run is now assured, unless some unforeseen occurrence, such as the fox going to ground, necessitates a draw for a fresh one; but in any case, owing to this marvellous knack of hitting off the line at the first check, our huntsman generally contrives to show a run some time during the day.

So much for the methods by which this William Shakespeare of the hunting field is wont to pursue his fox. But we have not done with him yet. What does he do on those bad scenting days which on the dry and stony Cotswold Hills are the rule rather than the exception? On such days, as well as hunting his fox, he humours his field. In the first place, unless he has distinct proof to the contrary, he invariably gives his fox credit for being a straight-necked one. He keeps moving on at a steady pace in the direction in which his instinct and knowledge lead him, even though there may be no scent, either on the ground or in the air, to guide the hounds. Every piece of good scenting ground—and he knows the capabilities of every field in this respect—is made the most of; "carrying" or dusty ploughs are scrupulously avoided. If he "lifts," it is done so quietly and cunningly that the majority of the riders are unaware of the fact; and the hounds never become wild and untractable. It is this free and generous method of hunting the fox that pleases his followers. Travess's casts are not made in cramped and stingy fashion, but a wide extent of country is covered even on a bad day; there is no rat-hunting. After a time all save a dozen sportsmen are left several fields behind. "They won't run to-day," is the general cry; "there is no hurry." But meantime some large grass fields are met with, or the huntsman brings the pack on to better terms with the fox, or maybe a fresh one jumps up, and away go the hounds for seven or eight minutes as hard as they can pelt. Only a dozen men know exactly what has happened. Most of the thrusters and all the *liver-men* have to gallop in earnest for half an hour to come up with the hunt; indeed, on many days they never see either huntsman or hounds again, and go tearing about the country cursing their luck in missing so fine a run! It is the old story of the hare and the tortoise. But herein lies the "humour" of it: the hare is pleased and the tortoise is pleased. The former, as represented by the field, has enjoyed a fine scamper, and lots of air (bother the currant jelly!) and exercise; the tortoise, on the other hand, has had a fine hunting run, and possibly by creeping slowly on for some hours it has killed its fox; whilst several good sportsmen have enjoyed an old-fashioned hunt in a wild country with a kill in the open.

Verbum sap: If you want to humour your field, you must leave them behind. It must not be done intentionally, however; the riders must be allowed, so to speak, to work out their own salvation in this respect.

Major de Freville's country as a whole is more suited to the "houndman" than for him who hunts to ride. The hills, save in one district, are so severe that hounds often beat horses; the result is, many are tempted to station themselves on the top of a hill, whence a wide view is obtainable, and trust to the hounds coming back after running a ring. Given the right sort of horse, however—short-backed, thoroughbred if possible, and with good enough manners to descend a steep place without boring and tearing his rider's arms almost out of their sockets—many a fine run may be seen in this wild district. Much of the arable land has gone back to grass, so that it is quite a fair scenting country; and the foxes are stronger and more straight-necked than in more civilised parts. One of the best days the writer ever had in his life was with these hounds. Meeting at Puesdown, they ran for an hour in the morning at a great pace, with an eight-mile point; whilst in the afternoon came a run of one-and-a-half hours, with a point of somewhere about ten miles.

With the exception of a small vale between Cheltenham and Tewkesbury, which is very good indeed, the Puesdown country is about the best, the undulations being less severe than in other parts.

On Thursdays Cirencester commands Mr. Miller's Braydon country. This country is a very great contrast to that which is ridden over on

Tuesdays and Wednesdays, and requires a very stout horse. It rides tremendously deep at times; and the fences, which come very frequently in a run, owing to the small size of the enclosures, are both big and blind. It is practically all grass. But there are several large woodlands, with deep clay rides, in which one is not unlikely to spend a part of Thursday; and these woods, owing in part to the shooting being let to Londoners, are none too plentifully provided with foxes. Wire, too, has sprung up in some parts of Mr. Miller's Braydon country. Few people have large enough studs to stand the wear and tear of this fine, wild country; consequently the fields are generally small. Sport, though not so good as it used to be, is still very fair, and to run down to Great Wood in the duke's country is sufficient to tax the powers of the finest weight-carrying hunter, whilst only the man with a quick eye to a country can live with hounds. It is often stated that blood horses are the best for galloping through deep ground. This is true in one way, though not on the whole. Thoroughbred horses are practically useless in this sort of country; their feet are often so small that they stick in the deep clay. A horse with small feet is no good at all in Braydon. A short-legged Irish hunter, about three parts bred, with tremendous strength in hocks and quarters, and biggish feet, is the sort the writer would choose. If up to quite two stone more than his rider's weight, and a safe and temperate fencer, he will carry you well up with hounds over any country. A fast horse is not required; for a racer that can do the mile on the flat at Newmarket in something under two minutes is reduced in really deep ground to an eight-mile-an-hour canter, and your short-legged horse from the Emerald Isle will leave him standing still in the Braydon Vale.

Some countries never ride really deep. The shires, for instance, though often said to be deep, will seldom let a horse in to any great extent—the ridge and furrow drains the field so well; and in that sort of deep ground which is met with in Leicestershire a thoroughbred one will gallop and "stay" all day. But a ride in Braydon or in the Bicester "Claydons" will convince us that a stouter stamp of horse is necessary to combat a deep, undrained clay country.

We must now leave the sporting Thursday country of the V.W.H. and turn to Friday.

Eastcourt, Crudwell, Oaksey, Brinkworth, Lea Schools—such are some of Lord Bathurst's Friday meets; and the pen can hardly write fast enough in singing the praises of this country. Strong, well-preserved coverts, sound grass fields, flying fences, sometimes set on a low bank, sometimes without a bank, varied by an occasional brook, with now and then a fence big enough to choke off all but the "customers"—such is the bill of fare for Fridays. To run from Stonehill Wood, *viâ* Charlton and Garsdon, to Redborn in the duke's country, as the hounds did on the first day of 1897, is, as "Brooksby" would say, "a line fit for a king, be that king but well minded and well mounted."

Stand on Garsdon Hill, and look down on the grassy vale mapped out below, and tell me, if you dare, that you ever saw a pleasanter stretch of country. How dear to the hunting man are green fields and sweet-scenting pastures, where the fences are fair and clean and the ditches broad and deep, where there is room to gallop and room to jump, and where, as he sails along on a well-bred horse or reclines perchance in a muddy ditch (Professor Raleigh! what a watery bathos!), he may often say to himself, "It is good for me to be here!" For when the hounds cross this country there are always "wigs on the green" in abundance; and in spite of barbed wire we may still sing with Horace,

> "Nec fortuitum spernere caespitem
> Leges sinebant,"

which, at the risk of offending all classical scholars, I must here translate: "Nor do the laws allow us to despise a chance tumble on the turf."

Round Oaksey, too, is a rare galloping ground. Should you be lucky enough to get a start from "Flistridge" and come down to the brook at a jumpable place, in less than ten minutes you will be, if not *in* Paradise, at all events as near as you are ever likely to be on this earth. This is literally true, for half way between "Flistridge" and Kemble Wood, and in the midst of Elysian grass fields, is a narrow strip of covert happily christened "Paradise."

219

Would that there was a larger extent of this sort of country, for it is not every Friday that hounds cross it! The duke's hounds have a happy knack of crossing it occasionally on a Monday, however, and on Thursdays Mr. Miller's hounds may drive a fox that way.

This district is not so easy for a stranger to ride his own line over as the Midlands; it is not half so stiff, but it is often cramped and trappy. But then you must "look before you leap" in most countries nowadays. In this Friday country wire is comparatively scarce. The fields run very large on this day, — quite two hundred horsemen are to be seen at favourite fixtures. About half this number would belong to the country, and the other half come from the duke's country and elsewhere. These Friday fields are as well mounted and well appointed as any in England. And to see a run one must have a good horse, — not necessarily an expensive one, for "good" and "expensive" are by no means synonymous terms with regard to horseflesh. It is with regret that we must add that foxes were decidedly scarce here last season (1897-8).

On Saturdays the Cirencester brigade will hunt with Mr. Miller. Fairford, Lechlade, Kempsford, and Water-Eaton are some of the meets. Here we have a totally different country from any yet considered. It is a wonderfully sporting one; and last season these hounds never had a bad Saturday, and often a 'clinker' resulted. Here again one can never anticipate what sort of ground will be traversed; but the best of it consists of a fine open country of grass and plough intermingled, the fields being intersected by small flying fences and exceptionally wide and deep ditches. "Snowstorm" — a small gorse half way between Fairford and Lechlade stations on the Great Western Railway — is a favourite draw. If a fox goes away you see men sitting down in their saddles and cramming at the fences as hard as their horses can gallop. There appears to be nothing to jump until you are close up to the fence; but nevertheless pace is required to clear them, for there is hardly a ditch anywhere round "Snowstorm" that is not ten feet wide and eight feet or more deep, and if you are unlucky your horse may have to clear fourteen feet. On the other hand, there is absolutely nothing that a horse going fast cannot clear almost without an effort if he jumps at all. So you may ride in confidence at every fence, and take it where you please. The depth of the ditch is what frightens a timid horse and, I may add, a timid rider; and if your horse stops dead, and then tries to jump it standing, you are very apt to tumble in.

A rare sporting country is this district; and as the horses and their riders know it, there are comparatively few falls. Round Kempsford and Lechlade the Thames and the canal are apt to get in the way, but once clear of these impediments a very open country is entered, either of grass and flying fences or light plough and stone walls. Another style of country is that round Hannington and Crouch. In old days, before wire was known, this used to be the best grass country in the V.W.H., but nowadays you must "look before you leap." With a good fox, however, hounds may take you into the best of the old Berkshire vale, and perhaps right up to the Swindon Hills. Round Water-Eaton is a fine grass country, good enough for anybody; but the increase of wire is becoming more and more difficult to combat in this as in other grazing districts of England.

The very varied bill of fare we have briefly sketched for a man hunting from Cirencester may include an occasional Wednesday with the Heythrop at "Bradwell Grove." It is not possible to reach the choicest part of this pleasant country by road from Cirencester, but some of the best of the stone-wall country of the Cotswold tableland is included in the Heythrop domain. Everybody who has been brought up to hunting has heard of "Jem Hills and Bradwell Grove": rare gallops this celebrated huntsman used to show over the wolds in days gone by; and on a good scenting day it requires a quick horse to live with these hounds. A fast and well-bred pack, established more than sixty years ago, they have been admirably presided over by Mr. Albert Brassey for close on a quarter of a century. Several pleasant vales intersect this country, notably the Bourton and the Gawcombe Vale; and there is excellent grass round Moreton-in-the-Marsh. As, however, the grass country of the Heythrop is too far from Cirencester to be reached by road, it hardly comes within our scope.

If hunting is doomed to extinction in the Midlands, owing to the growth of barbed wire, it is exceedingly unlikely ever to die out in the neighbourhood of Cirencester; for there is so much poor, unprofitable land on the Cotswold tableland and in the Braydon district that barbed wire and other evils of civilisation are not likely to interfere to deprive us of our national sport; Hunting men have but to be true to themselves, and avoid doing unnecessary damage, to see the sport carried on in the twentieth century as it has been in the past. If we conform to the unwritten laws of the chase, and pay for the damage we do, there will be no fear of fox-hunting dying out. England will be "Merrie England" still, even in the twentieth century; the glorious pastime, sole relic of the days of chivalry, will continue among us, cheering the life in our quiet country villages through the gloomy winter months;—if only we be true to ourselves, and do our uttermost to further the interests of the grandest sport on earth.

As I have given an account of a run over the walls, and as the Ciceter people set most store on a gallop over the stiff fences and grass enclosures of their vale, here follows a brief description in verse of the glories of fifty minutes on the grass. I have called it "The Thruster's Song," because on the whole I thoroughly agree with Shakespeare that

> "Valour is the chietest virtue, and
> Most dignifies the haver."

Hard riding and all sports which involve an element of danger are the best antidotes to that luxury and effeminacy which long periods of peace are apt to foster. What would become of the young men of the present day—those, I mean, who are in the habit of following the hounds—if hard riding were to become unfashionable? I cannot conceive anything more ridiculous than the sight of a couple of hundred well-mounted men riding day after day in a slow procession through gates, "craning" at the smallest obstacles, or dismounting and "leading over." No; hard riding is the best antidote in the world for the luxurious tendency of these days. A hundred years ago, when the sport of fox-hunting was in its infancy and modern conditions of pace were unknown, there was less need for this kind of recreation, "the image of war without its guilt, and only twenty-five per cent of its danger." For there was real fighting enough to be done in olden times; and amongst hunting folk, though

222

there was much drinking, there was little luxury. Therefore our fox-hunting ancestors were content to enjoy slow hunting runs, and small blame to them! But those who are fond of lamenting the modern spirit of the age, which prefers the forty minutes' burst over a severe country to a three hours' hunting run, are apt to lose sight of the fact that in these piping times of peace, without the risks of sport mankind is liable to degenerate towards effeminacy. For this reason in the following poem I have purposely taken up the cudgels for that somewhat unpopular class of sportsmen, the "thrusters" of the hunting field. They are unpopular with masters of hounds because they ride too close to the pack; but as a general rule they are the only people who ever see a really fast run. In Shakespeare's time hounds that went too fast for the rest of the pack were "trashed for over-topping," that is to say, they were handicapped by a strap attached to their necks. In the same way in every hunt nowadays there are half a dozen individuals who have reduced riding to hounds to such an art that no pack can get away from them in a moderately easy country. These "bruisers" of the hunting field ought to be made to carry three stone dead weight; they should be "trashed for overtopping." However, as Brooksby has tersely put it, "Some men hunt to ride and some ride to hunt; others, thank Heaven! double their fun by doing both." There are many, many fine riders in England who will not be denied in crossing a stiff country, and who at the same time are interested in the hounds and in the poetry of sport: men to whom the mysteries of scent and of woodcraft, as well as the breeding and management of hounds, are something more than a mere name: men who in after days recall with pleasure "how in glancing over the pack they have been gratified by the shining coat, the sparkling eye—sure symptoms of fitness for the fight;—how when thrown in to covert every hound has been hidden; how every sprig of gorse has bristled with motion; how when viewed away by the sharp-eyed whipper-in, the fox stole under the hedge; how the huntsman clapped round, and with a few toots of his horn brought them out in a body; how, without tying on the line, they 'flew to head'; how, when they got hold of it, they drove it, and with their heads up felt the scent on both sides of the fence; how with hardly a whimper they turned with him, till at the end of fifty minutes they threw up; how the patient huntsman stood still; how they made their own cast: and how when they came back on his line, their tongues doubled and they marked him for their own." To such good men and true I dedicate the following lines:—

A DAY IN THE VALE; OR, THE THRUSTER'S SONG.

You who've known the sweet enjoyment of a gallop in the vale, Comrades of the chase, I know you will not deem my subject stale. Stand with me once more beside the blackthorn or the golden gorse,— Don't forget to thank your stars you're mounted on a favourite horse; For the hounds dashed into covert with a zest that bodes a scent, And the glass is high and rising, clouded is the firmament. When the ground is soaked with moisture, when the wind is in the east Scent lies best,—the south wind doesn't suit the "thruster" in the least. Some there are who love to watch them with their noses on the ground; We prefer to see them flitting o'er the grass without a sound. We prefer the keen north-easter; ten to one the scent's "breast high"; With a south wind hounds can sometimes hunt a fox, but seldom fly. Hark! the whip has viewed him yonder; he's away, upon my word! If you want to steal a start, then fly the bullfinch like a bird; Gallop now your very hardest; turn him sharp, and jump the stile, Trot him at it—never mind the bough,—it's only smashed your tile! Now we're with them. See, they're tailing, from the fierceness of the pace, Up the hedgerow, o'er the meadow, 'cross the stubble see them race: Governor—by Belvoir Gambler,—he's the hound to "run to head," Tracing back to Rallywood, that fifty years ago was bred; Close behind comes Arrogant, by Acrobat; and Artful too; Rosy, bred by Pytchley Rockwood; Crusty, likewise staunch and true. Down a muddy lane, in mad excitement, but, alas! too late, Thunders half the field towards the portals of a friendly gate; Sees a dozen red-coats bobbing in the vale a mile ahead; Hears the huntsman's horn, and longs to catch those distant bits of red;— But in vain, for blind the fences, here a fall and there a "peck." Some one cries, "An awful place, sir; don't go there, you'll break   your neck." Not the stiff, unbroken fences, but the treacherous gaps we fear; "Though in front the post of honour, that of danger's in the rear." Forrard on, then forrard onwards, o'er the pasture, o'er the lea, Tossed about by ridge and furrow, rolling like a ship at sea; Stake and binder, timber, oxers, all are taken in our stride,— Better fifty

224

minutes' racing than a dawdling five hours' ride. I am not ashamed to own, with him who loves a steeplechase, That to me the charm in hunting is the ecstasy of *pace*,— This is what best schools the soldier, teaches us that we are men Born to bear the rough and tumble, wield the sword and not the pen. Some there are who dub hard riders worthless and a draghunt crew— Tailors who do all the damage, mounted on a spavined screw. Well, I grant you, hunting men are sometimes narrow-minded fools; Ignorant of all worth knowing, save what's learnt in riding-schools; Careless of the rights of others, scampering over growing crops, Smashing gates and making gaps and scattering wide the turnip tops;— But I hold that out of all the hunting fields throughout the land I could choose for active service a large-hearted, gallant band; I could choose six hundred red-coats, trained by riding in the van, Fit to go to Balaclava under brave Lord Cardigan. 'Tis the finest school, the chase, to teach contempt of cannon balls, If a man ride bravely onward, spite of endless rattling falls. And to be a first-rate sportsman, not a man who merely "rides," Is to be a perfect gentleman, and something more besides; Fearing neither man nor devil, kind, unselfish he must be, Born to lead when danger threatens—type of ancient chivalry. When you hear a "houndman" jeering at the "customers" in front, Saying they come out to ride a steeplechase and not to hunt, You may bet the "grapes are sour," the fellow's smoked his nerve away; Once he went as well as they do: "every dog will have his day." Though to ride about the roads in state may do your liver good, You see precious little "houndwork" either there or in the wood. He who loves to mark the work of hounds must ride beside the pack, Choosing his own line, or following others, if he's lost the knack. Lookers-on, I grant you, often see the best part of the game,— Still, to ride the roads and live with hounds are things not quite the same. Now a word to all those gallant chaps who love a hunting day: In bad times you know that farming is a trade that doesn't pay, Barbed wire's the cheapest kind of fence; the farmer can't afford Tempting post-and-rails and timber—for he's getting rather bored. Therefore, if we want to ride with our old devilry and dash, We must put our hands in pockets deep and shovel out the cash. When you want to hire a shooting you will gladly pay a "pony," Yet when asked to give it to the hounds you're apt to say you're "stony." Pay the piper, and the sport you love so well will flourish yet, Flourish in the dim hereafter; and its sun will never set. Help the noble cause of freedom; rich and poor together blend Hands and hearts for ever working for a great and glorious end.

CHAPTER XIV.

SPRING IN THE COTSWOLDS.

Whilst walking by the river one day in May I noticed a brood of wild ducks about a week old. The old ones are wonderfully tame at this time of year. The mother evidently disliked my intrusion, for she started off up stream, followed by her offspring, making towards a withybed a hundred yards or so higher up, where a secluded spring gives capital shelter for duck and other shy birds. What was my surprise a couple of hours later to see the same lot emerge from some rushes three-quarters of a mile up stream! They had circumvented a small waterfall, and the current is very strong in places. Part of the journey must have been done on dry land.

At the same moment that I startled this brood out of the rushes a moorhen swam slowly out, accompanied by her mate. It was evident, from her cries and her anxious behaviour, that she too had some young ones in the rushes; and soon two tiny little black balls of fur crawled out from the bank and made for the opposite shore. Either from blindness or fright they did not join their parents in mid stream, but hurried across to the opposite bank and scrambled on to the mud, followed by the old couple remonstrating with them on their foolishness. The mother then succeeded in persuading one of them to follow her to a place of safety underneath some overhanging boughs, but the other was left clinging to the bank, crying piteously. I went round by a bridge in the hope of being able to place the helpless little thing on the water; but, alas! by the time I got to the spot it was dead. The exertion of crossing the stream had been too much for it, for it was probably not twelve hours old.

When there are young ones about, moorhens will not dive to get out of your sight unless their children dive too. It is pretty to see them swimming on the down-stream side of their progeny, buoying them up in case the current should prove too strong and carry them down. If there are eggs still unhatched, the father, when disturbed, takes the little ones away to a safer spot, whilst the mother sticks to the nest. But they are rather stupid, for even the day after the eggs are hatched, on being disturbed by a casual passer-by, the old cock swims out into mid stream. He then calls to his tiny progeny to follow him, though they are utterly incapable of doing so, and generally come to hopeless grief in the attempt. Then the old ones are not very clever at finding children that have been frightened away from the nest. I marked one down on the opposite bank, and could see it crawling beneath some sticks; but the old bird kept swimming past the spot, and appeared to neither hear nor see the little ball of fur. Perhaps he was playing cunning; he may have imagined that the bird was invisible to me, and was trying to divert my attention from the spot.

Moorhens are always interesting to watch. With a pair of field-glasses an amusing and instructive half hour may often be spent by the stream in the breeding season.

I was much amused, while feeding some swans and a couple of wild ducks the other day, to notice that the mallard would attack the swans if they took any food that he fancied. One would have thought that such powerful birds as swans—one stroke of whose wings is supposed to be capable of breaking a man's leg—would not have stood any nonsense from an unusually diminutive mallard. But not a bit of it: the mallard ruled the roost; all the other birds, even the great swans, ran away from him when he attacked them from behind with his beak. This state of things continued for some days. But after a time the male swan got tired of the game; his patience was exhausted. Watching his opportunity he seized the pugnacious little mallard by the neck and gave him a thundering good shaking! It was most laughable to watch them. It is characteristic of swans that they are unable to look you in the face; and beautiful beyond all description as they appear to be in their proper element, meet them on dry land and they become hideous and uninteresting, scowling at you with an evil eye.

"THE "PILL" BRIDGE."

Sometimes as you are walking under the trees on the banks of the Coln you come across a little heap of chipped wood lying on the ground. Then you hear "tap, tap," in the branches above. It is the little nuthatch hard at work scooping out his home in the bark. He sways his body with every stroke of his beak, and is so busy he takes no notice of you. The nuthatch is very fond of filberts, as his name implies. You may see him in the autumn with a nut firmly fixed in a crevice in the bark of a hazel branch, and he taps away until he pierces the shell and gets at the kernel. Nuthatches, which are very plentiful hereabouts, are sometimes to be found in the forsaken homes of woodpeckers, which they plaster round with mud. The entrance to the hole in the tree is thus made small enough to suit them. Sometimes when I have disturbed a nuthatch at work at a hole in a tree, the little fellow would pop into the hole and peep out at me, never moving until I had departed.

Woodpeckers are somewhat uncommon here: I have not heard one in our garden by the river for a very long time, though a foolish farmer told me the other day that he had recently shot one. A mile or so away, at Barnsley Park, where the oaks thrive on a vein of clay soil, green woodpeckers may often be seen and heard. What more beautiful bird is there, even in the tropics, than the merry yaffel, with his emerald back and the red tuft on his head? The other two varieties of woodpeckers, the greater and lesser spotted, are occasionally met with on the Cotswolds. I do not know why we have so few green woodpeckers by the river, as there are plenty of old trees there; but these birds, which feed chiefly on the ground among the anthills, have a marked preference for such woods in the neighbourhood as contain an abundance of oak trees. The local name for these birds is "hic-wall," which Tom Peregrine pronounces "heckle." There is no more pleasing sound than the long, chattering note of the green woodpecker; it breaks so suddenly on the general silence of the woods, contrasting as it does in its loud, bell-like tones with the soft cooing of the doves and the songs of the other birds.

In various places along its course the river has long poles set across it; on these poles Tom Peregrine has placed traps for stoats, weasels, and other vermin. Recently, when we were fishing, he pointed out a great stoat caught in one of these traps with a water-rat in its mouth—a very strange occurrence, for the trap was only a small one, of the usual rabbit size, and the rat was almost as big as the stoat. There is so little room for the bodies of a stoat and a rat in one of these small iron traps that the betting must be at least a thousand to one against such an event happening. Unless we had seen it with our eyes we could not have believed it possible. The stoat, in chasing the rat along the pole, must have seized his prey at the very instant that the jaws of the trap snapped upon them both. They were quite dead when we found them.

Every one acquainted with gamekeepers' duties is well aware that the iron traps armed with teeth which are in general use throughout the country are a disgrace to nineteenth-century civilisation. It is a terrible experience to take a rabbit or any other animal out of one of these relics of barbarism. Sir Herbert Maxwell recently called the attention of game preservers and keepers to a patent trap which Colonel Coulson, of Newburgh, has just invented. Instead of teeth, the jaws of the new trap have pads of corrugated rubber, which grip as tightly and effectively as the old contrivance without breaking the bones or piercing the skin. I trust these traps will shortly supersede the old ones, so that a portion of the inevitable suffering of the furred denizens of our woods may be dispensed with.

In a hunting country where foxes occasionally find their way into vermin traps, Colonel Coulson's invention should be invaluable. Instead of having to be destroyed, or being killed by the hounds in covert, owing to a broken leg, it is ten to one that Master Reynard would be released very little the worse for his temporary confinement. Moreover, as Sir Herbert Maxwell points out, dog owners will be grateful to the inventor when their favourites accidentally find their way into one of these traps and are released without smashed bones and bleeding feet. Any kind of trap is but a diabolical contrivance at best, but these "humane patents" are a vast improvement, and do the work better than the old, as I can testify, having used them from the time Sir Herbert Maxwell first called attention to them, and being quite satisfied with them.

Badgers are almost as mysterious in their ways and habits as the otter. Nobody believes there are badgers about except those who look for their characteristic tracks about the fox-earths. Every now and then, however, a badger is dug out or discovered in some way in places where they were unheard of before. We have one here now.

A few years ago I saw a pack of foxhounds find a badger in Chearsley Spinneys in Oxfordshire. They hunted him round and round for about ten minutes. I saw him just in front of the hounds; a great, fine specimen he was too. As far as I remember, the hounds killed him in covert, and then went away on the line of a fox.

A year or two ago three fine young badgers were captured near Bourton-on-the-Water, on the Cotswolds. When I was shown them I was told they would not feed in confinement. Finding a large lobworm, I picked it up and gave it to one of them. He ate it with the utmost relish. His brown and grey little body shook with emotion when I spoke to him kindly—just as a dog trembles when you pet him. I am not certain, however, whether the badger trembled out of gratitude for the lobworm or out of rage and disgust at being confined in a cage.

Badgers would make delightful pets if they had a little less *scent*: nature, as everybody knows, has endowed them with this quality to a remarkable degree; they have the power of emitting or retaining it at their own discretion.

Badger-baiting with terriers is not an amusement which commends itself to humane sportsmen. It is hard luck on the terriers, even more than on the badger. The dogs have a very bad time if they go anywhere near him.

Talking of terriers, how endless are the instances of superhuman sagacity in dogs of all kinds! I once drove twenty-five miles from a place near Guildford in Surrey to Windsor. In the cart I took with me a little liver-coloured spaniel. When I had completed about half the journey I put the spaniel down for a run of a few miles: this was all she saw of the country. In Windsor, through some cause or other, I lost her; but when I arrived home a day or two afterwards, she had arrived there before me. It should be mentioned that the journey was not along a high-road, but by cross-country lanes. How on earth she got home first, unless she came back on my scent, then, finding herself near home, took a short cut across country, so as to be there before me, it is impossible to imagine.

How curious it is that all animals seem to know when Sunday comes round!

Fish and fowl are certainly much tamer on the seventh day of the week than on any other. We had a terrier that would never attempt to follow you when you were going to church so long as you had your Sunday clothes on; whilst even when he was following you on a week day, if you turned round and said "Church" in a decisive tone, he would trot straight back to the house. As far as we know he had no special training in this respect. This terrier, who was a rare one to tackle a fox, has on several occasions spent the best part of a week down a rabbit burrow. When dug out he seemed very little the worse for his escapade, though decidedly emaciated in appearance. Poor little fellow! he died a painless death not long ago from sheer old age. I was with him at the time, and did not even know he was ill until five minutes before he expired. The most obedient and faithful, as well as the bravest, little dog in the world, he could do anything but speak. How much we can learn from these little emblems of simplicity, gladness, and love. Implicit obedience and boundless faith in those set over us, to forgive and forget unto seventy times seven, to give gold for silver, nay, to sacrifice all and receive back nothing in return,—these are some of the lessons we may learn from creatures we call dumb. Perhaps they will have their reward. There is room in eternity for the souls of animals as well as of men; there is room for the London cab-horse after his life of hardship and cruel sacrifice; there is room for the innocent lamb that goes to the slaughter; there is room in those realms of infinity for every bird of the air and every beast of the field that either the necessity (that tyrant's plea) or the ignorance of man has condemned to torture, injustice, or neglect!

The most delightful of all dogs are those rough-haired Scotch deerhounds the author of "Waverley" loved so well. How timid and subdued are these trusty hounds on ordinary occasions! yet how fierce and relentless to pursue and slay their natural quarry, the antlered monarch of the glen! Once, in Savernake Forest, where the yaffels laugh all day amid the great oak trees, and the beech avenues, with their Gothic foliations and lichened trunks, are the finest in the world, a young, untried deerhound of ours slipped away unobserved and killed a hind "off his own bat." Though he had probably never seen a deer before, hereditary instinct was too strong, and he succumbed to temptation. Yet he would not harm a fox, for on another occasion, when I was out walking, accompanied by this hound and a fox-terrier, the latter bolted a large dog fox out of a drain. When the fox appeared the deerhound made after him, and, in his attempt to dodge, reynard was bowled over on to his back. But directly he was called, the deerhound came back to our heels, apparently not considering the vulpine race fair game. I will not vouch for the accuracy of the story, but our coachman asserts that he saw this deerhound at play with a fox in our kitchen garden,—not a tame fox, but a wild one. I believe, myself, that this actually did happen, as the man who witnessed the occurrence is thoroughly reliable.

There is no dog more knowing and sagacious in his own particular way than a well-trained retriever. What an immense addition to the pleasure of a day's partridge-shooting in September is the working of one of these delightful dogs! Only the other day, when I was sitting on the lawn, a retriever puppy came running up with something in his mouth, with which he seemed very pleased. He laid it at my feet with great care and tenderness, and I saw that it was a young pheasant about a fortnight old. It ran into the house, and was rescued unharmed a few hours afterwards by the keeper, who restored it to the hencoop from whence it came. One could not be angry with a dog that was unable to resist the temptation to retrieve, but yet would not harm the bird in the smallest degree.

One does not often see teams of oxen ploughing in the fields nowadays. Within a radius of a hundred miles of London town this is becoming a rare spectacle. They are still used sometimes in the Cotswolds, however, though the practice of using them must soon die out. Great, slow, lumbering animals they are, but very handsome and delightful beasts to look upon. A team of brown oxen adds a pleasing feature to the landscape.

As we come down the steep ascent which leads to our little hamlet, we often wonder why some of the cottage front doors are painted bright red and some a lovely deep blue. These different colours add a great deal of picturesqueness to the cottages; but is it possible that the owners have painted their doors red and blue for the sake of the charming distant effect it gives? These people have wonderfully good taste as a rule. The other day we noticed that some of the dreadful iron sheeting which is creeping into use in country places had been painted by a farmer a beautiful rich brown. It gave quite a pretty effect to the barn it adjoined. Every bit of colour is an improvement in the rather cold-looking upland scenery of the Cotswolds.

Cray-fishing is a very popular amusement among the villagers. These fresh-water lobsters abound in the gravelly reaches of the Coln. They are caught at night in small round nets, which are baited and let down to the bottom of the pools. The crayfish crawl into the nets to feed, and are hauled up by the dozen. Two men can take a couple of bucketfuls of them on any evening in September. Though much esteemed in Paris, where they fetch a high price as *écrevisse*, we must confess they are rather disappointing when served up. The village people, however, are very fond of them; and Tom Peregrine, the keeper, in his quaint way describes them as "very good pickings for dessert." As they eat a large number of very small trout, as well as ova, on the gravel spawning-beds, crayfish should not be allowed to become too numerous in a trout stream.

It is difficult to understand in what the great attraction of rook-shooting consists. Up to yesterday I had never shot a rook in my life. The accuracy with which some people can kill rooks with a rifle is very remarkable. I have seen my brother knock down five or six dozen without missing more than one or two birds the whole time. One would be thankful to die such an instantaneous death as these young rooks. They seem to drop to the shot without a flutter; down they come, as straight as a big stone dropped from a high wall. Like a lump of lead they fall into the nettles. They hardly ever move again. It is difficult work finding them in the thick undergrowth.

About eleven o'clock the evening after shooting the young rooks I was returning home from a neighbouring farmhouse when I heard the most lamentable sounds coming from the rookery. There seemed to be a funeral service going on in the big ash trees. Muffled cawings and piteous cries told me that the poor old rooks were mourning for their children. I cannot remember ever hearing rooks cawing at that time of night before. Saving the lark, "that scorner of the ground," which rises and sings in the skies an hour before sunrise, the rooks are the first birds to strike up at early dawn. One often notices this fact on sleepless nights. About 2.30 o'clock on a May morning a rook begins the grand concert with a solo in G flat; then a cock pheasant crows, or an owl hoots; moorhens begin to stir, and gradually the woodland orchestra works up to a tremendous burst of song, such as is never heard at any hour but that of sunrise.

> "Now the rich stream of music winds along,
> Deep, majestic, smooth, and strong,
> Through verdant vales."

How often one has heard this grand thanksgiving chorus of the birds at early dawn!

I wonder if the poor rooks caw all night long after the "slaughter of the innocents?" They were still at it when I went to bed at 12.30, and this was within two hours of their time of getting up.

> "Some say that e'en against that season cornea
> In which our Saviour's birth is celebrated,
> The bird of dawning singeth all night long."

Thus wrote Shakespeare of bold chanticleer; and perhaps the rooks when they are grieving for their lost ones, hold solemn requiem until the morning light and the cheering rays of the sun make them forget their woes.

It is difficult to understand what pleasure the farmers find in shooting young rooks with twelve-bore guns. Ours are always allowed a grand *battue* in the garden every year. They ask their friends out from Cirencester to assist. For an hour or so the shots have been rattling all round the house and on the sheds in the stable-yard. The horses are frightened out of their wits. Grown-up men ought to know better than to keep firing continually towards a house not two hundred yards away. A stray pellet might easily blind a man or a horse.

Farmers are sometimes very careless with their guns. Out partridge-shooting one is in mortal terror of the man on one's right, who invariably carries his gun at such a level that if it went off it would "rake" the whole line. If you tell one of these gentry that he is holding his gun in a dangerous way, he will only laugh, remarking possibly that you are getting very nervous. The best plan is not to ask these well-meaning, but highly dangerous fellows to shoot with you. Unfortunately it is probably the eldest son of the principal tenant on the manor who is the culprit. The best plan in such cases is to speak to the old man firmly, but courteously, asking him to try to dissuade his son from his dangerous practices.

It is amusing to watch the jackdaws when they come from the ivy-mantled fir trees to steal the food we throw every morning on to the lawn in front of the house for the pheasants, the pigeons, and other birds. They are the funniest rascals and the biggest thieves in Christendom. Alighting suddenly behind a cock pheasant, they snatch the food from him just as he imagines he has got it safely; and terribly astonished he always looks. Then these greedy daws will chase the smaller birds as they fly away with any dainty morsel, and compel them to give it up. A curiously mixed group assembles on the lawn each morning at eight o'clock in the winter. First of all there are the pheasants crowing loudly for their breakfast, then come the stately swans, several pinioned wild ducks, tame pigeons and wild and timid stock doves, four or five moorhens, any number of daws, as well as thrushes, blackbirds, starlings, house-sparrows, and finches. One day, having forgotten to feed them, I was astonished at hearing loud quacks proceeding from the dining-room, and was horrified to find that the ducks had come into the house to look for me and demand their grub.

Foxes give one a good deal of anxiety in May and June, when the cubs are about half grown. On arriving home to-day the first news I hear is that two dead cubs have been picked up: "one looks as if his head had been battered in, and the other appears to have been worried by a dog." This is the only information I can get from the keeper. It is really a serious blow; for if two have been found dead, how many others may not have died in their earth or in the woods?

Two seasons ago six dead cubs were picked up here; they had died from eating rooks which had been poisoned by some farmers. It took us a long time to get to the bottom of this affair, for no information is to be got out of Gloucestershire folk; you must ferret such matters out yourself.

There are still live cubs in the breeding-earth, for I heard them there this afternoon; so there is yet hope. But twenty acres of covert will not stand this sort of thing, considering that the hounds are "through" them once in three weeks, on an average, throughout the winter. Only one vixen survived at the end of last season, though another one has turned up since. We have two litters, fortunately. Where you have coverts handy to a stream of any kind, there will foxes congregate. They love water-rats and moorhens more than any other food.

A strange prejudice exists among hunting men against cleaning out artificial earths. There was never a greater fallacy. Fox-earths want looking to from time to time, say every ten years, for rabbits will render them practically useless by burrowing out in different places. A block is often formed in the drain by this burrowing, and the earth will have to be opened and the channel freed.

The best possible preventive measure against mange is to clear out your artificial earths every ten years. As for driving the foxes away by this practice, we cannot believe it. You cannot keep foxes from using a good artificial drain so long as it lies dry and secluded and the entrance is not too large. They prefer a small entrance, as they imagine dogs cannot follow them into a small hole.

A farmer made an earth in a hedgerow last year right away from any coverts, and, one would have thought, out of the beaten track of reynard's nightly prowls; yet the foxes took to this earth at the beginning of the hunting season, and they were soon quite established there.

There is no mystery about building a fox-drain. Reynard will take to any dry underground place that lies in a secluded spot. If it faces south—that is to say, if your earth runs in a half circle, with both entrances facing towards the south or south-west—so much the better. The entrance should not be more than about six inches square. Such a hole looks uncommonly small, no doubt, but a fox prefers it to a larger one. About half way through the passage a little chamber should be made, to tempt a vixen to lay up her cubs there. When there are lots of foxes and not too many earths, they will very soon begin to work a new drain, so long as it lies in a secluded spot and within easy distance of Master Reynard's skirmishing grounds.

We have lately made such an earth in a small covert, because the original earth is the wrong side of the River Coln. All the good country is on the opposite side of the river to that on which the old earth is situated. Foxes will seldom cross the stream when they are first found. It is hoped, therefore, that when they take to the new earth they will lie in the wood on the right side of the stream. We shall then close the old earth, and thus endeavour to get the foxes to run the good country. Much may be done to show sport by using a little strategy of this kind. Many a good stretch of grass country is lost to the hunt because the earths are badly distributed. It must be remembered that a fox when first found will usually go straight to his earth; finding that closed, he will make for the next earths he is in the habit of using.

The other day, while ferreting in the coverts previous to rabbit-shooting, the keeper bolted a huge fox out of one burrow and a cat out of the other. He also tells me that he once found a hare and a fox lying in their forms, within three yards of one another, in a small disused quarry. There is no doubt that, like jack among fish, the fox is friendly enough on some days, when his belly is full. He then "makes up to" rabbits and other animals, with the intent of "turning on them" when they least expect it. Without this treacherous sort of cunning, reynard would often have to go supperless to bed.

In those drains and earths where foxes are known to lie you will often see traces of rabbits. These little conies are wonderfully confiding in the way they use a fox-earth. It is difficult to believe that they live in the drain with the foxes, but they are exceedingly fond of making burrows with an entrance to an earth. They are a great nuisance in spoiling earths by this practice. Rabbits invariably establish themselves in fox-drains which have been temporarily deserted.

Foxes become very "cute" towards the end of the hunting season. They can hear hounds running at a distance of four or five miles on windy days. Knowing that the earths are stopped, they leave the bigger woods and hide themselves in out-of-the-way fields and hedgerows. Last season a fox was seen to leave our coverts, trot along the high-road, and ensconce himself among some laurels near the manor house. He was so easily seen where he lay in the shrubbery that a crowd of villagers stood watching him from the road. He knew the hounds would not draw this place, as it is quite small and bare, so here he stayed until dusk; then, having assured himself that the hounds had gone home, he jumped up and trotted back to the woods again.

A flock of sheep are not always frightened at a fox. The other day an old dog fox, the hero of many a good run in recent years from these coverts (an "old customer," in fact), was observed by the keeper and two other men trying to cross the river by means of a footbridge. A flock of sheep, doubtless taking him for a dog, were frustrating his endeavours to get across; directly he set foot on dry land they would bowl him over on to his back in the most unceremonious way. This game of romps went on for about ten minutes. Finally the fox, getting tired of trying to pass the sheep, trotted back over the footbridge. Fifty yards up stream a narrow fir pole is set across the water. The cunning old rascal made for this, and attempted to get to the other side; but the fates were against him. There was a strong wind blowing at the time, so that when he was half way across the pool, he was actually blown off sideways into the water. And a rare ducking he got! He gave the job up after this, and trotted back into the wood. This is a very curious occurrence, because the fox was perfectly healthy and strong. He is well known throughout the country, not only for his tremendous cheek, but also for the wonderful runs he has given from time to time. He will climb over a six-foot wire fence to gain entrance to a fowl-run belonging to an excellent sportsman, who, though not a hunting man, would never allow a fox to be killed. He is reported to have had fifty, fowls out of this place during the last few months. When caught in the act in broad daylight, the fox had to be hunted round and round the enclosure before he would leave, finally climbing up the wire fencing like a cat, instead of departing by the open door.

It is very rare that a mischievous fox, given to the destruction of poultry, is also a straight-necked one. Too often these gentry know no extent of country; they take refuge in the nearest farmyard when pressed by the hounds. At the end of a run we have seen them on the roof of houses and outbuildings time after time. On one occasion last season a hunted fox was discovered among the rafters in the roof of a very high barn. The "whipper-in" was sent up by means of a long ladder, eventually pulling him out of his hiding-place by his brush. Poor brute! perhaps he might have been spared after showing such marvellous strategy.

It speaks wonders for the good-nature and unselfishness of the farmer who owns the fowl-run above alluded to that he never would send in the vestige of a claim to the hunt secretary for the poultry he has lost from time to time. But he is one of the old-fashioned yeomen of Gloucestershire—a gentleman, if ever there was one—a type of the best sort of Englishman. Alas! that hard times have thinned the ranks of the old yeoman farmers of the Cotswolds! They are the very backbone of the country; we can ill afford to lose them, with their cheery, bluff manners and good-hearted natures.

Some of the people round about are not so scrupulous in the way of poultry claims. We have had to investigate a large number in, recent years. It is a difficult matter to distinguish *bonâ-fide* from "bogus" claims; they vary in amount from one to twenty pounds. Once only have we been foolish enough to rear a litter of cubs by hand, having obtained them from the big woods at Cirencester. Before the hunting season had commenced we had received claims of nineteen and fourteen pounds from neighbouring farmers for poultry and turkeys destroyed. One bailiff declared that the foxes were so bold they had fetched a young heifer that had died from the "bowssen" into the fox-covert. Whether the bailiff put it there or the foxes "fetched" it I know not, but the white, bleached skull may be seen hard by the earth to this day.

One of the claimants above named farms three hundred acres on strictly economical principles. He has allowed the land to go back to grass, and the only labour he employs on it is a one-legged boy, whom he pays "in kind." This boy arrived the other day with another poultry claim, when the following dialogue occurred: —

"I see you have got down sixteen young ducklings on the list?"

"Yaas, the jackdars fetched they."

"How do you know the jackdaws took them?" "'Cos maister said so."

"Do you shut up your fowls at night?"

"Yaas, we shuts the daar, but the farxes gets in. It be all weared out. There be great holes in the bowssen where they gets through and fetches them."

How can one pay poultry claims of this kind? It being absolutely impossible to verify these accounts properly, the only way is to take the general character of the claimant, paying according as you think him straightforward or the reverse. It is an insult to an honest man to offer him anything less than the amount he asks for; therefore claims which have every appearance of being *bonâ fide* should be settled in full. But the hunt can't afford it, one is told. In that case people ought to subscribe more. If men paid ten pounds for every hunter they owned, the income of most establishments would be more than doubled.

The farmers are wonderfully long-suffering on the whole, but they cannot be expected to welcome a whole multitude of strangers; nor can they allow large fields to ride over their land in these bad times without compensation of some sort. Slowly, but surely, a change is coming over our ideas of hunting rights and hunting courtesy; and the sooner we realise that we ought to pay for our hunting on the same scale as we do for shooting and fishing, the better will it be for all concerned.

Talking of hunting and foxes reminds me that a short time ago I went to investigate an earth to see if a vixen was laid down there. Finding no signs of any cubs, I was just going away when I saw a feather sticking out of the ground a few yards from the fox-earth. I pulled four young thrushes, a tiny rabbit, and two young water-rats out of this hole, and re-buried them. The cubs, it afterwards appeared, were laid up in a rabbit burrow some distance away. But the old vixen kept her larder near her old quarters, instead of burying her supplies for a rainy day close to the hole where she had her cubs. Perhaps she was meditating moving the litter to this earth on some future occasion.

I shall never forget discovering this litter. When looking down a rabbit-hole I heard a scuffle. A young cub came up to the mouth of the hole, saw me, and dashed back again into the earth. This was the smallest place I ever saw cubs laid up in. The vixen happened to be a very little one.

It is amusing to watch the cubs playing in the corn on a summer's evening. If you go up wind you can approach within ten yards of them. Round and round they gambol, tumbling each other over for all the world like young puppies. They take little notice of you at first; but after a time they suddenly stop playing, stare hard at you for half a minute, then bolt off helter-skelter into the forest of waving green wheat.

One word more about the scent of foxes. Not long ago a man wrote to the *Field* saying that he had proved by experiment that on the saturation or relative humidity of the air the hunter's hopes depend: in fact, he announced that he had solved the riddle of scent. It so happened that for some years the present writer had also been amusing himself with experiments of the same nature, and at one time entertained the hope that by means of the hygrometer he would arrive at a solution of the mystery. But alas! it was not to be. On several occasions when the air was well-nigh saturated, scent proved abominable. That the relative humidity of the air is not the all-important factor was often proved by the bad scent experienced just before rain and storms, when the hygrometer showed a saturation of considerably over ninety per cent. But there are undoubtedly other complications besides the evaporations from the soil and the relative humidity of the air to be considered in making an enquiry into the causes of good and bad scent. The amount of moisture in the ground, the state of the soil in reference to the all-important question of whether it carries or not, the temperature of the air, and last, but not by any means least, the condition of the quarry, be it fox, stag, or hare, are all questions of vital importance, complicating matters and preventing a solution of the mysteries of scent.

As the atmosphere is variable, so also must scent be variable. The two things are inseparably bound up with one another. For this reason, if after a period of rainy weather we have an anti-cyclone in the winter without severe frost, and an absence of bright sunny days, we can usually depend on a scent. Instead of the air rising, there is during an anti-cyclone, as we all know, a tendency towards a gentle down-flow of air or at all events a steady pressure, and this causes smoke, whether from a railway engine or a tobacco pipe, to hang in the air and scent to lie breast high.

Unfortunately the normal state of the atmospheric fluid is a rushing in of cold air and a rushing out or upwards of warmer air, causing unsettled variable equilibrium and unsettled variable scent. The barometer would be an absolutely reliable guide for the hunting man were it not for the complications already named above, complications which prevent either barometer or hygrometer from offering infallible indications of good or bad scenting days. However, scent often improves at night when the dew begins to form; and it may also suddenly improve at any time of day should the dew point be reached, owing to the temperature cooling to the point of saturation. This is always liable to occur at some time, on days on which the hygrometer shows us that there is over ninety per cent of moisture in the air. But here again radiation comes in to complicate matters; for clouds may check the formation of dew. It may safely be said, however, that other conditions being favourable, a fast run is likely to occur at any time of day should the dew point be reached. Thus the hygrometer is worthy to be studied on a hunting morning.

In May there is a good deal of weed-cutting to be done on a trout stream. Our plan is to have a couple of big field days about May 12th. The weeds on over two miles of water are all cut during that time. As they are not allowed to be sent down the stream, we get them out in several different places; they are then piled in heaps, and left to rot. The operation is repeated at the end of the fishing season. About a dozen scythes tied together are used. Two men hold the ends and walk up the stream, one on each side of the river, mowing as they go.

There is a certain amount of management required in weed-cutting. If much weed is left uncut, the millers grumble; if you cut them bare, there are no homes left for the fish. The last is the worse evil of the two. The millers are usually kind-hearted men, whilst poachers can commit fearful depredations in a small stream that has been cut too bare.

The way these limestone streams are netted is as follows: About two in the morning, when there is enough light to commence operations, a net is laid across the stream and pegged down at each end; the water is then beaten with long sticks both above and below the net. Nor is it difficult to drive the trout into the trap; they rush down helter-skelter, and, failing to see any net, they soon become hopelessly entangled in its meshes. The bobbing corks intimate to the poachers that there are some good trout in the net; one end is then unpegged, and the haul is made.

About ten trout would be a good catch. The operation is repeated four or five times, until some fifty fish have been bagged. The poachers then depart, taking care to remove all signs of their night's work, such as scales of fish, stray weeds, and bits of stick.

In weed-cutting by hand, instead of with the long knives, it is wonderful how many trout get cut by the scythes. There used to be several good fish killed this way at each annual cutting, when the men used to walk up the stream mowing as they went. One would have thought trout would have been able to avoid the scythes, being such quick, slippery animals.

Until the present season otters have seldom visited our parts of the Coln. Unfortunately, however, they have turned up, and are committing sad havoc among the fish. It is such a terribly easy stream for them to work. The water is very shallow, and the current is a slow one.

We are not well up in otter-hunting in these parts, there being no hounds within fifty miles. I have never seen an otter on the Coln. But one day, at a spot near which we have noticed the billet of an otter and some fishes' heads, I heard a noise in the water, and a huge wave seemed to indicate that something bigger than a Coln trout was proceeding up stream close to the bank all the way. On running up, of course I saw nothing. But half an hour afterwards I saw another big wave of the same kind. It was so close to me that if it had been a fish or a rat I must have seen him. I had a terrier with me, but of course he was unable to find an otter. A dog unbroken to the scent is worse than useless.

On another occasion I saw a water-vole running away from some larger animal under the opposite bank of the river. Some bushes prevented my seeing very well, but I am almost certain it was an otter. "A Son of the Marshes" mentions in one of his charming books that otters do kill water-rats. I was not aware of this fact until I read it in the book called "From Spring to Fall."

The broad shallow reach of the Coln in front of the manor house seems to be a favourite hunting-ground of the otter during his nocturnal rambles; for sometimes one is awakened at night by a tremendous tumult among the wild duck and moorhens that haunt the pool. They rush up and down, screaming and flapping their wings as if they were "daft."

A few weeks after writing the above we caught a beautiful female otter in a trap, weighing some seventeen pounds. I have regretted its capture ever since. Great as the number of trout they eat undoubtedly is, I do not intend to allow another otter to be trapped, unless they become too numerous. Such lovely, mysterious creatures are becoming far too scarce nowadays, and ought to be rigidly preserved. Last October we were shooting a withybed of two acres on the river bank, when the beaters suddenly began shouting, "An otter! An otter!" And sure enough a large dog otter ran straight down the line. This small withybed also contained three fine foxes and a good sprinkling of pheasants.

The number of water-voles in the banks of this stream seems to increase year by year. The damage they do is not great; but the millers and the farmers do not like them, because with their numerous holes they undermine the banks of the millpound, and the water finds its way through them on to the meadows. Country folk are very fond of an occasional rat hunt: they do lay themselves out to be hunted so tremendously. A rat will bolt out of his hole, dive half way across the stream, then, taking advantage of the tiniest bit of weed, he will come up to the surface, poke his nose out of the water and watch you intently. An inexperienced eye would never detect him. But if a stone is thrown at him, finding his subterfuge detected, he is apt to lose his head—either coming back towards you, and being obliged to come up for air before he reaches his hole, or else swimming boldly across to the opposite bank. In the latter case he is safe.

Tom Peregrine is a great hand at catching water-voles in a landing-net. He holds the net over the hole which leads to the water, and pokes his stick into the bank above. The rat bolts out into the net and is immediately landed. House-rats—great black brutes—live in the banks of the stream as well as water-voles. They are very much larger and less fascinating than the voles. To see one of the latter species crossing the stream with a long piece of grass in his mouth is a very pretty sight They are rodents, and somewhat resemble squirrels.

CHAPTER XV.

THE PROMISE OF MAY.

"Quis desiderio sit pudor aut modus
Tam cari capitis?"

HORACE.

About the middle of May the lovely, sweet-scenting lilac comes into bloom. It brightens up the old, time-worn barns, and relieves the monotony of grey stone walls and mossy roofs in the Cotswold village.

The prevailing colour of the Cotswold landscape may be said to be that of gold. The richest gold is that of the flaming marsh-marigolds in the water meadows during May; goldilocks and buttercups of all kinds are golden too, but of a slightly different and paler hue. Yellow charlock, beautiful to look upon, but hated by the farmers, takes possession of the wheat "grounds" in May, and holds the fields against all comers throughout the summer. In some parts it clothes the whole landscape like a sheet of saffron. Primroses and cowslips are of course paler still. The ubiquitous dandelion is likewise golden; then we have birdsfoot trefoil, ragwort, agrimony, silver-weed, celandine, tormentil, yellow iris, St. John's wort, and a host of other flowers of the same hue. In autumn comes the golden corn; and later on in mid winter we have pale jessamine and lichen thriving on the cottage walls. So throughout the year the Cotswolds are never without this colour of saffron or gold. Only the pockets of the natives lack it, I regret to say.

Every cottager takes a pride in his garden, for the flower shows which are held every year result in keen competition. A prize is always given for the prettiest garden among all the cottagers. This is an excellent plan; it brightens and beautifies the village street for eight months in the year. In May the rich brown and gold of the

248

gillyflower is seen on every side, and their fragrance is wafted far and wide by every breeze that blows.

Then there is a very pretty plant that covers some of the cottage walls at this time of year. It is the wistaria; in the distance you might take it for lilac, for the colours are almost identical.

Then come the roses—the beautiful June roses—the *nimium breves flores* of Horace. But the roses of the Cotswolds are not so short lived for all that Horace has sung: you may see them in the cottage gardens from the end of May until Christmas.

"SIDE VIEW OF MANOR HOUSE."

How cool an old house is in summer! The thick walls and the stone floors give them an almost icy feeling in the early morning. Even as I write my thermometer stands at 58° within, whilst the one out of doors registers 65° in the shade. This is the ideal temperature, neither too hot nor too cold. But it is not summer yet, only the fickle month of May.

Tom Peregrine is getting very anxious. He meets me every evening with the same story of trout rising all the way up the stream and nobody trying to catch them. I can see by his manner that he disapproves of my "muddling" over books and papers instead of trying to catch trout. He cannot understand it all. Meanwhile one sometimes asks oneself the question which Peregrine would also like to propound, only he dare not, Why and wherefore do we tread the perilous paths of literature instead of those pleasant paths by the river and through the wood? The only answer is this: The *daemon* prompts us to do these things, even as it prompted the men of old time.

> "There is a divinity that shapes our ends,
> Rough hew them how we will."

If there is such a thing as a "call" to any profession, there is a call to that of letters. So with an enthusiasm born of inexperience and delusive hope we embark as in a leaky and untrustworthy sailing ship, built, for ought we know, "in the eclipse, and rigged with curses dark," and at the mercy of every chance breeze are wafted by the winds of heaven through chaos and darkness into the boundless ocean of words and of books. When the waves run high they resemble nothing so much as lions with arched crests and flowing manes going to and fro seeking whom they may devour, or savage dogs rushing hither and thither foaming at the mouth; and when old Father Neptune lets loose his hungry sea-dogs of criticism, then look out for squalls!

But again the *daemon*, that still small voice echoing from the far-off shores of the ocean of time, whispers in our ear, "In the morning sow thy seed, and in the evening withhold not thine hand; for thou knowest not whether shall prosper, either this or that, or whether they both shall be alike good."

So we sow in weakness and in fear and trembling, "line upon line, line upon line; here a little and there a little," sometimes in mirth and laughter, sometimes in tears. Let us not ask to be raised in power. Let us resign all glory and honour and power to the Ancient of Days, prime source of the strength of wavering, weak mankind. Rather let us be thankful that by turning aside from "the clamour of the passing day" to tread the narrow paths of literature, however humble, however obscure our lot may have been, we gained an insight into the nobler destinies of the human soul, and learnt a lesson which might otherwise have been postponed until we were hovering on the threshold of Eternity.

In spite of complaints of east winds and night frosts, May is the nicest month in the year take it all in all. In London this is the case even more than in the country. The trees in the parks have then the real vivid green foliage of the country. There is a freshness about everything in London which only lasts through May. By June the smoke and dirt are beginning to spoil the tender, fresh greenery of the young leaves. In the early morning of May 12th, 1897, more than an inch of snow fell in the Cotswolds, but it was all gone by eight o'clock. In spite of the weather, May is "the brightest, merriest month of all the glad New Year." Everything is at its best. Man cannot be morose and ill-tempered in May. The "happy hills and pleasing shade" must needs "a momentary bliss bestow" on the saddest of us all. Look at yonder thoroughbred colt grazing peacefully in the paddock: if you had turned him out a month ago he would have galloped and fretted himself to death; but now that the grass is sweet and health-giving, he is content to nibble the young shoots all day long. What a lovely, satin-like coat he has, now that his winter garments are put off! There is a picture of health and symmetry! He has just reached the interesting age of four years, is dark chestnut in colour, and sixteen hands two and a half inches in height; grazing out there, he does not look anything like that size. Well-bred horses always look so much smaller than they really are, especially if they are of good shape and well proportioned. Alas! how few of them, even thoroughbreds, have the real make and shape necessary to carry weight across country, or to win races! You do not see many horses in a lifetime in whose shape the critical eye cannot detect a fault. We know the good points as well as the bad of this colt, for we have had him two years. Deep, sloping shoulders are his speciality; and they cover a multitude of sins. Legs of iron, with large, broad knees; plenty of flat bone below the knee, and pasterns neither too long nor too upright. Well ribbed up, he is at the same time rather "ragged-hipped," indicative of strength and weight-carrying power. How broad are his gaskins! how "well let down" he is! What great hocks he has! But, alas I as you view him from behind, you cannot help noticing that his hindlegs incline a little outwards, even as a cow's do—they are not absolutely straight, as they should be. Then as to his golden, un-docked tail: he carries it well—a fact which adds twenty pounds to his value; but, strange to say, it is not "well set on," as a thoroughbred's ought to be. He does not show the quality he ought in his hindquarters. Still his head, neck and crest are good, though his eye is not a large one. How much is he worth— twenty, fifty, a hundred, or two hundred pounds? Who can tell? Will he be a charger, a fourteen-stone hunter, or a London carriage horse? All depends how he takes to jumping. His height is against him,— sixteen hands two and a half inches is at least two inches too big for a hunter. Nevertheless, there are always the brilliant exceptions. Let us hope he will be the trump card in the pack.

Talking of horses, how admirable was that answer of Dr. Johnson's, when a lady asked him how on earth he allowed himself to describe the word *pastern* in his dictionary as the *knee* of a horse. "Ignorance, madam, pure ignorance," was his laconic reply. So great a man could well afford to confess utter ignorance of matters outside his own sphere. But how few of mankind are ever willing to own themselves mistaken about any subject under the sun, unless it be bimetallism or some equally unfashionable and abstruse (though not unimportant) problem of the day!

What beautiful shades of colour are noticeable in the trees in the early part of May! The ash, being so much later than the other trees, remains a pale light green, and shows up against the dark green chestnuts and the still darker firs. But what shall I say of the great spreading walnut whose branches hang right across the stream in our garden in the Cotswold Valley?

About the middle of May the walnut leaves resemble nothing so much as a mass of Virginia creeper when it is at its best in September. Beautiful, transparent leaves of gold, intermingled with red, glisten in the warm May sunshine,—the russet beauties of autumn combined with the fresh, bright loveliness of early spring!

Not till the very end of May will this walnut tree be in full leaf. He is the latest of all the trees. The young, tender leaves scent almost as sweetly as the verbena in the greenhouse. It is curious that ash trees, when they are close to a river, hang their branches down towards the water like the "weeping willows." Is this connected, I wonder, with the strange attraction water has for certain kinds of wood, by which the water-finder, armed with a hazel wand, is able to divine the presence of *aqua pura* hundreds of feet below the surface of the earth? What this strange art of rhabdomancy is I know not, but the "weeping" ash in our garden by the Coln is one of the most beautiful and shapely trees I ever saw. It will be an evil day when some cruel hurricane hurls it to the ground. We have lost many a fine tree in recent years, some through gales, but others, alas I by the hand of man.

A few years ago I discovered a spot about a quarter of a mile from my home which reminded me of the beautiful Eton playing-fields,

> "Where once my careless childhood stray'd,
> A stranger yet to pain."

It consisted of a few grass fields shut off by high hedges, and completely encircled by a number of fine elm trees of great age and lovely foliage. At one end a broad and shallow reach of the Coln completed the scene.

Having obtained a long lease of the place, I grubbed up the hedges, turned three small fields into one, and made a cricket ground in the midst. My object was to imitate as far as possible the "Upper Club" of the Eton playing-fields.

I had barely accomplished the work, the cricket ground had just been levelled, when the landlord's agent—or more probably his "mortgagee"—arrived on the scene, accompanied by a hard-headed, blustering timber merchant from Cheltenham. To my horror and dismay I was informed that, money being very scarce, they contemplated making a clean sweep of these grand old elms. On my expostulating, they merely suggested that cutting down the trees would be a great improvement, as the place would be opened up thereby and made healthier.

In the hope of warding off the evil day we offered to pay the price of some of the finest trees, although they could only legally be bought for the present proprietor's lifetime.

The contractor, however, rather than leave his work of destruction incomplete, put a ridiculous price on them. He refused to accept a larger sum than he could ever have cleared by cutting them down. This is what Cowper would have stigmatised as

> "disclaiming all regard
> For mercy and the common rights of man,"

and "conducting trade at the sword's point."

We then resolved to buy the farm. But the stars in their courses fought against us; we were unsuccessful in our attempt to purchase the freehold.

And so the contractor's men came with axes and saws and horses and carts. For days and weeks I was haunted by that hideous nightmare, the crash of groaning trees as they fell all around, soon to be stripped of all their glorious beauty. The cruel, blasphemous shouts of the men, as they made their long-suffering horses drag the huge, dismembered trunks across the beautifully levelled greensward of the cricket ground, were positively heart-rending. Ninety great elms did they strike down. A few were left, but of these the two finest came down in the great gale of March 1896.

> "Sic transit gloria mundi."

Trees are like old familiar friends, we cannot bear to lose them; every one that falls reminds us of "the days that are no more." Struck down in all the pride and beauty of their days, they remind us that

> "Those who once gave promise
> Of fruit for manhood's prime
> Have passed from us for ever,
> Gone home before their time."

They remind me that four of my greatest friends at school, ten short years ago, are long since dead. Like the trees felled by the woodman's axe, they were struck down by the sickle of the silent Reaper, even as the golden sheaves that are gathered into the beautiful barns. Other trees will spring up and shade the naked earth in the woods with their mantle of green: so, also,

> "Others will fill our places
> Dressed in the old light blue."

And just as in the woods fresh young saplings are daily springing up, so also the merry voices of happy, generous boys are ringing, as I write, in the old, old courts and cloisters by the silvery Thames; their merry laughter is echoed by the bare grey walls, whereon the names of those who have long been dust are chiselled in rude handwriting on the mouldering stone.

Hundreds we knew have gone down. The fatal bullet, the ravaging fever, the roaring torrent, and the sad sea waves; the slow, sure grip of consumption, the fall at polo, and the iron hoofs of the favourite hunter;—all claimed their victims.

Perhaps this is why we love to linger in the woods watching the rays of golden light reflected upon the warm, red earth, listening to the heavenly voices of the birds and the hopeful babbling of the brook. Those purple hills and distant bars of gold in the western sky at the soft twilight hour are rendered ever so much more beautiful when we dimly view them through a mist of tears.

And now your thoughts are taken back five short years; you are once more staying with your old Eton friend and Oxford comrade in his beautiful home in far-off Wales. All is joy and happiness in that lovely, romantic home, for in six weeks' time the young squire, the best and most popular fellow in the world, is to be married to the fair daughter of a neighbouring house. Is it possible that aught can happen in that short time to mar the heavenly happiness of those two twin souls? Alas for the gallant, chivalrous nature I Well might he have cried with his knightly ancestor of the "Round Table," "Me forethinketh this shall betide, but God may well foredoe destiny." He had gone down to the lake in the most beautiful and romantic part of his lovely home, taking with him, as was his wont, his fishing-rod and his gun. One shot was heard, and one only, on that ill-fated afternoon, and then all, save for the songs of the birds and the rippling of the deep waters of the lake, was wrapped in silence. Then followed the report—whispered through the party assembled to do honour to the future bride and bridegroom—that "Bill" was missing. Then came the agonising suspense and the eight hours' search throughout the long summer evening.

Late that night the father found the fair young form of his boy in a thick and tangled copse,—there it lay under the silent stars, the face upturned in its last appeal to heaven; and close by lay the deadly twelve-bore which had been the cause of all the misery and grief that followed.

> "Solemn before us
> Veiled the dark portal—
> Goal of all mortal.
> Stars silent rest o'er us;
> Graves under us silent."

He had evidently pursued game or vermin of some sort into the dense undergrowth of the wood, and in his haste had slipped and fallen over his gun, for the shot had just grazed his heart

Who that knew him will ever forget Bill Llewelyn, prince of good fellows, "truest of men in everything"? In all relations of life, as in the hunting field, he went as straight as a die.

The accidental discharge of a gun shortly after he came of age, and within a few weeks of his wedding day, has made the England of to-day the poorer by one of her most promising sons. Infinite charity! Infinite courage! Infinite truth! Infinite humility! Who could do justice in prose to those rare and godlike qualities? No: miserable, weak, and ineffectual though my gift of poesy may be, yet I will not let those qualities pass away from the minds of all, save the few that knew him well, without following in the footsteps (though at an immeasurable distance) of the divine author of "Lycidas," by endeavouring to render to his cherished memory "the meed of some melodious tear." For as time goes on, and the future unfolds to our view things we would have given worlds to have known long before, when the events that influenced our past actions and shaped our future destinies are seen through the dim vista of the shadowy, half-forgotten past, we must all learn the hard lesson which experience alone can teach, exclaiming with the "Preacher" the old, old words, "I returned, and saw under the sun that the race is not to the swift, nor the battle to the strong.... but time and chance happeneth to them all"

LINES IN MEMORY OF

WILLIAM DILLWYN LLEWELYN.

It may be chance,—I hold it truth,—
That of the friends I loved on earth
The ones who died in early youth
Were those of best and truest worth.

The swift, alas! the race must lose;
The battle goes against the strong,—
God wills it 'Tis for us to choose,
Whilst life is given, 'twixt right and wrong

'Tis not for us to count the cost
Of losing those we most do love;
He grudgeth not life's battle lost
Who wins a golden crown above.

And oft beneath the shades of night,
When tempests howl around these walls,
A vision steals upon my sight,
A footstep on the threshold falls.

I see once more that graceful form,

Once more that honest hand grasps mine.
Once more I hear above the storm
The voice I know so well is thine.

I see again an Eton boy,
A gentle boy, divinely taught,
And call to mind bow full of joy
In friendly rivalry we sought

The "playing-fields." Then, as I yield
To fancy's dreams, I see once more
The hero of the cricket field,
The oft-tried, trusty friend of yore.

What tender yearnings, fond regret,
These thoughts of early friendship bring!
None but the heartless can forget
'Mid summer days the friends of spring.

Now thoughts of Oxford fill my mind:
My Eton friend is with me still,
But changed—from boy to man; yet kind
And large of heart, and strong of will,

And blythe and gay. I recognise
The athletic form, the comely face,
The mild expression of the eyes,
The high-bred courtesy and grace.

Once more with patient skill we lure
The mighty salmon from the deep;
Once more we tread the boundless moor,
And wander up the mountain steep.

With gun in hand we scour the plain,
Together climb the rocky ways;
Regardless he of wind and rain
Who loved to "live laborious days."

I see again fair Penllergare,
Those woods and lakes you loved so well;
It seems but yesterday that there
I parted from you! Who can tell

The reason thou art gone before?
It is not given to us to know,
But doubtless thou wert needed more
Than we who mourn thee here below.

Life's noblest lesson day by day
Thy fair example nobly taught—
Self-sacrifice—to point the way
By which the hearts of men are brought

Nearer to God. This was thy task,
Humbly, unknowingly fulfilled;
And it were vain for us to ask
Why now thy voice is hushed and stilled.

O gallant spirit, generous heart!
If thou had'st lived in days gone by,
Thou would'st have loved to bear thy part
In glorious deeds of chivalry.

I make no apology for this digression, nor for unearthing from the bottom of my drawer lines that, written years ago, were never penned with any idea of publication. For was not the subject of those verses himself half a Cotswold man?

But now to return once more to the trees, the loss of which caused me to digress some pages back; there are compensations in all things. Not every one who becomes a sojourner among the Cotswold Hills is fated to undergo such a trial as the loss of these ninety elms. And, notwithstanding this severe lesson, I am still glad that I alighted on the spot from which I am now writing.

I have learnt to find pleasure in other directions now that my "Eton playing-fields" have passed away for ever. I have become infected by the spirit of the downs. I love the pure, bracing air and the boundless sense of space in the open hills as much as I ever loved the more concentrated charms of the valley. And even in the valley I have possessions of which no living man is able to deprive me. From my window I can see the silvery trout stream, which, after thousands of years of restless activity, is still slowly gliding down towards the sea; I can listen on summer nights to the murmuring waterfall at the bottom of the garden, the hooting of the owls, and the other sounds which break the awful silence of the night.

Nor can the hand of man disturb the glorious timber round the house; for it is "ornamental," and therefore safe from the hands of the despoiler. Storms are gradually levelling the ancient beech and ash trees in the woods, but it will be many a long day before the hand of nature has marred the beauty of what has always seemed to me to be one of the fairest spots on earth.

CHAPTER XVI.

SUMMER DAYS ON THE COTSWOLDS

"What more felicitie can fall to creature
Than to enjoy delight with libertie,
And to be lord of all the workes of Nature?"

E. SPENSER.

The finest days, when the trees are greenest, the sky bluest, and the clouds most snowy white are the days that come in the midst of bad weather. And just as there is no rest without toil, no peace without war, no true joy in life without grief, no enjoyment for the *blasé*, so there can be no lovely summer days without previous storms and rain, no sunshine till the tearful mists have passed away.

There had been a week's incessant rain; every wild flower and every blade of green grass was soaked with moisture, until it could no longer bear its load, and drooped to earth in sheer dismay. But last night there came a change: the sun went down beyond the purple hills like a ball of fire; eastwards the woods were painted with a reddish glow, and life and colour returned to everything that grows on the face of this beautiful earth.

"It seems a day
(I speak of one from many singled out),
One of those heavenly days which cannot die."
WORDSWORTH.

So it is pleasant to-day to wander over the fields; across the crisp stubbles, where the thistledown is crowding in the "stooks" of black oats; past stretches of uncut corn looking red and ripe under a burning sun. White oxeye daisies in masses and groups, lilac-tinted thistles, and bright scarlet poppies grow in profusion among the tall wheat stalks. A covey of partridges, about three parts grown, rise almost at our feet; for it is early August, and the deadly twelve-bore has not yet wrought havoc among the birds. On the right is a field of green turnips, well grown after the recent rains, and promising plenty of "cover" for sportsmen in September. In the hedgerow the lovely harebells have recovered from the soaking they endured, and their bell-shaped flowers of perfect blue peep out everywhere. The sweetest flower that grows up the hedgeside is the blue geranium, or meadow crane's-bill. The humble yarrow, purple knapweed, field scabious, thistles with bright purple heads, and St. John's wort with its clean-cut stars of burnished gold and its pellucid veins, form a natural border along the hedge, where wild clematis or traveller's joy entwines its rough leaf stalks round the young hazel branches and among the pink roses of the bramble.

By the roadside, where the dust blew before the rain and covered every green leaf with a coating of rich lime, there grow small shrubs of mallow with large flowers of pale purple or mauve; here, too, yellow bedstraw and bird's-foot lotus add their tinge of gold to the lush green grass, and the smaller bindweed, the lovely convolvulus, springs up on the barrenest spots, even creeping over the stone heaps that were left over from last winter's road mending.

Many another species of wild flower which, "born to blush unseen and waste its sweetness on the desert air," grows in the quiet Cotswold lanes might here be named; but even though at times one may feel, with Wordsworth,

> "To me the meanest flower that blows can give
> Thoughts that do often lie too deep for tears."

I will leave the humble wayside plants and descend into the vale. For it is along the back brook that the tallest and stateliest wild flowers may best be seen. The scythes mowed them all down in May, and again in July, in the broad "millpound," so that they do not grow so tall by the main stream; but the back brook, the natural course of the river before the mills were made, was left unmolested by the mowers, and is a mass of life and colour.

Here grows the graceful meadow-sweet, fair and tall, and white and fragrant; here the willow-herb, glorious with pink blossoms, rears its head high above your shoulders among the sword-flags and the green rushes and "segs"; the whole bank is a medley of white meadow-sweet, scorpion-grasses, forget-me-nots, pink willow-herbs, and lilac heads of mint all jumbled up together. Never was such a delightful confusion of colour! Great dock leaves two feet wide clothe the path by the water-side with all the splendour of malachite.

The breeze blows up stream, and the trout are rising incessantly, taking something small. They will not look at any artificial fly, even in the rippling breeze; there is nothing small enough in any fly-book to catch them this afternoon. But when the sun gets low, and the great brown moths come out and flutter over the water, the red palmer will catch a dish of fish. Willow trees—"withies" they call them hereabouts—grow along the brook-side. So white are the backs of their oval leaves that when the breeze turns them back, the woods by the river look bright and silvery. To-morrow, when the breeze has almost died away, only the tops of the willows will be silvered; the next day, if all be calm and still, all will be green as emerald. Such infinite variety is there in the woods! Not only do the tints change month by month, but day by day the colour varies; so that there is always something new, some fresh effect of light and shade to delight the eye of man in the quiet English country. Dotted about in the midst of the stream are little islands of forget-me nots. The lovely light blue is reflected everywhere in the water. Very beautiful are the scorpion-grasses both on the banks among the rushes and scattered about in mid stream.

The meadows are full of life. There are sounds sweet to the ear and sights pleasing to the eye. In the new-mown water-meadow grasshoppers—such hosts of them that they could never be numbered for multitude—are chirping and dancing merrily. "They make the field ring with their importunate chink, whilst the great cattle chew the cud and are silent. How like the great and little of mankind!" as Edmund Burke said years ago. By catching one of these "meagre, hopping insects of the hour," you will see that their backs are green as emerald and their bellies gold: some have a touch of purple over the eyes; their thighs, which are enormously developed for jumping purposes, have likewise a delicate tinge of purple.

Contrary to the saying of Izaak Walton, the trout do not seem to care much for grasshoppers nowadays, although perhaps they may relish them in streams where food is less plentiful. Our trout even prefer the tiny yellow frogs that are to be found in scores by the brook-side in early August. We have often offered them both in the deep "pill" below the garden; and though they would come with a dart and take the little frog, they merely looked at the grasshopper in astonishment, and seldom took one.

As we stand on the rustic bridge above the "pill" gazing down into the smooth flowing water, dark trout glide out of sight into their homes in the stonework under the hatch. These are the fish that rise not to the fly, but prey on their grandchildren, growing darker and lankier and bigger-headed every year. Wherever you find a deep hole and an ancient hatchway there you will also find these great black trout, always lying in a spot more or less inaccessible to the angler, and living for years until they die a natural death.

Was ever a place so full of fish as this "pill"? Looking down into the deeper water, where the great iron hooks are set to catch the poachers' nets, I could see dozens of trout of all sizes, but mostly small. At the tail of the pool are lots of small ones, rising with a gentle dimple. As the days became hotter and the stream ran down lower and lower, the trout left the long shallow reaches, and assembled here, where there is plenty of water and plenty of food.

Standing on the bridge by the ancient spiked gate bristling with sharp barbs of iron, like rusty spear and arrow-heads (our ancestors loved to protect their privacy with these terrible barriers), I listened to the waterfall three hundred yards higher up, with its ceaseless music; the afternoon sun was sparkling on the dimpling water, which runs swiftly here over a shallow reach of gravel—the favourite spawning-ground of the trout. There is no peep of river scenery I like so much as this. Thirty yards up stream a shapely ash tree hangs its branches, clothed with narrow sprays, right across the brook, the fantastic foliage almost touching the water. A little higher up some willows and an elm overhang from the other side.

There is something unspeakably striking about a country lane or a shallow, rippling brook overarched with a tracery of fretted foliage like the roof of an old Gothic building.

Who that has ever visited the village of Stoke Poges in Buckinghamshire will forget the lane by which he approached the home and last resting-place of the poet Gray? Perhaps you came from Eton, and after passing along a lane that is completely overhung with an avenue of splendid trees, where the thrushes sing among the branches as they sing nowhere else in that neighbourhood, you turned in at a little rustic gate. Straight in front of your eyes were very legibly written on grey stone three of the finest verses of the "Elegy." The monument itself is plain, not to say hideous, but the simple words inscribed thereon are unspeakably grand when read amongst the surroundings of "wood" and "rugged elm" and "yew-tree's shade," unchanged as they are after the lapse of a century and a half. The place, and more especially the lane, is a fitting abode for the spirit of the poet. One could almost hear the song of him who, "being dead, yet speaketh":

> "And the birds in the sunshine above
> Mingled their notes therewith, like voices of spirits departed."

LONGFELLOW.

Gray is a poet for whom, in common with most Englishmen, the present writer has a sincere respect. It has been said, however, of the "Elegy" by one critic that the subject of the poem gives it an unmerited popularity, and by another—and that quite recently—that it is the "high-water mark of mediocrity." Although Gray's own modest dictum was the foundation of the first of these harsh criticisms, we are unable to allow the truth of the one and must strongly protest against the other. It has been reported that Wolfe, the celebrated general, after reciting the "Elegy" on the eve of the assault on Quebec, declared that he would sooner have written such a poem than win a victory over the French. This was nearly a century and a half ago. Yet after so long a lapse of time the verses still retain their hold on the minds of all classes. In spite of the fact that Matthew Arnold and other admirers have declared that the "Elegy" was not Gray's masterpiece, yet it was this poem that brought a man who accomplished but a small amount of work into such lasting fame. From beginning to end, as Professor Raleigh says of Milton's work, the "Elegy" "is crowded with examples of felicitous and exquisite meaning given to the infallible word." Was ever a poem more frequently quoted or so universally plagiarised? In writing or speaking about the country and its inhabitants, if we would express ourselves as concisely as we possibly can, we are bound to quote the "Elegy"; it is invariably the shortest road to a terse expression of our meaning. Who can improve on "Far from the madding crowd's ignoble strife," or "The short and simple annals of the poor"? If Gray's "Elegy" is but "a mosaic of the felicities" of those who went before, let it be remembered that had he not laboriously pieced together that mosaic, these "felicities" would have been a sealed book to the majority of Englishmen. Not one man in a hundred now reads some of the authors from which they were culled. And as Landor said of Shakespeare, "He is more original than his originals." Even that strange individual, Samuel Johnson, who was accustomed whenever Gray's poetry was mentioned either to "crab" it directly or "damn it with faint praise," towards the end of his career admitted in his "Lives of the Poets" that "the churchyard abounds with images which find a mirror in every mind, and with sentiments to which every bosom returns an echo." But the chief value of the work seems really to lie in this: it has dignified the rural scenes and the honest rustics of England. It has invested every hoary-headed swain, every busy housewife, and every little churchyard in the country with a special dignity and a lasting charm. The traveller cannot look upon these scenes and faces without unconsciously connecting them with the lines he knows so well. Gray's "Elegy" will never be forgotten; for it has struck its roots deep in the national language and far down into the national heart.

Very similar to the quiet and leafy lane at Stoke Poges is the brook below the waterfall at A — — in the Cotswolds. On your left as you look up stream from the bridge of the "pill," a moss-grown gravel path runs alongside the water under a hanging wood of leafy elms and smooth-trunked beech trees, where the ringdoves coo all day. A tangled hedge filled with tall timber trees runs up the right-hand bank. Here the great convolvulus, queen of wild flowers, twists her bines among the hedge; the bell-shaped flowers are conspicuous everywhere, large and lily-white as the arum, so luxuriant is the growth of wild flowers by the brook-side.

A silver stream is the Coln hereabouts, the abode of fairies and fawns, and nymphs and dryads. But when the afternoon sun shines upon it, it becomes a stream of diamonds set in banks of emeralds, with an arched and groined roof of jasper, carved with foliations of graceful ash and willow, and over all a sky of sapphire sprinkled with clouds of pearl and opal. Later on towards evening there will be floods of golden light on the grass and on the beech trees up the eastern slope of the valley and on the bare red earth under the trees, red with fifty years' beech nuts. And later still, when the distant hills are dyed as if with archil, the sapphire sky will be striped with bars of gold and dotted with coals of fire; rubies and garnets, sardonyx and chrysolite will all be there, and the bluish green of beryl, the western sky as varied as felspar and changing colour as quickly as the chameleon. And as the day declines the last beams of the setting sun will find their way through the tracery of foliage that overhangs the brook, and the waters will be tinged with a rosy glow, even as in some ancestral hall or Gothic cathedral the sun at eventide pours through the blazoned windows and floods the interior with rays of soft, mysterious, coloured light.

I have been trying to describe one of the loveliest bits of miniature scenery on earth; yet how commonplace it all reads! Not a thousandth part of the beauty of this spot at sunset is here set down, yet little more can be said. How bitter to think that the true beauty of the trees, the path by the brook, and the sunlight on the water cannot be passed on for others to enjoy, cannot be stamped on paper, but must be seen to be realised! Truly, as Richard Jefferies says somewhere, there is a layer of thought in the human brain for which there are no words in any language. We cannot express a thousandth part of the beauty of the woods and the stream; we can but dimly feel it when we see it with our eyes.

"BELOW THE "PILL.""

Below the "pill"—for we have been gazing up stream—some sheep are lying under a gnarled willow on the left bank; some are nibbling at the lichen and moss on the trunk, others are standing about in pretty groups of three and four. One of them has just had a ducking. Trying to get a drink of water, he overbalanced himself and fell in. He walks about shaking himself, and doubtless feels very uncomfortable. Sheep do not care much for bathing in cold water. You have only to see the sheep-washing in the spring to realise how they dislike it. There is a place higher up the stream called the Washpool, where every day in May you can watch the men bundling the poor old sheep into the water, one after the other, and dipping them well, to free the wool from insects of all kinds. And how the trout enjoy the ticks that come from their thickly matted coats! One poor sheep is hopping about on the cricket field dead lame. Perhaps that leg he drags behind is broken! Why does not the farmer kill the poor brute? There is much misery of this kind caused in country places by the thoughtlessness of farmers. How much has yet to be learnt by the very men who love to describe the labourers as "them 'ere ignorant lower classes"! Alas! that these things can happen among the green fields and spreading elms and the heavenly sunshine of summer days! We should have more moral courage, and do as Carlyle bids us in his old solemn way: "But above all, where thou findest Ignorance, Stupidity, Brute-mindedness, attack it, I say; smite it, wisely, unwearily, and rest not while thou livest and it lives; but smite, smite in the name of God. The Highest God, as I understand it, does audibly so command thee, still audibly if thou hast ears to hear."

On the cricket pitch, a bare hundred yards away from the river bank, is a plentiful crop of dandelions, crow's-foot, clover, and, worst of all, enormous plantains. A gravel soil is very favourable to plantains, for stones work up and the grass dies. The dreadful plantain seems to thrive anywhere and everywhere, and on bare spots where grass cannot live he immediately appears. Rabbits have been making holes all over the pitch, and red spikes of sorrel, wonderfully rich and varied in colour, rise everywhere at the lower end of the field towards the river. The cricket ground has been somewhat neglected of late.

There is a great elm tree down close to the ground — the only tree that the winter gales had left to shade us on hot summer days. It came down suddenly, without the slightest warning; and underneath it that most careless of all keepers, Tom Peregrine, had left the large mowing-machine and the roller. So careless are some of these Gloucestershire folk that sooner than do as I had ordered and put the mowing-machine in the barn hard by, they must leave it in the open air and under this ill-fated tree. Down came my last beloved elm, smashing the mowing-machine and putting an end to all thoughts of cricket here this summer. It will be ages before the village carpenter will come with his timber cart and draw the tree away. A Gloucestershire man cannot do a job like this in under two years; they are always so busy, you see, in Gloucestershire — never a moment to spare to get anything done!

There was a time when the chief delight of summer lay in playing cricket. What ecstasy it was to be well set and scoring fast on the hard-baked ground (the harder the better), cutting to the boundary when the ball pitched short on the off, and driving her hard along the ground when they pitched one up! What could surpass the joy of scoring a century in those long summer days? Now we would as soon spend the holidays in the woods and by the busy trout stream, reading and taking note of the trees and the birds and the rippling of the waters as they flow onwards, ever onwards, towards the sea. There comes a time to all men, sooner or later, when we say to ourselves, *Cui bono?* In a few short years I shall no longer be able to hit the ball so hard, and in the "field" I am already becoming a trifle slow. Then do we take to ourselves pursuits that we can follow until the limbs are stiffened with age and the hair is white as snow.

Having spent the best years of life in the pursuit of pleasures that, however engrossing, nevertheless bore no real and lasting fruit, we finally fall back on interests that will last a lifetime, perhaps an eternity—for who knows how much of knowledge we shall take with us to another world? Aristotle was not far wrong when he described earthly happiness as a life of contemplation, with a moderate equipment of external good fortune and prosperity. There is no book so well worthy to be studied as the book of nature, no melodies like those of the field and fallow, wood and wold, and the still small voice of the busy streams labouring patiently onwards day by day.

In the fields beyond the river haymakers are busy with the second crop. Down to the ford comes a great yellow hay-cart, drawn by two strong horses, tandem fashion. One small boy alone is leading the big horses. Arriving at the ford, he jumps on to the leader's back and rides him through. The horses strain and "scaut," and the cart bumps over the deep ruts, nearly upsetting. Luckily there is no accident. So much is entrusted to these little farm lads of scarce fifteen years of age it is a wonder they do the work so well. From the tops of the firs comes the sound of pigeons winging their way from the "grove" to the "conygers" (the latter word means the "place of rabbits"; there are lots of woods so called in Gloucestershire). It is a curious piping sound that wood-pigeons make, and, not seeing the birds, you might think it came from the throat instead of the wings. One day two of us were looking at a wood-pigeon flying over, when we observed something drop from the skies and fall into the stream. On going up we saw that it was an egg she had dropped. There it lay at the bottom of the brook, apparently unbroken by the fall. Floating on the soft south wind, a heron flies over so quietly that unless he had given one of his characteristic croaks it was a hundred to one you did not see him pass. Many a heron and wild duck must pass over us unobserved on windy days. It is so difficult to observe when you are thinking. A man absorbed in reverie cannot see half the things that many country folk with less active brains never fail to observe. When we find people who live in the country unversed in the ways of birds, the knowledge of flowers and trees, and the habits of the simple country folk, we need not necessarily conclude that they are dull and empty-headed; the reverse is often the case. A man absorbed in business or serious affairs may love the country and yet know little of its real life. A good deal of time must be spent in acquiring this kind of knowledge, and it is not everybody who has the time or the opportunity to do it. If we come across a man with plenty of leisure, yet knowing nothing of what is going on around him, we may then perhaps have cause to complain of his dulness.

Mr. Aubrey De Vere relates an amusing story about Sir William Rowan Hamilton which exactly illustrates my meaning: "When he had soared into a high region of speculative thought he took no note of objects close by. A few days after our first meeting we walked together on a road, a part of which was overflowed by a river at its side. Our theme was the transcendental philosophy, of which he was a great admirer. I felt sure that he would not observe the flood, and made no remark on it. We walked straight on till the water was half way up to our knees. At last he exclaimed, 'What's this? We seem to be walking through a river. Had we not better return to the dry land?'"

There is a spot in the woods by the River Coln that is almost untrodden by man. It is the favourite resort of foxes. Nobody but myself and the earth-stopper has been there for years and years, save that when the hounds come the huntsman rides through and cheers the pack. It is in the conyger wood. No path leads through its quiet recesses, where ash and elm and larch and spruce, mostly self-sown, are mingled together, with a thick growth of elder spread beneath them. It was here, in an ancient, disused quarry, that the keeper pointed out not long since the secret dwelling-house of the kingfishers. A small crevice in the limestone rock, from which a disagreeable smell of dried fish bones issued forth, formed the outer entrance to the nest. One could not see the delicate structure itself, for it appeared to be several feet within the rock. A mass of powdered fish bones and the pungent odour from within were all the outward signs of the inner nest. By standing on a jutting ledge of the soft cretaceous rock, and holding on by another ledge, which appeared not unlikely to come down and crush you, one could peep into the hole and comfort oneself with the thought that one was nearer a kingfisher's nest than is usually vouchsafed to mortal man. It would be easy to get ladder and pickaxe and break open the rock until the nest was reached, but why disturb these lovely birds? They have built here year by year for centuries; even now some of this year's brood may be seen among the willows by the back brook.

From this quarry was dug in the year 1590 the stone to build the old manor house yonder. A few miles away toward Burford is the quarry from which men say Christopher Wren brought some of the stone to raise St. Paul's Cathedral. Yet the local people do not care a bit for this beautiful freestone of the Cotswold Hills. They want to bring granite from afar for their village crosses, and ugly blue slates for the roofs of the houses. At a parish council meeting the other day it was seriously proposed to erect a "Jubilee Hall" of *red* brick in our village. Anything for a change, you see; these people would not be mortal if they did not love a change. The pure grey limestone is commonplace hereabouts; I have actually heard it said that it will not last. Yet in every village stand the old Norman churches, built entirely of local stone, walls and roof; and many an old manor house as well lies in our midst, as good as it was three hundred years ago. To me, this limestone of the hills is one of the most beautiful features of the Cotswold country. I love to stand in a limestone quarry and mark the layers and ponderous blocks of clean white virgin rock — a tiny cleft in "the great stone floor which stretches over the face of the earth and under the limitless expanse of the sea." That solid cretaceous mass is but the remnants of the countless inhabitants of the old seas, — life changed into solid, hard rock; and even now, as the green grass and the sweet sainfoin spring up on the surface, feeding the flocks and herds that will soon in their turn feed mankind, earth is turning back again into life. Thus onwards in an endless cycle, even as the earth goes round, and the waters return to the place from whence they came, does nature's work go on; and when we consider these things, eternity and infinity lose part of their strangeness. Does it seem strange when we look upon this glorious country?—in May a sea of golden buttercups, in summer a sea of waving grass, and in the autumn a sea of golden corn; once it was a sea of salt water. And these great rounded banks, these hills and valleys, these billowy wolds,—could they but speak to us might tell strange things of the passing of the waters and of the inhabitants of the old ocean ages and ages ago; the mystery of the sea would be sung in every vale and echoed back by every rolling down.

A very wonderful matter it certainly is that the stone in which the whole history of the country-side is writ, not only in rolling downs and limestone streams, but even in church, tithe-barn, farm, and cottage, as well as in the walls and the roads and the very dust that blows upon them, should be nothing more nor less than a mass of dead animals that lived generation after generation, thousands of years ago, at the bottom of the sea.

There is silence in the woods—the drowsy silence of summer. Most of the birds have gone to the cornfields. An ash copse is never so full of birds as the denser woodlands, where the oaks grow stronger on a stiff clay soil. Here are no laughing yaffels, no cruel, murderous shrikes, and very few song-birds. Still, there are always the pigeons and the cushats, the wicked magpies and the screaming "jaypies," as the local people call the jays. Then, too, there are the birds down among the watercress and the brooklime in the clear pool below the spring, moorhens occasionally awakening the echoes by running down a weird chromatic scale or calling with their loud and mellow note to their friends and relations over at the brook; here, too, the softer croak of the mallard and the wild duck is also heard. A hawk, chasing some smaller bird, is darting and hovering over the tops of the firs, but, catching a glimpse of me, disappears from sight. Presently a little bird, with an eye keener even than the cruel hawk's, comes out from the hazels and perches on a post some ten yards away. It is a fly-catcher. As he sits he turns his eyes in every direction, on the look-out for dainty insects. He seems to have eyes at the back of his head, for instantly he sees a fly in the air right behind him, makes a dash, catches it, and flies on to the next post. He repeats the performance there, then once more changes his ground. When he has made another successful raid, he returns to his first post, always hunting in a chosen circuit, and always catching flies. He was here yesterday, and will be here again to-morrow. When you try to approach him, however, he flies away and hides himself in the firs.

If there are not many birds in the woods just now, still, there is always the beauty of the trees. How marvellous is the symmetry of form and colouring in the trunk and branches of a big ash tree! If you put mercury into a solution of nitrate of silver, and leave them for a few days to combine, the result will be a precipitation of silver in a lovely arborescent form, the *arbor Dianae*, beautiful beyond description. Such are my favourite ash trees when the summer sunshine sparkles on them. It is their bare, silvered trunks that give the special charm to these hanging woods. They stand out from dark recesses filled with alder and beech and ivy-mantled firs, rising in bold but graceful outline; columns of silver, touched here and there with the sad gold and green shades of lichen and moss. The moss that mingles with golden lichens is of a soft, velvety hue, like a mantle of half drapery on a beautiful white statue. And, oddly enough, though ferns do not grow on the limestone soil of the Cotswolds, yet on the first story so to speak of every big ash tree by the river, as well as on the pollard willows, there is a beautiful little fernery springing up out of the moss and lichen, which seems to thrive most when the lichen thrives—in the winter rather than in the summer. Then, too, the foliage of all kinds of trees and shrubs is not only different in form, but the minutest serrations vary; so that the leaves of two kinds of trees are no more alike than any two human faces are alike. The elm leaves are rough to the touch, like sandpaper, and their edges are clearly serrated; those of the beeches are smooth as parchment, and though the edges appear at first sight to be almost clean cut, they have very slight serrations, as if nature had rounded them with a blunt knife. The lobed ivy leaves are likewise highly polished, and they have sharp, pointed tips. The leaves of the common stinging-nettle ("'ettles" the labourers call them) have deep indents all round them. A great dock leaf, in which the chives have a strange resemblance to the arteries in the human frame, has small shallow indents all round it. Hazels are rough and almost round in form, save for a pointed tip at the end; they have ragged edges and ill-defined serrations. Everybody knows the sycamore from its five lobed leaves; and the chestnuts and oaks are, again, as different as possible. These are only a few instances; one might go on for a long time showing the endless variations of form in foliage.

Then there is the remarkable difference in colour and shade; not only are there a dozen different greens in one wood, but in one and the same beech you may see a marked contrast in the tone of its leaves. For about midsummer some trees put forth a second growth of foliage, so that there is the vivid yellow tint of the fresh shoots and the dark olive of the older leaves on one and the same branch. Of the rich autumnal shades I am not speaking; they would require a chapter to themselves.

There are other things to be noted in the woods besides the trees and the birds: lots of rabbits and squirrels, not to mention an occasional hedgehog. Squirrels are the most delightful of all the furred denizens of the woods. Running up the trees, with their long brushes straight out behind, they are not unlike miniature foxes. The slenderness of the twigs on which they manage to find support is one of the greatest wonders of the woods. The harmless hedgehog, as everybody is aware, rolls himself up into a lifeless ball of bristles on being disturbed. By staying quietly by him and addressing him in an encouraging tone, I lately induced a very large hedgehog to unroll himself and creep slowly along close to my feet.

It is very extraordinary how all wild animals, especially when young, can be won by kindness. I once came across a young hedgehog about three-parts grown; he was running about on the grass in front of the house in broad daylight, and kept poking his little nose into the earth searching for emmets and grubs. I made friends with him, dug him up some worms, and in less than half an hour he became as tame as possible. Tom Peregrine, the keeper, stood by and roared with laughter at his antics, saying he had never seen such a "comical job" in all his life. And it really was a curious sight. The hedgehog, with the merriest twinkle in his eyes, would take the worms out of my hand; and when I dangled them five or six inches off the ground, he would rear up on his hindlegs and snatch and grab until he secured them. Then he would sit up and scratch himself like a dog. He would allow me to take him up in my hands and stroke him, and yet not retire into his bristly shell. He ate a dozen worms and a bumble-bee straight off the reel, and then with all the gluttony of the pig tribe he went searching about for more food. I noticed that he ate the grass, in the same way as dogs do, for medicinal purposes. We put him into a large box with some hay in it, and as he still seemed hungry that evening, we gave him a couple of cockchafers from the kitchen, which he appeared to relish mightily. The little fellow was as happy as a king, crying and squeaking whenever we went to look at him, and hunting round the box for food. But, alas! we had overfed him. To our intense regret he died the next day from acute indigestion.

There are but few snakes or vipers in the district of which I am writing. But quite recently a man found a large trout about eighteen inches in length lying dead in the Coln, and protruding from the mouth of the fish was a large snake, also dead. The snake must have been swimming in the water (as they are known to do occasionally), and the trout being in a backwater, where food was scarce, must have seized the snake and choked himself in his efforts to bolt it This was a remarkable occurrence, because a Coln trout is most particular as to his bill of fare, and snakes are certainly not usually included in the list. There is such a plentiful supply of larvae, caddis, "stone-loach," fresh-water shrimps, crayfish, and other crustaceans, to say nothing of flies, minnows, and small fry, that a trout would very seldom attack a snake. A large lobworm, however, as every one knows, is a very attractive bait for any kind of fresh-water fish except pike.

Stoats with reddish-brown backs and yellow bellies may often be seen hunting the rabbits, and the little weasels may sometimes be drawn out of their holes in the walls if one makes a squeaking noise with the lips. Stoats usually hunt singly, weasels in packs and pairs.

But we must leave the woods, for the evening shadows are lengthening and the "golden evening brightens in the west." It is time to go up to the cornfields on the hill and see the sun set. I have said that there is no path through this wood; it is sacred to foxes.

They are not here now, however; they will not be back till all the corn is cut. The wheatfields are their summer quarters.

It is no easy matter to get out of a tangled wood in August. The stinging-nettles are seven feet high in places; we must hold our hands high above our heads and plough our way through them. When we finally emerge we are covered from head to foot with large prickly burrs from the seeding burdocks, as well as with the small round burrs of the goose-grass. Then

> "On and up where nature's heart
> Beats strong amid the hills."

As we pass onwards over the cornfields towards a piece of high ground from which it is our wont to watch the sun set, a silvery half-moon peeps out between the clouds. In the north-west the range of limestone hills is already tinged with purple. In the highest heaven are bars of distant cloud, so motionless that they appear to be sailing slowly against the wind. Lower down, dusky, smoke-like clouds, tinged here and there with a rosy hue, are flying rapidly onwards, ever onwards, in the sky. Later on the higher clouds will turn deep red, whilst brighter and brighter will glow the moon.

Yonder, twenty-five miles away, the old White Horse is just visible upon the distant chalk downs. Overhead the sky has the deep blue of mazarine, but westwards and south-west the colour is light olive green, gradually changing to an intensely bright yellow. Heavy banks of clouds are slowly rising in the south-west; the bleating of sheep at the ancient homestead half a mile away is the only sound to be heard. As the sun goes down to-night it resembles a great ship on fire amidst the breakers on a rockbound coast; for the western sky is dashed with fleecy clouds, like the spray that beats against the chalk cliffs on the shore of the mighty Atlantic; and amid the last plunges of the doomed vessel the spray is tinged redder and redder, ere with her human cargo she disappears amid the surf. But no sooner has she sunk into the abyss than the foam and the fierce breakers die away, and a wondrous calm broods over all things. In twenty minutes' time nothing is left in the western sky but a tiny bar of golden cloud that cannot yet quite die away, reminding me, as I still thought about the burning ship and her ill-fated crew, of

> "the golden key
> Which opes the palace of Eternity."

But eastwards, above the old legendary White Horse, the "Empress of the Night," serene and proudly pale, is driving her car across the darkening skies.

CHAPTER XVII.

AUTUMN.

I.

It is in the autumn that life in an old manor house on the Cotswolds has its greatest charm; for one of the chief characteristics of a house in the depths of the country surrounded by a broad manor is the game. The whole atmosphere of such a place savours of rabbits and hares and partridges. There may be no pheasant-rearing and comparatively little game of any kind, yet the place is, nevertheless, associated with sport with the gun. Ten to one there are guns, old and new, hanging up in the hall or the smoking-room, and perhaps fishing-rods too. There is a bond between the house and the fields around, and the connecting link is the game. Time was when the squire in these English villages lived on the produce of the estate: game, fish, and fowl, and the stock at the farm supplied his simple wants throughout the year. Huge game larders are yet to be seen in the lower regions of the manor house; you must pass through them to reach the still more ample wine cellars. Nearer London there is not much connection nowadays between the house and the land—you must walk on the roads; but away in the country it is over the broad fields that you roam. Even on a small manor of two thousand acres you may walk a dozen miles in an afternoon and not pass the boundary fence.

It is very surprising that there is not more demand for country houses in England when one considers that an extensive demesne may be rented at a price which is paid for a small flat in unfashionable Kensington. The local term in Gloucestershire for renting a manor is "holding the liberty"—the old Saxon word. The term is singularly expressive of the freedom possessed by the man who exchanges the life of the town or the villa for a manor in one of the remote counties. He who enjoys the sporting rights, with license (as the leases run) to hunt, fish, course, hawk, or sport without the labour and loss of farming the land, possesses all the pleasures of the squire's existence with few of its drawbacks and responsibilities. Yet many a fine old house in the country remains unlet because the life is considered a dull one by those who have not been brought up to it. With nature's book spread so amply before our eyes, the country is never dull. At no time of life is it too late to commence the study of this book of nature. The faculty of observation is one that is easily acquired. It is not a case of *nascitur non fit*. With tolerably good eyesight and a determination to learn, a man soon

> "Finds tongues in trees, books in the running brooks,
> Sermons in stones, and good in everything."

And the habit of observing once acquired, we can never lose it till we die.

Of course those who rent a place in preference to purchasing it miss one of the greatest and most useful privileges the country can confer—that of following in the footsteps of him who

> "Strove for sixty widow'd years to help his homelier brother
> man,
> Served the poor and built the cottage, rais'd the school and
> drained the fen."

These are the true delights of a country existence; and it is, I think, incumbent on the really rich men of England, if they have the welfare of the nation at heart, to hold a stake, however small, in the land, even at a sacrifice of income. I refer to men with incomes ranging from ten to a hundred thousand pounds per annum, who would not feel the loss of interest that would possibly accrue on an exchange of investment from "the elegant simplicity of the three per cents." to an agricultural estate in the country. They may be giving gold for silver in the transaction, but will be amply repaid in a thousand different ways. How infinitely preferable the existence of the poor countryman, even though times be hard, to that of the misguided being of whom it may be said:

> "Through life's dark road his sordid way he wends—
> An incarnation of fat dividends "!

A Cotswold Village; or, Country Life and Pursuits in Gloucestershire

C. SPRAGUE.

It is probable that the bicycle will cause a larger demand for remote country houses. To the writer, who, previous to this summer, had never experienced the poetry of motion which a bicycle coasting downhill, with a smooth road and a favourable wind, undoubtedly constitutes, the invention seems of the greatest utility. It brings places sixty miles apart within our immediate neighbourhood. Let the south wind blow, and we can be at quaint old Tewkesbury, thirty miles away, in less than three hours. A northerly gale will land us at the "Blowing-stone" and the old White House of Berkshire with less labour than it takes to walk a mile. Yet in the old days these twenty miles were a great gulf fixed between the Gloucestershire natives and the "chaw-bacons" over the boundary. Their very language is as different as possible. To this day the villagers who went to the last "scouring of the horse" and saw the old-fashioned backsword play, talk of the expedition with as much pride as if they had made a pilgrimage to the Antipodes.

As September draws nigh and the days rapidly shorten, the merry hum of the thrashing machine is heard all day long. The sound comes from the homestead across the road, and buzzes in my ears as I sit and write by the open window. How wonderful the evolution of the thrashing machine! How rough-and-ready the primitive methods of our forefathers! First of all there was the Eastern method of spreading the sheaves on a floor of clay, and allowing horses and oxen to trample on the wheat and tread out the corn. Not less ancient was the use of the old-fashioned flail—an instrument only discarded within the memory of living man. Yet what a wonderful difference there is between the work accomplished in a day with the flails and the daily output of the modern thrashing machine!

In the porch of the manor house, amid an accumulation of old traps and other curious odds and ends there hangs an ancient and much-worn flail. Two stout sticks, the handstaff and the swingle, attached to each other by a strong band of gut, constitute its simple mechanism. The wheat having been strewn on the barn floor, the labourer held the handstaff in both hands, swung it over his head, and brought the swingle down horizontally on to the heads of ripe corn. Contrast this fearfully laborious process with the bustling, hurrying machine of to-day. And yet with all this improvement the corn can scarcely be thrashed out at a profit. So out of joint are the times and seasons that the foreigner is allowed to cut out the home producer. Half the life of the country-side has gone, and no man dare whisper "Protection."

Even in these bad times the man with a head on his shoulders above the average of his neighbours comes forth to show what can be done with energy and pluck. Twenty years ago a labouring man, who "by crook or by hook" had saved a hundred pounds, bought a thrashing machine (probably second-hand) He took it round to the various farms, and did the thrashing at so much per day. By and by he had saved enough money to take a farm. A few years later he had two thrashing machines travelling the country, and in this poor district is now esteemed a wealthy man. I always found him an excellent game-preserver and a most straightforward fellow. Another farming neighbour of mine, however, was always talking about his ignorance and lack of caste. All classes, from the peer to the peasant, seem to resent a man's pushing his way from what they are pleased to consider a lower station into their own.

In the autumn gipsies are to be seen travelling the roads, or sitting round the camp fire, on their way to the various "feasts" or harvest festivals. "Have you got the old gipsy blood in your veins?" I asked the other day of a gang I met on their way to Quenington feast "Always gipsies, ever since we can remember," was the reply. Fathers, grandfathers were just the same, — always living in the open air, winter and summer, and always moving about with the vans. In the winter hawking is their occupation. "Oh no! they never felt the cold in winter; they could light the fire in the van if they wanted it."

Although many of the farmers here have given up treating their men to a spread after the harvest is gathered in, there is still a certain amount of rejoicing. The villagers have a little money over from extra pay during the harvest, so that the gipsies do not do badly by going the round of the villages at this time. The village churches are decorated in a very delightful manner for these feasts: such huge apples, carrots, and turnips in the windows and strewn about in odd places; lots of golden barley all round the pulpit and the font; and perhaps there will be bunches of grapes, such as grow wild on the cottage walls, hung round the pulpit. Then what could look prettier against the white carved stone than the russet and gold leaves of the Virginia creeper? and these they freely use in the decorations. If one wants to see good taste displayed in these days, one must go to simple country places to find it. At Christmas the old Gothic fane is hung with festoons of ivy and of yew in the old fashion of our forefathers.

I paid a visit to my old friend John Brown the other day, as I thought he would be able to tell me something about the harvest feasts of bygone days. He is a dear old man of some seventy-eight summers, though somewhat of the *laudator temporis acti* school; but what good-nature and sense of humour there is in the good, honest face!

"Fifty year ago 'twere all mirth and jollity," he replied to our enquiry as to the old times. "There was four feasts in the year for us folk. First of all there was the sower's feast,—that would be about the end of April; then came the sheep-shearer's feast,—there'd be about fifteen of us as would sit down after sheep-shearing, and we'd be singing best part of the night, and plenty to eat and drink; next came the feast for the reapers, when the corn was cut about August; and, last of all, the harvest home in September. Ah! those were good times fifty years ago. My father and I have rented this cottage eighty-six years come Michaelmas; and my father's grandfather lived in that 'ere housen, up that 'tuer' there, nigh on a hundred years afore that. I planted them ash trees in the grove, and I mind when those firs was put in, near seventy years ago. Ah! there *was* some foxes about in those days; trout, too, in the 'bruk'—it were full of them. You'll have very few 'lets' for hunting this season; 'twill be a mild time again. Last night were Hollandtide eve, and where the wind is at Hollandtide there it will stick best part of the winter. I've minded it every year, and never was wrong yet The wind is south-west to-day, and you'll have no 'lets' for hunting this time."

"Lets" appear to be hindrances to hunting in the shape of frosts. It is an Anglo-Saxon word, seldom used nowadays, though it is found in the dictionary; and our English Prayer Book has the words "we are sore let and hindered in running the race," etc. Shakespeare too employs it to signify a "check" with the hounds.

As I left, and thanked John Brown for his information, he handed me a little bit of paper, whereon was written: "to John Brown 1 day minding the edge at the picked cloos 2s three days doto," etc. I found that this was his little account for mending the hedge at the "picket close."

"AN OLD-FASHION LABOURING COUPLE."

A fine stamp of humanity is the Cotswold labourer; and may his shadow never grow less.

> "Princes and lords may flourish or may fade,
> A breath can make them, as a breath has made;
> But a bold peasantry, their country's pride,
> When once destroyed can never be supplied."

Fresh and health-giving is the breeze on the wolds in autumn, like the driest and oldest iced champagne. In the rough grass fields tough, wiry bents, thistles with purple flowers, and the remnants of oxeye daisies on brittle stalks rise almost to the height of your knees. Lovely blue bell-flowers grow in patches; golden ragwort, two sorts of field scabious, yellow toad-flax, and occasionally some white campion remain almost into winter. Where the grass is shorter masses of shrivelled wild thyme may be seen. The charlock brightens the landscape with its mass of colour among the turnips until the end of November, if the season be fairly mild. But the hedges and trees are the glory of "the happy autumn fields." The traveller's joy gleams in the September sunlight as the feathery awns lengthen on its seed vessels. What could be more beautiful! Later on it becomes the "old man's beard," and the hedges will be white with the snowy down right up to Christmas, until the winter frosts have once more scattered the seeds along the hedgerow. Of a rich russet tint are the maple leaves in every copse and fence. On the blackthorn hang the purple sloeberries, like small damsons, luscious and covered with bloom. Tart are they to the taste, like the crab-apples which abound in the hedges. These fruits are picked by the poor people and made into wine. Crab-apples may be seen on the trees as late as January. Blackberries are found in extraordinary numbers on this limestone soil, and the hedges are full of elder-berries, as well as the little black fruit of the privet. Add to these the red berries of the hawthorn or the may, the hips and haws, the brown nuts and the succulent berries of the yew, and we have an extraordinary variety of fruits and bird food. Woodbine or wild honeysuckle may often be picked during October as well as in the spring. By the river the trout grow darker and more lanky day by day as the nights lengthen. The water is very, very clear. "You might as well throw your 'at in as try to catch them," says Tom Peregrine. The willows are gold as well as silver now, for some of the leaves have turned; while others still show white downy backs when the breeze ruffles them. In the garden by the brook-side the tall willow-herbs are seeding; the pods are bursting, and the gossamer-like, grey down—the "silver mist" of Tennyson—is conspicuous all along the brook. The water-mint and scorpion-grasses remain far into November, and the former scents more sweetly as the season wanes. But

> "Heavily hangs the broad sunflower,
>   Over its grave in the earth so chilly;
> Heavily hangs the hollyhock;
>   Heavily hangs the tiger lily."

An old wild duck that left the garden last spring to rear her progeny in a more secluded spot half a mile up stream has returned to us. Every morning her ten young ones pitch down into the water in front of the house, and remain until they are disturbed; then, with loud quacks and tumultuous flappings, they rise in a long string and fly right away for several miles, often returning at nightfall. Such wild birds are far more interesting as occasional visitors to your garden than the fancy fowl of strange shape and colouring often to be seen on ornamental water. A teal came during the autumn of 1897 to the sanctuary in front of the house, attracted by the decoys; she stayed six weeks with us, taking daily exercise in the skies at an immense height, and circling round and round. Unfortunately, when the weeds were cut, she left us, never to return.

By the end of October almost all our summer birds have left us. First of all, in August, went the cuckoo, seeking a winter resort in the north of Africa. The swifts were the next to go. After a brief stay of scarce three months they disappeared as suddenly in August as they came in May. The long-tailed swallows and the white-throated martins were with us for six months, but about the middle of October they were no more seen. All have gone southwards towards the Afric shore, seeking warmth and days of endless sunshine. Gone, too, the blackcap, the redstart, and the little fly-catcher; vanishing in the dark night, they gathered in legions and sped across the seas. One night towards the end of September, whilst walking in the road, I heard such a loud, rushing sound in front, beyond a turning of the lane, that I imagined a thrashing machine was coming round the corner among the big elm trees. But on approaching the spot, I found the noise was nothing more nor less than the chattering and clattering of an immense concourse of starlings. The roar of their wings when they were disturbed in the trees could be heard half a mile away. Although a few starlings remain round the eaves of the houses throughout the winter, vast flocks of them assemble at this time in the fields, and some doubtless travel southwards and westwards in search of warmer quarters. The other evening a large flock of lapwings, or common plover, gave a very fine display—a sort of serpentine dance to the tune of the setting sun, all for my edification. They could not quite make up their minds to settle on a brown ploughed field. No sooner had they touched the ground than they would rise again with shrill cries, flash here and flash there, faster and faster, but all in perfect time and all in perfect order—now flying in long drawn out lines, now in battalions; bowing here, bowing there; now they would "right about turn" and curtsey to the sun. A thousand trained ballet dancer; could not have been in better time. It was as if all joined hands, dressed in green and white; for at every turn a thousand white breasts gleamed in the purple sunset. The restless call of the birds added a peculiar charm to the scene in the darkening twilight.

Of our winter visitants that come to take the place of the summer migrants the fieldfare is the commonest and most familiar. Ere the leaf is off the ash and the beeches are tinged with russet and gold, flocks of these handsome birds leave their homes in the ice-bound north, and fly southwards to England and the sunny shores of France. Such a *rara avis* as the grey phalarope—a wading bird like the sandpiper—occasionally finds its way to the Cotswolds. Wild geese, curlews, and wimbrels with sharp, snipe-like beaks, are shot occasionally by the farmers. A few woodcocks, snipe, and wildfowl also visit us. In the winter the short-eared owls come; they are rarer than their long-eared relatives, who stay with us all the year. The common barn owl, of a white, creamy colour, is the screech owl that we hear on summer nights. Brown owls are the ones that hoot; they do not screech.

Curiously enough I missed the corncrake's well-known call in the meadows by the river in the springtime of 1897; and not one was bagged in September by the partridge-shooters. This is the first year they have been absent. I always looked for their pleasing croak in May by the trout stream, and invariably shot several while partridge-shooting in former years.

The earthquake of 1895 was very severely felt in the Cotswolds. Next to an earthquake a bad thunderstorm is the most awe inspiring of all things to mortals. During last autumn the Cotswold district was visited by a thunderstorm of short duration, but great severity. A gale was blowing from the south; thunder and lightning came up from the same direction, and, travelling at an immense speed, passed rapidly over our house about ten p.m. The shocks became louder and louder; and whilst five or six of us were watching the lightning from a large window in the hall, there was a deafening report as of a dozen canons exploding simultaneously at close quarters. At the same time a flame of blue fire of intense brilliancy seemed to fall like a meteor a few yards in front of our eyes. At first we were sure the house had been struck, so that the first impulse was to rush out of doors; but the succeeding report being much less severe, confidence was restored. The general conclusion was that a thunderbolt had fallen, and, missing the house by a few yards, had disappeared in the earth. A search next morning on the lawn did not throw any light on the matter. Probably, if there was a thunderbolt, it fell into the river; for it is well known that water is a great conductor of the electric fluid, and thunderstorms often seem to follow the course of a stream. The summer lightning, which kept the sky in a blaze of light for two hours after the storm had passed away, was the finest I remember.

It is a pity mankind is so little addicted to being out of doors after sunset. Some of the most beautiful drives and walks I have ever enjoyed have been those taken at night. Driving out one evening from Cirencester, the road on either side was illuminated with the fairy lights of countless glow-worms. It is the female insect that is usually responsible for this wonderful green signal taper; the males seldom use it. Whereas the former is merely an apterous creeping grub, the latter is an insect provided with wings. Flying about at night, he is guided to his mate by the light she puts forth; and it is a peculiar characteristic of the male glow-worm, that his eyes are so placed that he is unable to view any object that is not immediately beneath him.

It is early in summer that these wonderful lights are to be seen; June is the best month for observing them. During July and August glow-worms seem to migrate to warmer quarters in sheltered banks and holes, nor is their light visible to the eye after June is out, save on very warm evenings, and then only in a lesser degree.

The glow-worms on this particular night were so numerous as to remind one of the fireflies in the tropics. At no place are these lovely insects more numerous and resplendent than at Kandy in Ceylon. Myriads of them flit about in the cool evening atmosphere, giving the appearance of countless meteors darting in different directions across the sky.

In the clear Cotswold atmosphere very brilliant meteors are observable at certain seasons of the year. Never shall I forget the strange variety of phenomena witnessed whilst driving homewards one evening in autumn from the railway station seven miles away. There had been a time of stormy, unsettled weather for some weeks previously, and the meteorological conditions were in a very disturbed state. But as I started homewards the stars were shining brightly, whilst far away in the western sky, beyond the rolling downs and bleak plains of the Cotswold Hills, shone forth the strange, mysterious, zodiacal light, towering upwards into a point among the stars, and shaped in the form of a cone. It was the first occasion this curious, unexplained phenomenon had ever come under my notice, and it was awe inspiring enough in itself. But before I had gone more than two miles of my solitary journey, great black clouds came up behind me from the south, and I knew I was racing with the storm. Then, as "the great organ of eternity began to play" and the ominous murmurs of distant thunder broke the silence of the night, a stiff breeze from the south seemed to come from behind and pass me, as if travelling quicker than my fast-trotting nag. Like a whisper from the grave it rustled in the brown, lifeless leaves that still lingered on the trees, making me wish I was nearer the old house that I knew was ready to welcome me five miles on in the little valley, nestling under the sheltering hill. And soon more clouds seemed to spring up suddenly, north, south, east, and west, where ten minutes before the sky had been clear and starry. And the sheet lightning began to play over them with a continuous flow of silvery radiance, north answering south, and east giving back to west the reflected glory of the mighty electric fluid. But the centre of the heavens was still clear and free from cloud, so that there yet remained a large open space in front of me, wherein the stars shone brighter than ever. And as I gazed forward and upward, and urged the willing horse into a twelve-mile-an-hour trot, the open space in the heavens revealed the glories of the finest display of fireworks I have ever seen. First of all two or three smaller stars shot across the hemisphere and disappeared into eternal space. But suddenly a brilliant light, like an enormous rocket, appeared in the western sky, far above the clouds. First it moved in a steady flight, hovering like a kestrel above us; then, with a flash which startled me out of my wits and brought my horse to a standstill, it rushed apparently towards us, and finally disappeared behind the clouds. It was some time before either horse or driver regained the nerve which had for a time forsaken them; and even then I was inclined to attribute this wonderful meteoric shower to a display of fireworks in a neighbouring village, so close to us had this last rocket-like shooting star appeared to be. A meteor which is sufficiently brilliant to frighten a horse and make him stop dead is of rare occurrence. I was thankful when I reached home in safety that I had not only won my race against the storm, but that I had seen no more atmospheric phenomena of so startling a nature.

In addition to the wonders of the heaven there are many other interesting features connected with a drive or walk by the light of the stars or the moon. A Cotswold village seen by moonlight is even more picturesque than it is by day. The old, gabled manor houses are a delightful picture on a cold, frosty night in winter; if most of the rooms are lit up, they give one the idea of endless hospitality and cheerfulness when viewed from without. To walk by a stream such as the Coln on such a night is for the time like being in fairyland. Every eddy and ripple is transformed into a crystal stream, sparkling with a thousand diamonds. The sound of the waters as they gurgle and bubble over the stones on the shallows seems for all the world like children's voices plaintively repeating over and over again the old strain:

> "I chatter, chatter as I flow
> To join the brimming river,
> For men may come and men may go,
> But I go on for ever."

Now is the time to discover the haunts of wild duck and other shy birds like the teal and the heron. In frosty weather many of these visitors come and go without our being any the wiser, unless we are out at night. Before sunrise they will be far, far away, and will probably never return any more. Time after time we have been startled by a flight of duck rising abruptly from the stream, in places where by day one would never dream of looking for them. Foxes, too, may be seen within a stone's throw of the house on a moonlight evening. They love to prowl around on the chance of a dainty morsel, such as a fat duck or a semi-domestic moorhen. Nor will they take any notice of you at such a time.

I made a midnight expedition once last hunting season to see that the "earths" were properly stopped in some small coverts situated on a bleak and lonely spot on the Cotswold Hills. On the way I had to pass close to a large barrow. Weird indeed looked the old time-worn stone that has stood for thousands of years at the end of this old burial mound. A small wood close by rejoices in the name of "Deadman's Acre." The moon was casting a ghastly light over the great moss-grown stone and the deserted wolds. The words of Ossian rose to my lips as I wondered what manner of men lay buried here. "We shall pass away like a dream. Our tombs will be lost on the heath. The hunter shall not know the place of our rest. Give us the song of other years. Let the night pass away on the sound, and morning return with joy." Then, as the rustling wind spoke in the lifeless leaves of the beeches, the plain seemed to be peopled with strange phantasies—the ghosts of the heroes of old. And a voice came back to me on the whispering breeze:

> "Thou, too, must share our fate; for human life is short.
> Soon will thy tomb be hid, and the grass grow rank on thy grave."

MACPHERSON'S *Ossian*.

And sometimes when I have been up on the hills by night, and, looking away over the broad vale stretched out below, have seen in the distance the gliding lights of some Great Western express—a trusty weight-carrier bearing through the darkness its precious burden of humanity—I thought of the time when the old seas ran here. And then there seemed to come from the direction of the old White Horse and Wayland Smith's cave the faint murmuring sound of the "Blowing-stone" ("King Alfred's bugle-horn")—that summoner of men to arms a thousand years ago, like the beacons of later days that "shone on Beachy Head"; and I felt like a man standing at the prow of a mighty liner, "homeward bound," on some fine though dark and starless evening, when no sound breaks upon his ear but the monotonous beating of the screw and the ceaseless flow of unfathomed waters, save that ever and anon in the far distance the moaning foghorn sounds its note of warning; whilst as he stands "forward" and inhales the pure health-giving salt distilled from balmy vapours that rise everlastingly from the surface of the deep, nothing is visible to the eye—straining westward for a glimpse of white chalk cliffs, or eastward, perhaps, for the first peep of dawn—save the intermittent flash from the lighthouse tower, and the signals glowing weird and fiery that reveal in the misty darkness those softly gliding phantasies, the ships that pass in the night.

II.

In nine years out of ten autumn lingers on until the death of the old year; then, with the advent of the new, our English winter begins in earnest.

It is Christmas Day, and so lovely is the weather that I am sitting on the terrace watching the warm, grateful sun gradually disappearing through the grey ash trunks in the hanging wood beyond the river. The birds are singing with all the promise of an early spring. There is scarcely a breath of wind stirring, and one might almost imagine it to be April. Tom Peregrine, clad in his best Sunday homespun, passes along his well-worn track through the rough grass beyond the water, intent on visiting his vermin traps, or bent on some form of destruction,—for he is never happy unless he is killing. My old friend, the one-legged cock pheasant, who for the third year in succession has contrived to escape our annual battue, comes up to my feet to take the bread I offer. When he was flushed by the beaten there was no need to call "Spare him," for with all the cunning of a veteran he towered straight into the skies and passed over the guns out of shot. Two fantail pigeons of purest white, sitting in a dark yew tree that overhangs the stream a hundred yards away, make the prettiest picture in the world against the dusky foliage.

Splash!—a great brown trout rolls in the shallow water like a porpoise in the sea. A two-pounder in this little stream makes as much fuss as a twenty-pound salmon in the mighty Tweed.

Hark! was that a lamb bleating down in old Mr. Peregrine's meadow? It was: the first lamb, herald of the spring that is to be. May its little life be as peaceful as this its first birthday: less stormy than the life of that Lamb whose birth all people celebrate to-day.

The rooks are cawing, and a faint cry of plover comes from the hill.

Soft and grey is the winter sky, but behold! round the sun in the west there arises a perfect solar halo, very similar to an ordinary rainbow, but smaller in its arc and fainter in its hues of yellow and rose—a very beautiful phenomenon, and one seldom to be seen in England. Halos of this nature are supposed to arise from the double refraction of the rays from the sun as the light passes through thin clouds, or from the transmission of light through particles of ice. It lingers a full quarter of an hour, and then dies away. Does this bode rough weather? Surely the cruel Boreas and the frost will not come suddenly on us after this lovely, mild Christmas! Listen to the Christmas bells ringing two miles away at Barnsley village I we can never tire of the sound here, for it is only on very still days that it reaches us across the wolds.

"Hark! In the air, around, above,
  The Angelic Music soars and swells,
And, in the Garden that I love
  I hear the sound of Christmas Bells.

"From hamlet, hollow, village, height,
  The silvery Message seems to start,
And far away its notes to-night
  Are surging through the city's heart.

"Assurance clear to those who fret
  O'er vanished Faith and feelings fled,
That not in English homes is yet
  Tradition dumb, or Reverence dead.

"Now onward floats the sacred tale,
  Past leafless woodlands, freezing rills;
It wakes from sleep the silent vale,
  It skims the mere, it scales the hills;

"And rippling on up rings of space,
  Sounds faint and fainter as more high,
Till mortal ear no more may trace
  The music homeward to the sky.

"To courtly roof and rustic cot
  Old comrades wend from far and wide;
Now is the ancient feud forgot,
  The growing grudge is laid aside.

"Peace and goodwill 'twixt rich and poor!
  Goodwill and peace 'twixt class and class!
Let old with new, let Prince with boor
  Send round the bowl, and drain the glass!"

ALFRED AUSTIN.

I have culled these lines from the poet laureate's charming "Christmas Carol," as they are both singularly beautiful and singularly appropriate to our Cotswold village.

I take the liberty of saying that in our little hamlet there *is* peace and goodwill 'twixt rich and poor at Christmas-time.

> "Now is the ancient feud forgot,
> The growing grudge is laid aside."

Our humble rejoicings during this last Christmas were very similar to those of a hundred years ago. They included a grand smoking concert at the club, during which the mummers gave an admirable performance of their old play, of which more anon; then a big feed for every man, woman, and child of the hamlet (about a hundred souls) was held in the manor house; added to which we received visits from carol singers and musicians of all kinds to the number of seventy-two, reckoning up the total aggregate of the different bands, all of whom were welcomed, for Christmas comes but once a year, after all, and "the more the merrier" should be our motto at this time. So from villages three and four miles away came bands of children to sing the old, old songs. The brass band, including old grey-haired men who fifty years ago with strings and wood-wind led the psalmody at Chedworth Church, come too, and play inside the hall. We do not brew at home nowadays. Even such old-fashioned Conservatives as old Mr. Peregrine, senior, have at length given up the custom, so we cannot, like Sir Roger, allow a greater quantity of malt to our small beer at Christmas; but we take good care to order in some four or five eighteen-gallon casks at this time. Let it be added that we never saw any man the worse for drink in consequence of this apparent indiscretion. But then, we have a butler of the old school.

When we held our Yuletide revels in the manor house, and the old walls rang with the laughter and merriment of the whole hamlet (for farmers as well as labourers honoured us), it occurred to me that the bigotphones, which had been lying by in a cupboard for about a twelvemonth, might amuse the company. Bigotphones, I must explain to those readers who are uninitiated, are delightfully simple contrivances fitted with reed mouthpieces—exact representations in

295

mockery of the various instruments that make up a brass band—but composed of strong cardboard, and dependent solely on the judicious application of the human lips and the skilful modulation of the human voice for their effect. These being produced, an impromptu band was formed: young Peregrine seized the bassoon, the carter took the clarionet, the shepherd the French horn, the cowman the trombone, and, seated at the piano, I myself conducted the orchestra. Never before have I been so astonished as I was by the unexpected musical ability displayed. No matter what tune I struck up, that heterogeneous orchestra played it as if they had been doing nothing else all their lives. "The British Grenadiers," "The Eton Boating Song," "Two Lovely Black Eyes" (solo, young Peregrine on the bassoon), "A Fine Hunting Day,"—all and sundry were performed in perfect time and without a false note. Singularly enough, it is very difficult for the voice to "go flat" on the bigotphone. Then, not content with these popular songs we inaugurated a dance. Now could be seen the beautiful and accomplished Miss Peregrine doing the light fantastic round the stone floor of the hall to the tune of "See me dance the polka"; then, too, the stately Mrs. Peregrine insisted on our playing "Sir Roger de Coverley," and it was danced with that pomp and ceremony which such occasions alone are wont to show. None of your "kitchen lancers" for us hamlet folk; we leave that kind of thing to the swells and nobs. Tom Peregrine alone was baffled. Whilst his family in general were bowing there, curtseying here, clapping hands and "passing under to the right" in the usual "Sir Roger" style, he stood in grey homespun of the best material (I never yet saw a Cotswold man in a vulgar chessboard suit), and as he stood he marvelled greatly, exclaiming now and then, "Well, I never; this is something new to be sure!" "I never saw such things in all my life, never!" He would not dance; but, seizing one of the bigotphones, he blew into it until I was in some anxiety lest he should have an apoplectic fit I need scarcely say he failed to produce a single note.

Thus our Yuletide festivities passed away, all enjoying themselves immensely, and thus was sealed the bond of fellowship and of goodwill 'twixt class and class for the coming year.

Whilst the younger folks danced, the fathers of the hamlet walked on tiptoe with fearful tread around the house, looking at the faded family portraits. I was pleased to find that what they liked best was the ancient armour; for said they, "Doubtless squire wore that in the old battles hereabouts, when Oliver Cromwell was round these parts." On my pointing out the picture of the man who built the house three hundred years ago, they surrounded it, and gazed at the features for a great length of time; indeed, I feared that they would never come away, so fascinated were they by this relic of antiquity, illustrating the ancient though simple annals of their village.

I persuaded the head of our mummer troop to write out their play as it was handed down to him by his predecessors. This he did in a fine bold hand on four sides of foolscap. Unfortunately the literary quality of the lines is so poor that they are hardly worth reproducing, except as a specimen of the poetry of very early times handed down by oral tradition. Suffice it to say that the *dramatis personae* are five in number—viz., Father Christmas, Saint George, a Turkish Knight, the Doctor, and an Old Woman. All are dressed in paper flimsies of various shapes and colours. First of all enters Father Christmas.

> "In comes I old Father Christmas,
> Welcome in or welcome not,
> Sometimes cold and sometimes hot.
> I hope Father Christmas will never be forgot," etc.

Then Saint George comes in, and after a great deal of bragging he fights the "most dreadful battle that ever was known," his adversary being the knight "just come from Turkey-land," with the inevitable result that the Turkish knight falls. This brings in the Doctor, who suggests the following remedies:—

> "Give him a bucket of dry hot ashes to eat,
> Groom him down with a bezom stick,
> And give him a yard and a half of pump water to drink."

For these offices he mentions that his fee is fifty guineas, but he will take ten pounds, adding:

> "I can cure the itchy pitchy,
> Palsy, and the gout;
> Pains within or pains without;
> A broken leg or a broken arm,
> Or a broken limb of any sort.
> I cured old Mother Roundabout," etc.

He declares that he is not one of those "quack doctors who go about from house to house telling you more lies in one half-hour than what you can find true in seven years."

So the knight just come from Turkey-land is resuscitated and sent back to his own country.

Last of all the old woman speaks:

> "In comes I old Betsy Bub;
> On my shoulder I carry my tub,
> And in my hand a dripping-pan.
> Don't you think I'm a jolly old man?
>
> Now last Christmas my father killed a fat hog,
> And my mother made black-puddings enough to choke a dog,
> And they hung them up with a pudden string
> Till the fat dropped out and the maggots crawled in," etc.

The mummers' play, of which the above is a very brief *résumé*, lasts about half an hour, and includes many songs of a topical nature.

Yes, Christmas is Christmas still in the heart of old England. We are apt to talk of the good old days that are no more, lamenting the customs and country sports that have passed away; but let us not forget that two hundred years hence, when we who are living now will have long passed "that bourne from which no traveller returns," our descendants, as they sit round their hearths at Yuletide, may in the same way regret the grand old times when good Victoria—the greatest monarch of all ages—was Queen of England; those times when during the London season fair ladies and gallant men might be seen on Drawing-room days driving down St James's Street in grand carriages, drawn by magnificent horses, with servants in cocked hats and wigs and gold lace; when the rural villages of merrie England were cheered throughout the dreary winter months by the sound of horse and hound, and by the sight of beautiful ladies and red-coated sportsmen, mounted on blood horses, careering over the country, clearing hedges and ditches of fabulous height and width; when every man, woman, and child in the village turned out to see the "meet," and the peer and the peasant were for the day on an equal footing, bound together by an extraordinary devotion to the chase of "that little red rover" which men called the fox—now, alas! extinct, as the mammoth or the bear, owing to barbed wire and the abolition of the horse; when to such an extent were games and sports a part of our national life that half London flocked to see two elevens of cricketers (including a champion "nine" feet high called Grace) fighting their mimic battle arrayed in white flannels and curiously coloured caps, at a place called Lords, the exact site of which is now, alas I lost in the sea of houses; when as an absolute fact the first news men turned to on opening their daily papers in the morning was the column devoted to cricket, football, or horse-racing; when in the good old days, before electricity and the motor-car caused the finest specimen of the brute creation to become virtually extinct (although a few may still be seen at the Zoological Gardens), horse-racing for a cup and a small fortune in gold was only second to cricket and football in the estimation of all merrie Englanders—the only races now indulged in being those of flying machines to Mars and back twice a day. Two hundred years hence, I say, the Victorian era—time of blessed peace and unexampled prosperity—will be pronounced by all unprejudiced judges as the true days of merrie England. Let us, then, though not unmindful of the past, pin our faith firmly on the present and the future. *Carpe diem* should be our motto in these fleeting times, and, above all, progress, not retrogression. Let us, as the old, old sound of the village bells comes to us over the rolling downs this New Year's eve, recall to mind

> ".... the primal sympathy
> Which having been must ever be."

Let our hearts warm to the battle cry of advancing civilisation and the attainment of the ideal humanity, soaring upwards step by step, re-echoing the prayer contained in those lilting stanzas with which Tennyson greets the New Year:

"Ring out the old, ring in the new;
   Ring happy bells across the snow:
   The year is going, let him go;
Ring out the false, ring in the true.

"Ring out the grief that saps the mind,
   For those that here we see no more
   Ring out the feud of rich and poor,
Ring in redress to all mankind.

"Ring out false pride in place and blood,
   The civic slander and the spite;
   Ring in the love of truth and right;
Ring in the common love of good.

"Ring out old shapes of foul disease;
   Ring out the narrowing lust of gold;
   Ring out the thousand wars of old,
Ring in the thousand years of peace.

"Ring in the valiant man and free,
   The larger heart, the kindlier hand;
   Ring out the darkness of the land.
Ring in the Christ that is to be."

CHAPTER XVIII.

WHEN THE SUN GOES DOWN.

"I saw Eternity the other night
Like a great ring of pure and endless light,
  All calm, as it was bright:—
And round beneath it, time in hours, days, years,
  Driven by the spheres,
Like a vast shadow moved, in which the world
  And all her train were hurl'd."

HENRY VAUGHAN.

It is the end of May; a bright, rainless, and at times bitterly cold month it has been. But now the chill east wind has almost died away. Summer has come at last. Once more I am making for the Downs. Very seldom am I there at this period of the year; but before going away for several months, I bethought me that I would go and inspect the improvements at the fox-covert, stopping on my way at the "Jubilee" gorse covert we lately planted, to see if there is a litter of cubs there this year. Across the fields we go, ankle deep in buttercups and clover at one moment, then up the hedge to avoid treading the half-grown barley. We are so accustomed to take a bee-line across these shooting grounds of ours that we quite forget that the farmer would not thank us for trampling down his crops at the end of May. But soon we are on the Downs, well out of harm's way and far removed from highroads and footpaths. What a glorious panorama lies all around! Why do we not come here oftener in summer?—the country is ten times more lovely then than it is in the shooting season. A field of sainfoin in June, with its glorious blossoms of pink, is one of the prettiest sights in all creation. Seen in the distance, amid a setting of green wheatfields and verdant pastures, it ripples in the garish light of the summer sun like a lake of rubies.

> "Land and sea
> Give themselves up to jollity;
> And with the heart of May
> Doth every beast keep holiday."

Ah! there will be lots of foxes when the hounds come to the fox-covert next October. The unpleasant smell at the mouth of the earth tells us that there are cubs there; and as we stand over it we can hear them playing down below in the bowels of mother earth. Very distinct, too, are the tracks—*traffic*, the keeper calls them—leading by sundry well-trodden paths to the dell below—a nice sunny dell, facing south-west, where in spring the violets and primroses grow among the spreading elder. These cubs were not born here. Their mother brought them from an old hollow stump of a tree by the river, half a mile away. When she found her lair discovered by an angler who happened to pass that way, she brought them across the river by the narrow footbridge right up here on to the hill. The cubs from the tree have disappeared, so no doubt these are the ones. Well, there are lots of rabbits for them; the little fellows are popping about all over the place.

How tame all wild animals become in the summer!—all except the ones we want to circumvent—magpies, jays, stoats, and such small deer. Lapwings fly round us, crying restlessly, "Go away, go away!" Their shrill treble accents remind one of a baby's squall. Pigeons and ringdoves, partridges and hares seem to be plentiful "as blackberries in September." A gorgeous cock pheasant crows and jumps up close to us, followed by his mate. This is a pleasing sight up here, for they are wild birds. There has been no rearing done in these copses on the hills within the memory of man.

Tom Peregrine suddenly appears out of a hedge, where he has been watching the antics of the cubs at the mouth of the fox-earth. He has grown very serious of late, and tells you repeatedly that there is going to be another big European war shortly. Let us hope his gloomy forebodings are doomed to disappointment. Surely, surely at the end of this marvellous nineteenth century, when there are so many men in the world who have learnt the difficult lessons of life in a way that they have never been learnt before, nations are no longer obliged to behave like children, or worse still, with their petty jealousies and bickerings and growlings, "like dogs that delight to bark and bite."

Tom Peregrine, having done but little work for many months, is now making himself really useful, for a change, by copying out parts of this great work; and, to do him justice, he writes a capital, clear hand. He is very anxious to become secretary to "some great gentleman," he says. If any of my readers require a sporting secretary, I can confidently recommend him as a man of "plain sense rather than of much learning, of a sociable temper, and one that understands a little of backgammon." There is no fear of his "insulting you with Latin and Greek at your own table." He would have suited Sir Roger capitally for a chaplain, I often tell him; and though he hasn't a notion who Sir Roger may be, he thoroughly enjoys the joke.

The fox-covert presents a strange appearance. It is full of young spruce trees, and the lower branches have been lopped down, but not cut through or killed. Under each tree there is now a grand hiding-place for foxes and rabbits—a sort of big umbrella turned topsy-turvy. The rabbits appreciate the pains we have been at; but I fear the foxes, for whom it was intended, at present look on the shelter with suspicion. They dislike the gum which oozes continually from the gashes in the bark; it sticks to their coats, and gives an unpleasant sensation when they roll. They cannot keep their beautiful coats sleek and glossy, as is their invariable rule, as long as their is any gum sticking to them.

How clearly we can see the Swindon Hills in the bright evening atmosphere! They must be more than twenty miles away. The grand old White Horse, making the spot where long, long ago the Danes were vanquished in fight, is not visible; but he is scarcely to be seen at all now, as the lazy Berkshire people have neglected their duty. He really must be scoured again this summer; he is a national institution. Londoners take a much greater interest in him than do the honest folk who live bang under his nose.

We must continue our excavations at Ladbarrow copse yonder. Men say it is the largest barrow in the county, full of "golden coffins" and all sorts of priceless antiquities! At present all we have discovered are some bones, with which we stuffed our pockets. When we arrived home, however, they were found to have belonged to a poor old sheep-dog that was buried there. But see! the setting sun is tinging the tops of the slender, shapely ash trees in yonder emerald copse. The whole plain is changing from a vast arena of golden splendour to a mysterious shadowy land of dreams. A fierce light still reveals every object on the hill towards the east; but westwards beneath yon purple ridge all is wrapped in dim, ambiguous shade.

It is sad to think that I alone of mortal men should be here to see this glorious panorama. It seems such a waste of nature's bounteous store that night after night this wondrous spectacle should be solemnly displayed, with no better gallery than a stray shepherd, who, as he "homeward plods his weary way," cares little for the grand drama that is being performed entirely for his benefit. Nature is indeed prodigal of her charms in out-of-the-way country places.

Sometimes whilst walking over these remote fields on summer evenings, I have stopped to ask myself this question: Is it possible that these exquisite wild flowers, these groves and dells of verdant tracery, these birds with their priceless music, and these wondrous, ineffable effects of light and shade which form part of the everyday pageant of English rural scenery are doomed "to waste their sweetness on the desert air"? Is it possible (to go further afield) that those lovely scenes in Wales—the fairy glens near Bettws-y-Coed, or the luxuriant valleys of Carmarthen, further south, where silvery Towey flows below the stately ruins of Dynevor Castle; those romantic reaches on the Wye, from Chepstow to the frowning hills of Brecon; those solitary, but unspeakably grand, mountains and passes of the Highlands, such as Glencoe, Ben Nevis, or those of the scarcely explored Hebrides; those smiling waters of the lovely Trossachs; those countless spots in the "Emerald Isle" that the tourist has never seen, whether in fertile Wicklow or among the whispering woods and weird waters of the west; those gorgeous forests of Ceylon; those interminable jungles of the beautiful East, with their unknown depths of tropical splendour;—is it possible that these scenes of wondrous beauty are inhabited and enjoyed by nothing more than is visible to our limited mortal gaze?

I believed, as a boy, and with a romance still unsubdued by time I would yet fain believe, that when the soul of man escapes from the poor tenement of clay in which it has been pent up for some threescore years and ten, it has not far to go. I would fain believe that heaven is not only above us, but, in some form or other entirely beyond our mortal ken, all around us, in every beautiful thing we see; that these hills and vales, these woods of delicately wrought fan-tracery groining, these mazes of golden light when the sun goes down, are peopled not alone by human flesh and blood. "There are also terrestrial bodies, and bodies celestial. But the glory of the celestial is one, and the glory of the terrestrial is another."

Who can imagine the shape or form of the immortal soul? As I walked over those golden fields to-night it seemed as if there were spirits all around me—glorious, bright spirits of the dead—invisible, intangible, like rays of pure light, in the clear atmosphere of those Elysian fields. I cannot but believe that there arise from the secret parts of this beautiful earth, at dawn of day and at eventide, other voices besides the ineffable songs of birds, the rustling murmurs that whisper in the woods, and the plaintive babbling of the brooks—hymns of unknown depths of harmony, impossible to describe, because impossible to imagine—crying night and day: "Blessing, and honour, and glory, and power be unto Him that sitteth upon the throne and unto the Lamb for ever and ever."

Yes, dear reader,

> "Though inland far we be,
> Our souls have sight of that immortal sea
> Which brought us hither."

When the sun goes down, if you will turn for a little while from the noise and clamour of the busy world, you shall list to those voices ringing, ringing in your ears. Words of comfort shall you hear at eventide, "and sorrow and sadness shall be no more,"—even though, as the years roll on, perforce you cry, with Wordsworth:

> "What though the radiance which was once so bright
> Be now for ever taken from my sight,
> Though nothing can bring back the hour

Of splendour in the grass, of glory in the flower,
> We will grieve not, rather find
> Strength in what remains behind;
> In the primal sympathy
> Which having been must ever be;
> In the soothing thoughts that spring
> Out of human suffering;
> In the faith that looks through death,
> In years that bring the philosophic mind."

THE END.

APPENDIX.

GEORGE RIDLER'S OVEN.

(Note from the papers of the Gloucestershire Society)

It is now generally understood that the words of this song have a hidden meaning which was only known to the members of the Gloucestershire Society, whose foundation dates from the year 1657. This was three years before the restoration of Charles II. and when the people were growing weary of the rule of Oliver Cromwell. The Society consisted of Loyalists, whose object in combining was to be prepared to aid in the restoration of the ancient constitution of the kingdom whenever a favourable opportunity should present itself. The Cavalier or Royalist party were supported by the Roman Catholics of the old and influential families of the kingdom; and some of the Dissenters, who were disgusted with the treatment they received from Cromwell, occasionally lent them a kind of passive aid. Taking these considerations as the keynote to the song, attempts have been made to discover the meaning which was originally attached to its leading words. It is difficult at the present time to give a clear explanation of all its points. The following, however, is consistent throughout, and is, we believe, correct: —

> "The stwuns that built Gaarge Ridler's oven,
> And thauy qeum from the Bleakeney's Quaar;
> And Gaarge he wur a jolly ould mon,
> And his yead it graw'd above his yare."

By "George Ridler" was meant King Charles I. The "oven" was the Cavalier party. The "stwuns" which built the oven, and which "came out of the Blakeney Quaar," were the immediate followers of the Marquis of Worcester, who held out to the last steadfastly for the royal cause at Raglan Castle, which was not surrendered till 1646, and was, in fact, the last stronghold retained for the king. "His head did grow above his hair" was an allusion to the crown, the head of the State, and which the king wore "above his hair."

> "One thing of Gaarge Ridler's I must commend,
> And that wur vor a notable theng;
> He mead his braags avoore he died,
> Wi' any dree brothers his zons zshou'd zeng."

This meant that the king, "before he died," boasted that notwithstanding his present adversity, the ancient constitution of the kingdom was so good and its vitality so great that it would surpass and outlive any other form of government, whether republican, despotic, or protective.

> "There's Dick the treble and John the mean
> (Let every mon zing in his auwn pleace);
> And Gaarge he wur the elder brother,
> And therevoore he would zing the beass."

"Dick the treble, Jack the mean, and George the bass" meant the three parts of the British constitution—King, Lords, and Commons. The injunction to "let every man sing in his own place" was intended as a warning to each of the three estates of the realm to preserve its proper position and not to attempt to encroach on each other's prerogative.

> "Mine hostess's moid (and her neaum 'twur Nell),
> A pretty wench, and I lov'd her well;
> I lov'd her well—good reauzon why,
> Because zshe lov'd my dog and I."

"Mine hostess's moid" was an allusion to the queen, who was a Roman Catholic; and her maid, the Church. The singer, we must suppose, was one of the leaders of the party, and his "dog" a companion or faithful official of the Society; and the song was sung on occasions when the members met together socially: and thus, as the Roman Catholics were Royalists, the allusion to the mutual attachment between the "maid" and "my dog and I" is plain and consistent.

> "My dog has gotten zitch a trick
> To visit moids when thauy be zick;

> When thauy be zick and like to die,
> Oh, thether gwoes my dog and I."

The "dog"—that is, the official or devoted member of the Society—
had "a trick of visiting maids when they were sick." The meaning
here was that when any of the members were in distress, or
desponding, or likely to give up the royal cause in despair, the
officials or active members visited, consoled, and assisted them.

> "My dog is good to catch a hen,—
> A duck and goose is vood vor men;
> And where good company I spy,
> Oh, thether gwoes my dog and I."

The "dog," the official or agent of the Society, was "good to catch a
hen," a "duck," or a "goose"—that is, any who were well affected to
the royal cause of whatever party; wherever "good company I spy,
Oh, thither go my dog and I"—to enlist members into the Society.

> "My mwother told I when I wur young,
> If I did vollow the strong beer pwoot,
> That drenk would pruv my auverdrow,
> And meauk me wear a thzreadbare cwoat."

"The good ale-tap" was an allusion, under cover of a similarity in the
sound of the words "ale" and "aisle," to the Church, of which it was
dangerous at that time to be an avowed follower, and so the
members were cautioned that indiscretion would lead to their
discovery and "overthrow."

> "When I hev dree zixpences under my thumb,
> Oh, then I be welcome wherever I qeum
> But when I have none, oh, then I pass by,—
> 'Tis poverty pearts good company."

The allusion here is to those unfaithful supporters of the royal cause
who "welcomed" the members of the Society when it appeared to be
prospering, but "parted" from them in adversity, probably referring
ironically to those lukewarm and changeable Dissenters who veered
about, for and against, as Cromwell favoured or contemned them.
Such could always be had wherever there were "three sixpence-

under the thumb"; but "poverty" easily parted such "good company."

> "When I gwoes dead, as it may hap,
> My greauve shall be under the good yeal tap;
> In vouled earmes there wool us lie,
> Cheek by jowl, my dog and I."

"If I should die," etc.—an expression of the singer's wish that if he should die he may be buried with his faithful companion (as representing the principles of the Society) under the good aisles of the church, thus evincing his loyalty and attachment to the good old constitution and to Church and king even in death.

INDEX

Abbey, Edwin
Ablington Manor
Acman Street
Aethelhum, the Saxon
Agriculture
Alder tree
Aldsworth and Oliver Cromwell
Alfred, King
Amphitheatre, Roman
Ampney Park
Angelus, the
Antiquity, charm of
Arbor Diana
Architecture, Elizabethan
Aristotle
Arlington Row
Artificial fox-earths
Austin, Alfred

Badgers
Bampton-in-the-Bush
Barnby, Joseph
Barns, tithe
Barometer
Barrows, ancient
Bathurst family
Bathurst, Lord
Battues
Bazley, Sir Thomas
Bettws-y-Coed
Bibury Races
Bibury village
Bigotphones
Blowing-stone, the

CPSIA information can be obtained
at www.ICGtesting.com
Printed in the USA
BVHW081229080223
658130BV00005B/34

11/9/15